THE INNER SANCTUM

City Council

Newcastle Libraries and Information Service

 0845 002 0336

Due for return	Due for return	Due for return

Please return this item to any of Newcastle's Libraries by the last date shown above. ff not requested by another customer the loan can be renewed, you can do this by phone, post or in person. **Charges may be made for late returns.**

Mark Guidi is the chief football writer at the *Sunday Mail* and has been with Scotland's biggest-selling newspaper since 1995. He also works for Radio Clyde's *Superscoreboard* team. He is the author of *You Can Call Me Stan: The Stiliyan Petrov Story*, *Oranje and Blue: The Arthur Numan Story* and *Tormented: The Andy McLaren Story*. He lives with his wife Anne and their three daughters, Eva, Sophia and Claudia.

THE
INNER
SANCTUM

The Secrets Behind Celtic's 1997–98 Title Win

MARK GUIDI

MAINSTREAM
PUBLISHING

EDINBURGH AND LONDON

First published in Great Britain in 2008 by
MAINSTREAM PUBLISHING COMPANY
(EDINBURGH) LTD
7 Albany Street
Edinburgh EH1 3UG

ISBN 9781845963583

All photos © Scottish Daily Record and Sunday Mail Ltd,
except where stated

A catalogue record for this book is available
from the British Library

Typeset in Caslon and Gill Sans

Printed in Great Britain by
Clays Ltd, St Ives plc

Acknowledgements

I would like to thank Mainstream for publishing this book, particularly Bill Campbell and Peter MacKenzie. Thanks to the excellent editorial team of Paul Murphy and Graeme Blaikie. Also to Fiona Atherton for her hard work.

Many thanks to Brian McSweeney, who helped me bring this together. It would not have been possible without his input.

Thanks to Billy McNeill for contributing a foreword to this book. Thomas Jordan and Ewan Smith were also invaluable, as they helped track down players from the 1998 squad. Thanks to Jordan Costello and Michael Oliver Jnr for helping with the research.

To David McKie for casting his expert eye over it. To Peter McLean for his help.

Thanks to my sports editor at the *Sunday Mail*, George Cheyne.

There would have been no book if the 1998 coaching staff and players had not been willing to cooperate, so thanks to them all for giving up their time to share their memories. It is much appreciated. Also, thanks to Eileen O'Donnell for speaking to me at such a difficult time for her and her family.

Contents

	Foreword by Billy McNeill MBE	9
one	Finding a Manager	13
two	Building a Team	27
three	The Worst Possible Start	45
four	Europe – A Turning Point	57
five	A Winning Streak	69
six	Internal War	83
seven	Losing to Rangers	91
eight	Keeping the Title Hopes Alive	99
nine	Coca-Cola Cup Triumph	105
ten	Celebrating Success	113
eleven	Ne'erday Victory	123
twelve	Phil O'Donnell	139
thirteen	The Get-out	151
fourteen	The Run-in	161
fifteen	A Wasted Opportunity	173
sixteen	One in a Row	181
seventeen	The Aftermath	199
eighteen	The Main Men	215
nineteen	Back to Square One	225
	Results from the 1997–98 season	239

Foreword

I was at Easter Road for the opening league game of the 1997–98 season and watched Hibs defeat Celtic 2–1. I left Edinburgh later that afternoon thinking that Rangers would go on to achieve ten in a row. I felt quite down at the thought.

As much as I wasn't a part of the set-up at Parkhead any more, the forthcoming season had tremendous significance for me, as I had been part of the team that won nine titles with Celtic from 1966 to 1974. I knew that every player who had contributed something during that period would want that record preserved. Every Celtic supporter was also filled with dread at the prospect of Rangers beating our proud achievement.

First and foremost, the reason we won our titles was down to Jock Stein. He returned to the club and really galvanised us. We won the Scottish Cup in 1965, and he then took us away for a summer tour of America, a trip that lasted five and a half weeks but set the foundations for the following nine league championships. We came back a determined bunch and had real pride in our work to do well for Celtic and our supporters.

The first title in 1966 is the one that sticks out for me. It was the first title many of the squad had ever won, and it gave us all a taste for more. We never looked back from then on and went on to win the European Cup the following year. Some people might think it became easier to win the league with every passing season, but I believe each one became harder, no doubt about that.

That's why I had so much respect for Walter Smith and his players when they won nine championships from 1989 to 1997. They won their titles in a different fashion from us, as they entered into the transfer market and had the financial muscle to sign virtually any player in Britain. They did sign fabulous players, such as Brian Laudrup, Paul Gascoigne, Mark Hateley and Jörg Albertz. Of course, the nucleus of their squad was Scottish, with Richard Gough, Ally McCoist, Andy Goram, John Brown, Ian Durrant and Stuart McCall all making major contributions.

In contrast, much of our pride was down to the fact that we all came from within a 35-mile radius of Celtic Park, and, apart from a couple of players, we all came through the ranks.

During the season Rangers were going for ten, whenever I was asked about the significance of the campaign, I used to try to play it down and say it didn't bother me. Believe me, it did. It mattered a lot. There was no way we wanted Rangers to overtake our record. We didn't want them having the bragging rights and going down in the annals of football history.

Wim Jansen was the man selected by Fergus McCann to stop it from happening. He came in and had to start from scratch. He had a dreadful start but gradually got things together as the new signings arrived and made their mark. I think it really was a squad effort that season, but Craig Burley, Marc Rieper, Jackie McNamara, Simon Donnelly, Tom Boyd, Jonathan Gould, Henrik Larsson and Alan Stubbs all played very well.

It was no surprise to me that Wim took time to find his feet. It's not until you manage either half of the Old Firm that you realise the pressure and expectation levels involved. It's frightening, but it's also wonderful. Old Firm games, in particular, really get to you, in a different way from all other games. When I was manager, I used to get to Parkhead before ten in the morning, and as soon as I walked down the tunnel for a look at the empty stadium the ground would be talking to me. The 'Jungle' would be staring back at me, and I dared not let it down.

When I was manager of Manchester City, Tony Book was on the coaching staff, and he used to go on and on about the derby game against Manchester United. My first taste of one was at Maine Road. After the game, Tony asked me how it compared to an Old Firm game, and I told him it didn't even come close. I said the Manchester derby was like a 'Gala Day'. I arranged tickets for a midweek Old Firm game at Parkhead and took Tony along to show him exactly what I meant. As ever, the atmosphere was electric. As we drove back down the road, Tony didn't open his mouth until we were past Motherwell. 'Billy, I've never seen anything like that in my life.'

It spoke volumes for Wim and his players that they were able to bounce back from losing the first Old Firm game of the season. That 1–0 defeat at Ibrox really could have left them with no way back, but they rallied and picked up results. In my opinion, the turning point came when they defeated Rangers 2–0 in the New Year fixture. Wonderful strikes from Craig Burley and Paul Lambert sealed the win.

That crucial victory helped take Celtic towards the league title away to Dunfermline on the second-last day of the season. A win was required, and it looked good when Simon Donnelly scored. Craig Faulconbridge levelled, and I left Fife that afternoon deflated. I couldn't have felt any worse had I actually been the manager. As I drove home, the reservations I had on the opening day of the season resurfaced.

It was still in Celtic's hands, and they had one more chance to wrap it up. St Johnstone were the visitors to Parkhead, and goals from Henrik Larsson and Harald Brattbakk clinched the three points and the title. What a feeling.

I was manager of Celtic when Rangers won the first of their nine titles, but I take great pride in the fact that I won the championship in 1988 with Celtic to stop them winning that year, as Graeme Souness had led them to the title the previous season. Had we not won the league in our centenary year, it could well have been 11 in a row for Rangers!

I know the Lisbon Lions were all thrilled with the 1998 win: pleased for Wim and his players and relieved our record hadn't been surpassed. I suppose it was meant to be that both sides share this wonderful record.

It was nice to see Murdo MacLeod beside Wim. I signed Murdo for Celtic, and I was pleased to see him back for such an important season. It meant so much to Murdo. Davie Hay also made a significant contribution that season.

I shook Wim's hand after the game and offered my congratulations. Naturally, he was delighted, and it was a pity he felt the need to resign a couple of days later. Wim is a lovely man and will always have a proud place in Celtic's history books. I didn't used to like him because he played in the Feyenoord side that defeated us in the 1970 European Cup final! But, in many ways, he made up for that by winning the title in 1998.

Billy McNeill

one

Finding a Manager

On 2 May 1997, Celtic sacked Tommy Burns. It was a Friday evening and rumours had been rife since lunchtime that he was about to be dismissed. By the time it was made official at around 8.35 p.m., approximately 1,500 Celtic fans had gathered outside Parkhead to find out exactly what was going on. Surrounded by four security guards, Burns said nothing; he just waved at the fans as he left through the front door. His three-year contract expired on 13 July, and Celtic released a statement declaring their intention to pay him for its remaining eleven weeks.

Despite attractive and entertaining football, his time as manager came to an end because he and his players couldn't stop Rangers' dominance during his three years in charge. In a major shock, Celtic had just lost to First Division side Falkirk in the semi-final of the Scottish Cup, and Parkhead supremo Fergus McCann decided Burns was not the man to lead his club any longer. Indeed, in the aftermath of that result, Burns had been ready to resign but was talked out of it after a chance meeting with an old friend from Glasgow's Gallowgate. Burns had also told Billy Stark, his number two, that he was quitting before he changed his mind. But it was only a matter of time before the decision was made for him.

It was a turbulent time, and Burns wasn't the only one to lose his job. McCann was also unhappy with members of the board, and less than a week before he bulleted Burns, director Willie Haughey was also shown the door. Club secretary Dominic Keane resigned in protest at Haughey's dismissal. Celts in crisis? Well, were they ever in anything else during the previous decade?

The Falkirk result was the final nail in Burns's coffin, but it was likely that he would have been sacked regardless. From very early into his career as Celtic manager, there was no eye contact between him and McCann, their relationship having broken down within months of him accepting McCann's offer to come on board in the summer of 1994. One of the few things they could agree on was their disappointment in seeing Rangers reign supreme. Walter Smith's side were just about to clinch their ninth league title in a row and managed to do so on 7 May 1997. Brian Laudrup scored with a header against Dundee United at Tannadice to give the Ibrox club their most satisfying moment since they had won the European Cup-Winners' Cup in 1972 after a 3–2 victory against Moscow Dynamo in the Nou Camp stadium, Barcelona. On the same night that Rangers clinched the title, Celtic drew 0–0 at home to Kilmarnock. Stark was caretaker manager.

Rangers had always been in the shadow of their great rivals on two fronts: Celtic were the first British side to win the European Cup after their 2–1 victory against Inter Milan in Lisbon; and Jock Stein's side had a vice-like grip on the domestic game as they racked up nine titles on the trot from 1966 until 1974. But Laudrup's goal released one monkey from their backs and allowed Rangers the latest bragging rights.

McCann knew he had to respond and decided to completely restructure the 'football department' of Celtic Football Club. He was going to appoint a head coach to take charge of the day-to-day duties of coaching the players on the training field with full responsibility for team selection and, ultimately, results on a match day. But, in a Continental style, there would be a general manager, a new role at Parkhead, created by McCann to relieve the head coach of having to deal with player contracts and transfer negotiations. Burns had often become embroiled in such matters, which had led to countless disagreements and heated arguments between the chairman and manager.

Most of the Celtic squad were sorry to see Burns go.

Tom Boyd: 'We should have defeated Falkirk in the cup semi-final. We had a good team and should never have allowed them two chances. I remember Tommy Burns being very upset after that game and rightly so. If we had won, it would have given us a Scottish Cup final against Kilmarnock. Had we got there and won the cup, I'm sure Fergus McCann would have given Tommy one more year in the job. Fergus would argue Tommy had three seasons and that was long enough. I don't agree. I think managers deserve longer, providing that they show they are on the right track.

'Tommy had a lot to contend with when he became Celtic boss. He was up against Rangers, and they had an established squad and an open chequebook. We also had to play for one season at Hampden Park to allow for the redevelopment of Celtic Park. That didn't help Tommy's case.

'Sir Alex Ferguson was given five years to get it right at Manchester United, and he has repaid the club over and over again. However, had Sir Alex been working in the managerial climate of today, stretching back a decade, then he wouldn't be in that job. Davie Moyes has also rewarded Everton for their belief in him.

'I felt sorry for Tommy. However, for his own sake, maybe he was better to get away from the club that summer. When I see Tommy now, we have a laugh and a joke about what it was like under Fergus back then, but at the time it was no laughing matter.'

Alan Stubbs became the record transfer signing when he joined from Bolton Wanderers for £3.5 million in June 1996. Burns had hoped the ball-playing, composed central defender – tipped for a fine career at international level with England – would enhance the back-line, but Stubbs didn't make the impact in his first season that he and Burns had hoped for.

Alan Stubbs: 'I was so sorry Tommy didn't win the title in 1997. He wanted us to play the "Celtic way", and I think the team only suffered one defeat in the league the season before I arrived, yet it still wasn't enough. I was devastated when he lost his job. He wore his heart on his sleeve, and I'm sure if he was given the chance to do it all again, he would change things. I don't think he would allow himself to get too wrapped up in it all again. He used to carry the weight of the whole club and the expectation of every fan on his shoulders, and when we lost a game he gave the impression he was personally responsible and owed thousands of Celtic fans an apology. In managerial terms, he was a young man when he took over, and I think it would have been a different story had he been in charge five years later.'

McCann made it clear that he was willing to break with tradition and appoint a manager who had never played for the club or had an affinity with it, perhaps through Irish roots. McCann was determined to appoint the best man for the job and not the best 'Celtic' man for the job.

McCann certainly did away with tradition when he appointed the club's general manager on 21 June. Lawyer and broadcaster Jock Brown was handed the task of being the middleman between the football department and the boardroom. He would be responsible for contract and transfer negotiations. The head coach would also report to him to discuss transfer targets and leave Brown to attempt to conclude the deals.

Many Celtic supporters greeted Brown's appointment with trepidation. Being the brother of the then Scotland manager Craig Brown was not a problem. But certain elements of the Parkhead support felt that Brown displayed a bias towards Rangers, or a dislike of Celtic, and threatened to hand back their season tickets. (For what it's worth, Jock didn't grow up supporting Rangers or Celtic.) Brown had to appeal for calm and to be given time to prove he could do a good job for Celtic.

Brown's first task was to appoint a head coach. Davie Hay was already at the club, having worked there under Burns. He was the only survivor from that era, as Billy Stark had resigned as assistant manager a couple of weeks after Burns was sacked. Murdo

MacLeod – manager of Partick Thistle the previous season – was brought in to take over the role of reserve team manager on 24 June. John Clark – a Lisbon Lion – was brought in as kit controller. MacLeod was delighted to be back at Celtic Park.

Murdo MacLeod: 'I had just returned from a family holiday and didn't know what the future held. However, right out of the blue, Davie Hay phoned me at the house on the Thursday night. Davie was acting general manager of Celtic and was helping Fergus McCann to recruit coaching staff. We briefly discussed what it was about and then agreed to meet at a hotel near Glasgow Airport to discuss it in more detail. The meeting was good, and I had a lot of respect for Davie. He was my manager at Celtic, and I'll never forget winning the title on the final day of the season in 1986, and also the Scottish Cup final in 1985.

'The offer from Davie on behalf of Celtic was for me to join the coaching staff in some capacity. Because a first-team head coach was still to be appointed, Davie couldn't give me a precise job description. Depending on the thoughts of the new head coach, I could have ended up as reserve team boss or assistant head coach. I asked Davie for time to think it over. The prospect of going back to Celtic appealed, not least because of the magnitude of the season ahead. However, the money wasn't great, and I wanted to discuss it in detail with my family.

'A couple of days after I met Davie, Jock Brown was appointed as Celtic's general manager. Jock was immediately on the phone, as he agreed with Davie's decision to offer me a job. We arranged to meet for further discussions. Davie also came along with Jock. I was impressed with their plans and agreed to join. So, with what was at stake in the new season, in terms of attempting to stop Rangers from completing ten in a row, I wasn't going to throw away the opportunity to make a positive impression on a new head coach and a chance of working with the first team.

'You couldn't wipe the smile from my face. It was a fantastic feeling to be back at Celtic. I'd always hoped to return but never thought I'd be given the chance. The following day, a press conference was called to announce my arrival, and I posed for photos with Davie, Jock and John Clark, the Lisbon Lion who'd agreed to come to the club.'

Davie Hay: 'I was sad to see Tommy Burns leave us. It was unfortunate for him to be up against such a talented, exceptional Rangers team. But Tommy's teams did manage to play entertaining football and gave the fans some memorable moments. However, he suffered because of the success across the city, and Fergus McCann felt it was time for a change of manager. Tommy had been in charge for three years, and Rangers had just clinched nine championships on the trot.

'There was a lot of upheaval going on, and apart from needing to find Tommy's successor there was also the need to rebuild the team. Paul McStay was retiring, Pierre van Hooijdonk had been sold to Nottingham Forest, and Paolo Di Canio and Jorge Cadete wanted to leave because of a dispute over an increased financial contract they felt they were entitled to. But that wasn't my main concern. I was appointed interim manager but wasn't given any input by Fergus McCann over the appointment of the new manager. That might seem strange to some, but it's the way it was. However, I was allowed to bring in someone to be a part of the coaching set-up, and there really wasn't any time to waste.

'Murdo MacLeod was an up-and-coming coach and had been manager at Partick Thistle. He had played for me when I had been manager of Celtic, and he was a winner at that time and had gone on to pick up more experience abroad when he moved to Borussia Dortmund. I felt he had the credentials to come in and play some kind of role in the new regime. I phoned Murdo and we agreed to meet. The meeting went fairly well, and I had a feeling he would come on board once we got one or two minor things sorted out. Another meeting was arranged, but in the interim Jock Brown was appointed as general manager, a new role created by McCann as part of his vision for the way ahead.'

Although MacLeod was a vital component of the backroom team, Brown's priority was to appoint a successor to Burns.

McCann already had a list he was working his way through. From names put to him by agents making contact to recommend one of their clients, McCann's search had taken him all around the world. But now Brown was in charge of working his way through the rest of the candidates in a bid to get a quality coach on board.

Sir Bobby Robson was the man Celtic had expressed most interest in. He was in charge of Barcelona at the time and had a certain José Mourinho as his assistant, but the former England boss was stepping down at the end of the season to make way for Louis van Gaal.

Speaking in his autobiography after that event, Robson recalled how he came close to becoming the manager of Celtic in the summer of 1997. But there were other names under consideration. Brown used his contacts in the game, along with the knowledge of his brother Craig, to research potential appointments, digging into every detail of their background as a football person and a human being to make sure they ticked all the required boxes. However, Robson continued to be the main focus of attention, although Brown always insisted that he never spoke to him. That, of course, doesn't mean to say that no one from Celtic spoke to the respected former England manager.

An incredible list of 38 names appeared in the media linked to the Celtic job that summer. Most of the time, Celtic would refuse to give an off-the-record 'steer' as to whether a name a reporter had been given as being in the frame for the job was 'under consideration'. This led to the likes of Artur Jorge, Joe Kinnear, Stuart Baxter, Anghel Iordănescu, John Toshack, Wim van Hanegem, Christoph Daum, Gigi Maifredi and Nevio Scala being mentioned as being on the shortlist of candidates.

On 1 July, Robson officially ruled himself out of a move to Parkhead after he accepted an offer to 'move upstairs' at the Nou Camp. This was a serious blow to Celtic, and it left them in a bit of a panic. However, despite the task of trying to stop Rangers, and McCann having a reputation of being difficult to work for, there was no shortage of people wanting the job. On the same day, Celtic sold defender Brian O'Neil to Roy Aitken's Aberdeen for £750,000.

Wim Jansen's name was put forward and added to the list, albeit not very high up. However, as other names above him were scored off the list for a variety of reasons, Wim's credentials became more appealing. The Dutchman had an outstanding CV as a player. He was capped sixty-five times by Holland and had appeared in two World Cup finals, in 1974 against West Germany and in 1978 against Argentina. His name was first mentioned in the media on 26 June, and it was revealed that he was keen to land the job but wasn't sure if he was being seriously considered. Spanish side Tenerife were also said to be interested in him.

It was vital to get someone in. After Burns was sacked, McCann had stated that Celtic might well start the new season without a manager, and he would hold out for the right man to lead the club. But that just wasn't possible and exposed how naive McCann was in football matters. The players started pre-season training on 25 June and were disappointed not to have a successor to Burns in place.

Apart from there not being a manager, there was also the absence of club captain Paul McStay. On 16 May, McStay had announced his retirement from football. The Celtic skipper had an ankle injury and couldn't carry on after 15 years in the first team. He had made six hundred and seventy-seven appearances for the club, won three league titles and been capped seventy-three times by his country.

Meanwhile, Burns – having knocked back the chance to manage Reading – accepted an offer from Kenny Dalglish to become first-team coach at Newcastle United. Newcastle were immediately linked with a move for unsettled Celtic striker Paolo Di Canio, signed by Burns from AC Milan for £1 million a year earlier.

It wasn't unusual for Celtic to be attracting negative headlines. Of course, it was convenient for those with blinkers on to blame the media, but, in truth, the club didn't help itself, especially in regard to situations such as the Di Canio contract saga.

Across the city, Rangers appeared to be fine tuning an already well-run unit and had spent more than £14 million attracting players such as Lorenzo Amoruso, Sergio Porrini, Jonas Thern and Marco Negri to Ibrox. Brian Laudrup had looked set to quit that summer to join Ajax in a £6 million transfer but had changed his mind and opted to stay in Scotland. This was another boost for Celtic's rivals.

The Celtic players were desperate for a manager to be appointed.

Tom Boyd: 'For three or four weeks after Tommy's departure, the speculation surrounding who his replacement was going to be was crazy. There was no stability at the club, and we started pre-season training without a manager. Considering it was to be such an important season in the history of Celtic, that wasn't ideal. We were meant to be a big club, but we weren't acting like one. The players knew the season was all about stopping Rangers winning another title. We had to protect the history of Celtic Football Club. We were focused but needed a manager to give us proper guidance.'

Morten Wieghorst: 'Things were not great at the club. In fact, it would be more accurate to say it was chaotic. We tried to keep it calm in the dressing-room and switch off from what was going on off the park, but it wasn't easy. We just wanted a manager to be appointed so we could move on and try to bring some form of stability to the place. Slowly but surely, things got together and a bit of calm was restored, and we were then able to focus on the job ahead. I think Murdo also has to take a lot of credit, as he came in and tried to reassure the players that things would work out fine and that there would be plenty to be positive about once the new manager was in place.'

Murdo MacLeod: 'McCann and Brown worked behind the scenes to bring in a new head coach. In the meantime, I was in charge of pre-season training for the first team, and Willie McStay assisted me. We had a good bunch of lads to work with, but the squad lacked quality, experience and depth. Paul McStay had just retired and was going to be a major loss to the midfield engine room. Peter Grant was ready to leave to pursue a career in England. On top of that, Paolo Di Canio was in the huff, training on his own in Italy and refusing to come back because of a wages dispute with McCann. Jorge Cadete also had a problem and was allowed to remain in Portugal, away from our training, on medical grounds. Add all of that to the fact that there was no head coach in place, and it didn't make for the most stable of environments to work in. But I couldn't allow any of that stuff to get in the way of our preparation. I had to be professional, send out the right signals to the players and make sure that they were as fit as they possibly could be for the arrival of the new gaffer.

'During the first few days, I was none the wiser as to the situation with the appointment of a new gaffer. I was never consulted – not kept in the "loop". That was fair enough, I suppose. However, I did receive a phone call from a third party – someone with no official connection to Celtic – to tell me that Sir Bobby Robson had been approached about taking over at Celtic and was very keen to accept. During the same conversation, I was also told that he was aware of my position at Celtic and was happy for me to work as his number two that season. I was delighted with that news. It was great to know I was wanted and was going to have a role at the highest level.

'For reasons unknown to me, Robson never was appointed, and we had to set off for our pre-season camp in Holland without a manager. The players were unsettled with this. They were fed up seeing the club being criticised in the media for taking so long to appoint a replacement for Tommy Burns. Having witnessed Rangers winning nine in a row to equal Celtic's long-standing record, they were in a depressed state of mind and needed to know what direction we were going in very quickly.

'Rico Annoni always managed to smile. Perhaps, being a foreigner, he didn't realise the full extent of what was going on and just how important a season it was going to be for Celtic. He asked me if I was to be known as "Boss" with a smile on his face.

'Our pre-season training camp was in the south of Holland,

on the outskirts of Arnhem. It was a top base, often used by the Dutch national team. My only thoughts were to make sure that the players' fitness continued to get up to speed and that none of them tried to undermine our preparations by breaking any curfews and sneaking out for a few drinks. But we had a good bunch of lads, and I knew the senior professionals such as Tom Boyd, Alan Stubbs, Peter Grant, Gordon Marshall, Tosh McKinlay, Andy Thom, Tommy Johnson, Morten Wieghorst and Phil O'Donnell wouldn't attempt to pull the wool over my eyes. The last thing I or the club needed was any negative stories appearing about breaches of discipline.'

Given his experience and contacts in the game, you would have thought that Hay would have been asked for advice on a managerial appointment, but that wasn't the case.

Davie Hay: 'I had applied for the general manager's job and went through the interview process. I felt I conducted myself well and that I had the credentials to fulfil the role well, but McCann thought otherwise. I was disappointed not to get it, but the next day I had moved on from that and got my head down to make sure I would be a help to Jock and the football club. There was no hangover about not getting the job. Jock would act as the link between the football department and the boardroom. He would be responsible for helping to bring in a new head coach and from then on would conduct all transfer negotiations for players coming to Parkhead and going out the door. Jock had plenty to be getting on with. Not only was he trying to conclude a deal for a new gaffer, he was also dealing with the complications of the Paolo Di Canio and Jorge Cadete cases.

'Celtic had been linked with many names as possible head coaches, but I genuinely had no idea what was going on. I was never consulted, never asked for an opinion. The name doing the rounds inside the stadium was Bobby Robson. He appeared to be a clear favourite but that was never confirmed to me. Many names appeared in the media as being in with a chance of becoming manager, but I never knew the ones that were genuine contenders. What was decided was that I'd be given a promotion to become assistant general manager, an appointment I was delighted to accept.

'On the day the players returned for pre-season training, there was still no head coach in place. Murdo took the training, and when the squad set off a few days later for their training camp in Holland the situation was still the same. By that stage, Wim's name had been mentioned in the newspapers as a possibility. On the day we flew into Schipol Airport in Amsterdam, it became clear that Wim was the man Celtic were in pursuit of and that negotiations were well underway. That, however, was never confirmed to me by anyone at the club.'

On the morning Celtic flew into Amsterdam, one newspaper claimed that Jansen's appointment was imminent. On 3 July – just two days after Robson announced that he was staying at Barcelona – Celtic appointed fifty-year-old Jansen. After coaching spells in Saudi Arabia and Japan, Jansen was delighted to land the job and was prepared to meet the challenge of ending the Ibrox domination head on.

MacLeod was officially told about the appointment in a phone call that night to the camp in Holland. He then relayed the information to the players, and there was a sense of relief that the uncertainty was finally over. But Murdo had never met Wim before, and some of the players had a look of 'Wim who?' on their faces, which was perhaps understandable after the club had been linked with some household names. However, Murdo and a few of the senior players were aware of Wim's achievements in the game and that he had won the European Cup with Feyenoord in 1970 and had also played in World Cup finals with Holland. With that kind of CV, the team was willing to give the new man their full cooperation and effort.

The press didn't view Jansen's appointment as a masterstroke, and they believed that Walter Smith and his squad would go on to win the title once again and set a new record. But Jansen's close friend Johan Cruyff congratulated Celtic on making such a clever appointment.

With his curly hair and unimposing appearance, Jansen left Glasgow to join up with the squad in Arnhem. His task of restoring the glory days to Celtic Park was up and running.

Wim Jansen: 'I was invited by Jock Brown to speak to him about the Celtic job. A few days later, I was on my way to Glasgow. I was excited about the prospect of becoming the head coach of Celtic. It was definitely a job I wanted. Celtic is a huge club with a proud history. It is a club for its people. It reminded me of Feyenoord. I liked that kind of club.

'I was delighted to be offered the job. I conducted all of the negotiations myself. I did not have an agent. I had an agent as a player, but as a coach I felt I didn't need one. Ideally, I would have been appointed four or five weeks earlier. But this was the situation I found myself in, and I had to get on with it. I just wanted to get to the training camp as quickly as possible. There was not a second to waste.'

Davie Hay: 'Wim's appointment was confirmed to me by Jock. I was in Holland with Murdo and the squad, and was told that Wim would make his way out there to join us. By that point, we'd been there two days, and it was a relief for the players that the uncertainty that had surrounded the club for more than two months was now at an end.

'I flew home to conduct a piece of business and then flew back out to join Wim and Murdo in Holland. I only planned to stay for one night, but Wim wanted me there for longer and insisted that I stay on. I think that I only had one pair of socks and one pair of pants with me, but I showered well for the rest of the week!'

two

Building a Team

Now that the uncertainty was over, the players knew the real work was about to begin. Some of them had underachieved when Tommy Burns was in charge, and this was their chance to start with a clean slate and impress the new boss.

On the morning that Wim arrived back in his homeland at the pre-season camp, MacLeod took the training session. The new head coach stood on the sidelines and observed for a while. Then, halfway through the session, he was brought over by Jock to be introduced to Murdo and the players. Wim shook each and every one of them warmly by the hand. From the first moment Murdo met Wim, he had respect for him, as he had achieved plenty in the game. It was now McLeod's job to bring the Dutchman up to speed with the fitness of the squad and the standard of player he had to work with.

MacLeod also wanted to know what his future was under Jansen. He was only a temporary first-team coach, and Jansen had the final say on the role he would occupy. But MacLeod had no immediate targets about trying to win the Dutchman's respect in a bid to secure the number-two job. He had the attitude that he'd go about his business in a professional manner and would let things progress naturally – he didn't want to force the issue.

If he landed the job, great; if not, he'd keep his head held high and get on with the role that he was appointed to.

Jock Brown flew back to Scotland to conduct business from there. Davie Hay remained at the training camp to assist Wim and Murdo. They had a meeting immediately after training to discuss with Wim the challenge that lay ahead in trying to stop Rangers. Wim was conscious of the significance of the season ahead but, understandably, wasn't totally aware of just how much it would mean to so many people. An intelligent man, he quickly took it all in and knew exactly what was required.

Signing targets were also discussed at that meeting. Hay was chief scout during Tommy's reign as manager and had assembled a lengthy list of players he thought would enhance the squad. Names such as Craig Burley, Stéphane Mahé and Darren Jackson were on that list, and MacLeod suggested bringing John Collins back to the club from Monaco. Paul Lambert's name was also mentioned in that initial conversation, and Davie Hay got on the case, dealing with the player's then agent, Jim Melrose.

Wim had his ideas, and the first name he came up with was that of Henrik Larsson. Larsson was Wim's premier target, and Jock was told to pursue him. Wim knew the player from working together at Feyenoord, and they had a good relationship.

Another topic of conversation late into Jansen's first night in Holland was the need for a top-class striker, and it was decided that they would go for Pierre van Hooijdonk. Pierre had left the club six months earlier to join Nottingham Forest for around £4 million, but they had been relegated, and his preference was to return to Scotland instead of playing in England's second tier.

Pierre was on holiday in his home town of Breda at that time and travelled to Arnhem for a meeting with Jansen. Van Hooijdonk was a popular player in the dressing-room and with the fans, but a row with McCann over an improved contract had led to the Dutch internationalist moving to the City Ground. McCann regularly fell out with players over cash at that time: Di Canio and Cadete were also in dispute over their weekly wage.

Pierre listened to Jansen's plans and wanted to be a part of the new set-up. He had left Celtic Park with only a Scottish Cup-winners' medal to show for his time north of the border, and he wanted to return to help the club win the title.

Murdo MacLeod: 'We put Pierre's name to Jock, but we were quickly told that Fergus would not be in favour of bringing him back to the club. We were also told that John Collins was earning an excellent salary at Monaco and that we would not be able to compete with the kind of money he was on. It was frustrating to hear early on that signing targets were being ruled out. However, there was positive news in that the ball was rolling to bring in Henrik, Stéphane, Craig and Darren.

'It was of paramount importance that we brought in top players. Rangers had Brian Laudrup, Paul Gascoigne, Ally McCoist, Stuart McCall, Ian Durrant and Ian Ferguson on board. They were in the winning habit and knew exactly what it took to cope with the demands of being successful under the non-stop glare of the Old Firm spotlight.

'Walter Smith had also been given a significant budget to strengthen his squad and had spent millions bringing in three Italians – Lorenzo Amoruso, Marco Negri and Sergio Porrini. He also signed talented Swedish midfielder Jonas Thern from AS Roma on a Bosman. It was game on, and, at that stage, we were well behind them and had a mountain to climb without the proper footwear. The backroom staff, however, were up for the challenge, and we had to filter it through to the players that we could win the title.'

It was at this time that Davie Hay's football knowledge became vital. Having worked with Tommy Burns, he knew the strengths and weaknesses of every player. Although Burns suspected that he would be sacked several months before McCann chopped him, he still hoped to be kept on and had compiled a list with Hay on prospective summer signing targets. As a result, Jansen and MacLeod leaned heavily on Hay for information and on any progress that might have been made on players wanting to join the club. Hay knew

Celtic didn't have a squad capable of mounting a serious challenge to win the league. At least seven players had to be brought in, and more would be required if Di Canio and Cadete left.

Wim really wanted the pair to stay. He knew they had talent, and if they were in the right frame of mind, they would be assets on the pitch. Hay had been involved in bringing both to Celtic and had spoken to Bobby Robson about Cadete. Robson had worked with him at Sporting Lisbon and had given the player a glowing reference. But during the summer after Rangers had won their nine in a row, Cadete was reported to have developed psychological problems and was signed off work at Celtic by a Portuguese doctor.

Paolo joined Celtic later in their pre-season tour for a couple of games in Ireland, but it was easy to tell that his heart was no longer in it. He felt he had a verbal agreement with McCann for an improved contract but had nothing in writing. McCann denied that such an agreement was ever discussed.

The priority, however, was to bring in new players. In the past, Hay had recommended players to Burns. Now, he had to identify players that would fit into the team without much time to settle. He had to get the balance absolutely perfect.

Davie Hay: 'A lengthy list of potential signing targets had been assembled when Tommy was in charge. I was involved in putting that list together, having done many scouting missions, and I recommended a few of those targets to Wim.

'In the past, I had identified players, such as the "Three Amigos" [van Hooijdonk, Di Canio and Cadete], and Tommy had made the final decision. This time, however, was different. It wasn't just about looking at a player and assessing if he was good enough to play for Celtic and able to cope with the pressures that would bring. It was now about identifying a player that could fit into the team. It wasn't a case of bringing in players to supplement the squad. It was about building a new team. There was a lot more to it.

'We went about our business and pursued Darren Jackson, Stéphane Mahé and Craig Burley. Those names were on the list of the previous manager, and Wim trusted my judgement on them. It was good to know Wim had every faith in my suggestions, and much of that was down to the foreign mentality. Abroad, unlike in Scotland, the head coach is there to train the players and choose the team and tactics, but in many instances he is given the players he has to work with. It's a scenario they are comfortable with. Wim certainly was.

'From my point of view, I've always believed in being strong with your recommendations. If it is your job to scout for players for a football club, then you have to be decisive. That's why I always had a "Yes" or "No" answer for managers when it came to players. If I believed in a player, I would say, "Sign him," whereas some chief scouts would protect themselves and say to the manager, "Aye, the player is worth you taking a look at." For me, that's a total cop out.

'Wim had total trust in me and never questioned my judgement. But I have to admit, I had nothing to do with one of the greatest pieces of transfer business ever done by the club, that of Henrik Larsson for £650,000. Wim made it a priority for Jock to get Henrik. Wim had worked with him at Feyenoord and wanted to bring him to Parkhead. Under normal circumstances, it was a transfer that would have taken a couple of days to finalise, but Henrik was in the middle of a contract dispute with his Dutch club, and that delayed the transfer by a couple of weeks. I suppose, though, he was worth the wait!'

Jansen was impressed with MacLeod and Hay from the first meeting and knew that he had people around him with talent whom he could trust.

Wim Jansen: 'Murdo and Davie were a big help. I had to lean on them often, and they were always there for me. I knew from our first meeting together at the training camp in Holland that we could work well as a "threesome". Davie was very important. He'd been working as Celtic's chief scout and had some excellent contacts. He also had a list of players he thought would improve the squad. With Murdo, we worked through the list, and I added a few ideas of my own. Jock Brown would then do the paperwork to complete the signings.

'Apart from not having time on our side, we also didn't have a lot of money to spend. Murdo, Davie and I spoke about the players we had and the positions we urgently needed to strengthen. We were excited about the challenge, and the more time we spent together the more our confidence grew. But when you do not have the money you want to properly challenge your opponents, then it is not easy. You can't get good players for small, small money. But we had to try to do this. I didn't ask so much about budgets for players when I met with Celtic to speak about the job. I felt it was not the most important thing to speak about at that time.'

Celtic's first game under Jansen was a pre-season clash against Dutch amateur side FC Beatrix. Played on a Saturday night in front of no more than 1,000 spectators, they recorded a massive 21–0 victory. Jansen allowed himself to be guided by MacLeod that night, as he preferred to take on the role of observer.

Jansen liked the way MacLeod handled affairs during their three days working together, and on the Sunday afternoon he called the former midfield powerhouse for a meeting after they had eaten lunch with the players. Wim wasted no time in asking MacLeod if he wanted to become his assistant manager. Macleod was delighted to accept the offer. It was a special moment, and an honour for MacLeod to be asked by Wim to work with him in such an important season in the history of Celtic Football Club.

MacLeod: 'I'd won league titles with Celtic and played for Scotland in the 1990 World Cup finals in Italy, but Wim asking me to be his assistant is one of the most memorable moments I have from my time in the game. He must have felt I could be an asset and that I had the respect of the players, which was vital. I'll always be grateful to Wim for entrusting me with that role.

'Wim had a couple of things he wanted to put me right on, and the first thing was that he didn't want me standing at the edge of the technical area, shouting at the players. During the game against Beatrix, I was out on the touchline, asking the boys not to let their standards slip and to keep going. Alan Stubbs was pinging passes here, there and everywhere, and I wanted that to be the case until the final whistle. Wim said that we would sit together in the dugout. If changes needed to be made or instructions relayed to the players, we would discuss it, and one of us would quietly stand up and tell the players our thoughts.

'I couldn't wait to get on the phone to tell Mhairi and our daughters the good news. My wife was chuffed to bits. If there was one club the whole family would have chosen for me to go and work for, then it would have been Celtic, but it's not often that dreams become a reality.

'I knew I would learn from Wim, and working with him was an education. We hit it off together, although he was a different manager from what we would expect in the Scottish game. He never shouted and bawled, and he never swore. It was different from what I was used to, and the players also found it a little bit strange at first. For example, after we lost a pre-season friendly, I expected him to read the riot act, but Wim remained calm and told the players to go away and have a think about their contribution to the game. The whole group would then speak about it the next day. It was quite funny, but you could see the logic in it. From early on, I could see he had great knowledge of the game and a great eye for quickly sussing out players' strengths and weaknesses.'

Apart from assembling a backroom team, Jansen had to appoint a captain. Peter Grant and Alan Stubbs had filled in the previous season when Paul McStay was injured, but there was also a clear shout for giving the armband and responsibility to Tom Boyd. Able to occupy a number of positions in defence, Boyd was going to play every week. He was also an experienced internationalist and had the respect of the dressing-room.

Grant was looking to move on and several English clubs were interested in him, and Stubbs wasn't totally settled at Celtic and had asked to leave the previous season for personal reasons. Jansen discussed the situation with MacLeod and Hay, and they all agreed that Boyd was the sensible selection.

Tom Boyd: 'Wim was appointed, and, like most of the boys, I hadn't a clue who he was. I had no idea what he had achieved as a manager, and his appointment came as a big surprise to me. Wim made me captain, and it was an honour – one of the proudest moments of my career to follow in the footsteps of legends such as Billy McNeill and Danny McGrain.'

Wim was happy with a number of the squad but also knew that he had to get players in. Paul Lambert was another signing target they were desperate to land. Lambert had helped win the European Cup for Borussia Dortmund just a few months earlier, and there was no doubt that he would bring many positive attributes to the club. He was unsettled in Germany, and the indications were that he would be happy to come back to Scotland to play for Celtic. The details were passed on to Jock Brown.

Wim knew that a dominant centre-half was required, and Marc Rieper's name came up in a conversation with Hay and MacLeod. Rieper had plenty of experience from playing with Denmark and was with West Ham in the English Premiership. Wim fancied him, but he knew that Harry Redknapp would be in no rush to sell. Again, Rieper's details were passed to Jock.

That Gianluca Vialli might be willing to move to Parkhead came as a bit of a shock. Agents had indicated that he would be interested in playing in Scottish football and that he was aware of Celtic. But the salary was going to be around £1 million a year, and Wim questioned whether Vialli, after a successful career with Juventus and Italy, would still have the necessary hunger to do well. However, his name was not discarded, and Jock made further checks. Karl-Heinz Riedle was also suggested, and Wim decided he wanted to pursue him. Again, though, word came back from Jock that he was too expensive.

A different name seemed to be mentioned every day as a signing target for Jansen. Giovanni van Bronckhorst – then at Feyenoord who went on to sign for Rangers the following summer – was linked with the club. Others, such as Orlando Trustfull of Sheffield Wednesday and Inter Milan's Swiss midfielder Ciriaco Sforza, also rated mentions. Powerful Dutch defender Ulrich van Gobbel was the next name reported to be interesting Jansen, and he was then joined on the list of possibilities by England veteran Peter Beardsley.

As it was, the first player to arrive under Jansen's tenure was Darren Jackson. The Scotland striker, who could also play in midfield, joined from Hibs in a £1.25 million deal on 12 July. Wim didn't know anything about Jackson, but MacLeod and Hay told him that he was one of the best players in the country at that time and that he had an appetite for success. He could play up front or as a midfielder, and he had plenty of aggression.

Jackson had been at Hibs for five years after moving to Easter Road from Dundee United and was to turn 31 later in July. But he wasn't the most popular of players with the Celtic supporters, and his signing didn't go down too well. Jackson knew that he had a job on his hands to work things in his favour and change the fans' opinion of him as a footballer.

Darren Jackson: 'I didn't grow up a Celtic man, and when I signed I felt I had to win over the Celtic fans, as I had a hate-hate relationship with them. But I wasn't liked by most opposition fans. I know that I irritated fans, but I'd also like to think it was because of my ability. But it was a challenge I was looking forward to. I had to win the Hibs fans over when I signed there and managed to do so. I felt confident I'd also make a good impression on the Celtic fans. Celtic fans prefer to see their "own" wearing the jersey, but I knew that as long as I gave my all they'd be satisfied.

'The initial interest from Celtic came when Tommy Burns was in charge. My agent, Raymond Sparkes, knew Tommy was interested, and I told Raymond to relay a message that I'd love to sign for the club. A few weeks later, Tommy was sacked by Celtic, and I thought the chance had passed me by. I was almost 31 and was desperate for the chance to play for a club like Celtic. I was so disappointed.

'But Celtic started to appoint people into different roles at the club before they unveiled the new manager, and John Clark came in to look after the kit room. John had tried to sign me for Cowdenbeath years earlier, so I knew he liked me. Murdo MacLeod was appointed to the coaching staff, and we were teammates at Hibs. So, I felt there was still a wee chance.

'When Wim Jansen was appointed, there was talk that I was on his list. My name must have been put to him by Davie Hay and Murdo, and he agreed to sign me. Hibs accepted a bid of around £1 million, and I was on my way. I never met Wim before I signed. Raymond met with Jock Brown and Eric Riley and sorted my terms on a three-year contract to become Wim's first signing. My move was confirmed on a Saturday morning, and that's when I was paraded to the media. I knew I wasn't the big signing the fans wanted, and I was apprehensive. I was asked to go out onto the front steps of Celtic Park, as a few hundred fans had gathered. I stood for photos and held a Celtic scarf above my head, but some fans weren't happy with me joining the club and there were a few boos. It wasn't nice to hear.

'So, there was no doubt that I had a challenge on my hands, and I was determined to prove a point. I didn't want to prove the doubters wrong – it was more a case of wanting to prove Wim and the football department right for signing me.

'I never felt strange walking into the Celtic dressing-room. Several of the players were in the Scotland squad, and it was just a case of blending in. After a few days, I went away with the squad to a tournament in Ireland. I was told to room with Paolo Di Canio and was delighted. Paolo was in dispute with Celtic, and he often arrived into the room in a bad mood, his fiery temper ready to come to the fore. I tried to calm him down, and I often told him that I wanted him to stay, as I would have loved the chance to play with him, the chance to watch him entertain on the field.

'At least I got to see him in action in the hotel room, which was also entertaining. He used to do sit-ups and press-ups – that's when he wasn't on his mobile phone. In the conversations I had with him, he told me he loved it at Celtic and loved the fact he was adored by 50,000 fans every week, fans who idolised his every move.'

The day before Jackson signed, Celtic were publicly linked with Henrik Larsson, although the player's name had been given to Brown by Jansen on his first day at the club. It was to take another two weeks before the Swedish striker finally got the chance to move to Glasgow and start an amazing seven-year association during which he achieved legendary status.

Before Larsson arrived, there was plenty more activity, with McCann pulling out the chequebook on a few occasions to enhance the playing squad and give Jansen a fighting chance of winning the title. Players already at the club were involved in contract negotiations, and despite the fact that it was widely known that Celtic were in the market for a left-back, Tosh McKinlay signed a two-year extension to his contract on 7 July. The following day, Celtic defeated FC Veere 8–0 in the next game of their Dutch tour.

Celtic then moved to Ireland to continue their preparations for the new season with a three-game tournament. Despite Di Canio joining them, they didn't manage to win a game. They lost 3–2 to Derry City and were booed off the pitch by the travelling fans. They then drew 2–2 with PSV Eindhoven and drew 1–1 with St Patrick's in their final 90 minutes on 18 July. On their return from Ireland, MacLeod was officially announced as Jansen's assistant manager.

The next seven days was a busy time in the transfer market, and the squad began to take shape. Craig Burley signed from Chelsea on 24 July in a £2.5-million deal. Celtic knew the Scotland internationalist would give them strength and presence in the engine room. Craig had a bit of stature about him, which was required after the loss of Paul McStay. He wasn't a regular for Chelsea, and he needed to play week in, week out to make sure he was part of the Scotland set-up. It was thought that he could help Celtic to win silverware.

Craig Burley: 'I had been on the list of the two previous Celtic managers before Wim arrived. Lou Macari tried to sign me when he was in charge. He phoned me one Sunday afternoon when I was at home, and I thought it was someone at the wind-up and told him to fuck off. I was a kid at that time and didn't fancy moving back to Scotland. I really wanted to try and make my mark in England. Tommy Burns was also interested, but, again, my first choice was to stay with Chelsea.

'It then got serious when Wim took over. He wouldn't have known who I was and would have been going on the recommendation of Murdo and Davie. Again, my preference was to stay with Chelsea, but Ruud Gullit had just left me out of the 1997 FA Cup-final victory against Middlesbrough. I was angry at that decision. Chelsea had offered me a new four-year contract and a testimonial. The testimonial didn't mean much, to be honest. Kerry Dixon was a total legend at Chelsea, and I think less than 5,000 fans turned up for his testimonial, so you can imagine how many would have turned up for mine!

'The call came in that I could speak to Celtic after they had agreed a fee of around £2.5 million with Chelsea. I had other options – Martin O'Neill wanted to take me to Leicester and Gordon Strachan made it clear that he wanted me to play for him at Coventry. I beat both of them to it at Celtic!

'The truth is that I really didn't want to play football in Scotland. England was always my thing, and that stemmed from my uncle George playing most of his career down there. I really had mixed feelings about my move to Celtic, and so did Sheryl. But Celtic offered me a five-year deal and a good hike in my weekly wage.

'I had no idea about the nine-in-a-row stuff. I really didn't. Yes, I was brought up in Cumnock, but I never had the slightest bit of interest in the Old Firm or the religious baggage that came with it all. I never gave a shit about any of that stuff. I played football morning and afternoon from when I was at primary school, and I was only interested in the team I was playing for. The only senior games I went to see were the ones my dad, Tom, took me to. He was a linesman, and I'd go with him to his games.

'The day I was to sign, I couldn't find Celtic Park. I didn't know Glasgow and had no idea where the stadium was. And the day went from bad to worse. Sheryl was with me, and she sat in the Jock Stein Lounge as I went about my media duties, doing interviews with telly, radio and the papers to publicise my signing. I also posed for photos. I think that I was away for near enough two hours. Sheryl was left on her own, which I thought was unprofessional. When I eventually found her, she was in tears and asked me if I could call off the transfer. She didn't want to be at Celtic and didn't want to move back to Scotland. She was also from Cumnock but enjoyed living in England. I wasn't overly enamoured, either. I really questioned myself about the move, and I would have called it off if I could have. But I had signed the contract and had to get on with it.

'So, the club didn't appear to be putting too much effort into helping me and my family settle, and the fans weren't jumping through hoops at my signing. The Celtic fans were unsure of me, and there were mixed opinions about them signing me for such a large fee.

'But the time was right to get away from Chelsea and try something different. So, I went from an arrogant Dutchman in Gullit to a Dutchman I'd never heard of in Wim. But I could tell from our first meeting that Wim was a nice man, although I had yet to form an opinion of him as a manager.'

Celtic felt it was important to get some players in who knew the Scottish game. The management team was not against bringing in foreigners, but they had to gel quickly, so it was important to sign as many English-speaking players and ones that wouldn't need time to adjust to the pace and charged atmosphere of the Scottish Premier League.

Jansen was still desperate to bring in Larsson, but his contractual situation was causing a delay. Wim knew he'd get him; it would just take time. Jansen assured MacLeod and Hay the guy would be worth the wait. Larsson signed 24 hours after Burley.

Jansen also wanted to keep Paolo Di Canio, which he made clear to Jock Brown. However, the problems between Di Canio and the club were deep-rooted, and the coaching staff never really believed that they would be resolved to the point that the player would rejoin the squad in the proper frame of mind for such an important campaign.

The search for new players continued. Jansen was encouraged by Brown, where possible, to target players with a re-sale value, which was fair enough. That was one of the reasons why Kieron Dyer was targeted by Jansen a few weeks into the season. Dyer was just 18 and playing regularly in the Ipswich first team. He was an energetic midfielder, and Jansen thought he would be a great signing for Celtic. The fee would have been in the region of £2 million, and Wim thought that it was a worthwhile investment, as Dyer could come to Scotland, further his career and reputation, and be sold back down to England for at least double the price Celtic had paid for his services. However, Jansen's recommendation was not backed by his employers, and a move to bring Dyer to Celtic was never sanctioned. Around 18 months later, the young player moved to Newcastle in a deal in the region of £6 million, and he then won a call-up to the full England squad. It was the opinion of the football staff at Celtic that not going for Kieron was a wasted opportunity and demonstrated a lack of foresight.

Players continued to be linked with a move to Parkhead. The latest was striker Marcio Santos, a £3-million rated Brazilian playing for Ajax. It also emerged that Manchester City were keen to take Tommy Johnson away from Parkhead on a loan deal. And left-back Stéphane Mahé was signed in a £500,000 transfer from French side Rennes.

Stéphane Mahé: 'It was a huge step for me to come to Scotland. I knew no one there, I couldn't speak a word of the language, and when I looked around the leagues, there weren't a lot of French players anywhere. I was one of the first to move over from France, and I was nervous. But from the second I arrived in Scotland to the day I left, I had a terrific time. I had just left Rennes and was a bit unhappy. I needed something else, something to give me my spark back again, and Celtic was the perfect fit for me. It was like falling in love again. Everything about Scotland and about Celtic excited me. I came over to speak with Wim Jansen, and when he showed me the vast stadium, I thought, "Wow, this really is a great club."

'As each day passed and I learned more and more about the incredible history of Celtic, I fell more and more in love with it. The language of football is universal, and we had such a friendly, spirited squad of players in my first season that you couldn't fail but settle in. The passion the fans have for their club is unrivalled. I can't think of anywhere else in the world that can claim to have fans like Scotland does. Here was a club with 60,000 fans who don't turn on you after a bad performance. They don't boo you, and they don't make you feel unhappy. It's not in the Scottish nature to do that.

'Wim Jansen was also a big help to me. The first thing you want from a coach is to know that he wants you, that he *really* wants you in his team. He made that clear when he had signing talks. Then you want an ambitious and determined man. He was certainly that. He came with a clear goal in mind – to stop Rangers from creating history by winning ten in a row. He brought in so many new faces, they all settled quickly, and we gelled into a great side that was clearly going places.'

But the real drama in the transfer market was just around the corner. The messy Di Canio affair eventually came to an end on 6 August when he was transferred to Premiership side Sheffield Wednesday in a deal worth around £3 million in cash to Celtic and Dutch winger Regi Blinker moving to Parkhead from Hillsborough. The transfer was more or less thrashed out in an Amsterdam hotel four days earlier when Celtic officials met with Wednesday boss David Pleat and his directors. The Italian winger had been AWOL since 19 July, the night he shook his teammates by the hand in the Celtic home dressing-room and told them that he was returning to his homeland, never to play for Celtic again. Di Canio was fined by the club for leaving without permission, but he did not care and said he would go to court to challenge the deduction from his wage packet.

He left Glasgow Airport with a parting shot aimed at Jock Brown, saying: 'Jock Brown is trying to turn the Celtic fans against me. It is nearly impossible for us to beat Rangers this season, as they have two good teams, and we don't even have one.'

The transfer soon took on even more significance. Jock Brown angered the media and was accused of misleading them, as the night before Paolo Di Canio signed for Sheffield Wednesday the Celtic general manager had repeatedly insisted that the player would not be sold. His justification for this assertion was that the player was 'traded' to Wednesday and was not a direct transfer, as Regi Blinker was part of the deal. Brown, a former journalist and broadcaster, had many friends in the media until that day. He lost the respect of a number of former friends and colleagues. To put it simply, quite a few in the media felt he could not be trusted when giving out information in his role as general manager.

Signs of Brown's way of working were visible the previous week when Henrik Larsson was paraded at his media conference in the Parkhead boardroom. Always keen to take centre stage and speak when not directly spoken to, the general manager waxed lyrical about how Larsson had demonstrated that he knew all about Celtic and the proud history of the club when they'd met in the early stages of the contract negotiations. With reference to Brown's comments, Larsson was then asked by a journalist to expand on what he knew about Celtic, and the Swede was honest enough to admit that he wasn't sure what Brown was talking about, as he knew next to nothing about the club.

The press conference at Parkhead to introduce Blinker should have been about the player's move to the Hoops. Instead, Brown was given a hard time by the media and asked to explain his words the day before about Di Canio's situation. Clearly fidgeting and then banging his fist on the table in front of him, Brown insisted that he had not misled anyone and that instead it was the media's fault for not wording their questions to him carefully enough. Blinker was completely bewildered watching the drama unfold.

Regi Blinker: 'My career at Sheffield Wednesday started well, and I scored two goals on my debut in a 3–2 defeat against Aston Villa. David Pleat signed me, but he had Orlando Trustfull and later Benito Carbone in the squad, and he looked upon us as luxury players. Unfortunately, David only played with one luxury player in his starting line-up.

'I wasn't too happy at Sheffield, and Wim Jansen found out. I don't know how, but I was told he was keen to sign me. Part of the reason was because he had taken me to Feyenoord when I was just sixteen and had given me a five-year contract the following year. I played in the 1993 Feyenoord title-winning side under Wim van Hanegem. Wim Jansen was technical director that season.

'I got a call to say Wednesday had given me permission to speak to Celtic. My first thought was that Celtic were a big club, but the Scottish Premier League would not test me enough, and that it would be quite easy from week to week. It was a natural thought to have.

'Discussions must have taken place at the other end, with Paolo Di Canio going the other way. I don't know why, but the deal was complicated, and it meant Celtic holed me up in a room for two days in the Glasgow hotel One Devonshire Gardens, until they could announce my signing. I remember going out for a walk one afternoon during that time, and I made my way along Great Western Road. I got to the junction at the Botanic Gardens and turned left towards Maryhill Road. There was nothing much to see, and it made me think that there wasn't a lot in Glasgow and that it was quite a boring city. Of course, had I turned right that day and gone down Byres Road, my initial outlook would have been so different.

'Eventually, Paolo Di Canio sorted out his contract, allowing me to conclude my move to Celtic. I was introduced to the home support for the first time when I came on the pitch during a midweek friendly against Roma. I was given an excellent reception, and as I looked around the stadium it hit me just how big a club I was joining. I met Paolo a couple of times in Sheffield when I was back to finalise my removal arrangements, and we spoke about Celtic. He told me it was a big club and a special club. At that time, I didn't realise the full extent of the ten-in-a-row implications. Why should I? It didn't make a big impression on me at first, but after a couple of weeks I was in no doubt what it meant to the fans on both sides of the city.'

Di Canio's departure left Rico Annoni as the sole Italian at the club. The two players were friends, and the Celtic coaches thought that the defender would try to arrange a ticket out of the club. But Annoni stayed and went on to enhance his cult status with the Celtic fans, although he rarely featured in Jansen's starting line-up during the season.

Rico Annoni: 'When Paolo left, perhaps some people thought I would want to go back to Italy. Yes, we were both Italian, but we had different characters. I wanted to stay in Glasgow and try to do something for Celtic. Glasgow is a great city, and I miss staying there. My daughter, Sederica, misses it and tries to go back as often as she can. It was an interesting period in my life, for reasons on and off the park. I found the whole Catholic and Protestant thing fascinating. I am Catholic, but never had any problems with the Protestant people. I had respect for them and their feelings. I think Glasgow has a nice society.'

Jansen was still keen to bring people in. He thought that it was important to sign a goalkeeper, and Jonathan Gould joined the club on a free transfer from Bradford on 2 August as competition for Gordon Marshall and Stewart Kerr. With the signing of the new keeper, Jansen was one step closer to creating a squad that would be ready for the challenges of the new season.

three

The Worst Possible Start

Forty-eight hours after signing Gould, the league season started for Celtic in a live Sky television clash against Hibs at Easter Road. It was supposed to be the day a marker was laid down under the new manager, a day when Rangers would find out that they had a major fight on their hands to win the tenth title they so craved. Celtic wore their bumble-bee strip of yellow and black hoops, but there was little buzz from them. Hibs were all over the top of them, not giving their opponents a minute's peace from the kick-off.

Self-confessed Celtic fan Chic Charnley ran the show from start to finish. The Hibs midfielder had a terrific game, a performance that started a campaign for him to be included in Craig Brown's Scotland squad. Full of natural talent, Charnley swaggered about the pitch, slowing the play down and speeding up the tempo when required. Hibs took the lead in the 20th minute. Tony Rougier raced down the left wing, sent over a low cross and Lee Power was there to knock the ball past Marshall from close range.

The equaliser came nine minutes later when Malky Mackay rose above the Hibees' defence to bullet a header past Ólafur Gottskálksson. Mackay split his head open in the process after a clash of heads with Brian Welsh. The towering defender got bandaged up and came back on.

Celtic introduced Henrik Larsson in the 58th minute for his debut. Celtic looked the likelier side to score at that stage, and Tommy Johnson and Darren Jackson both came close. Stevie Crawford then hit the crossbar for Hibs before Charnley scored the winner – and it was a disaster for Larsson. He was short with a pass intended for Jackson, and Charnley intercepted about 30 yards from goal. He strode forward, lined up a shot and then sent a powerful left-foot drive in on Marshall. The ball swerved and found its way past the Celtic keeper. Charnley deserved his goal, and Hibs merited the three points. It was the first win the Easter Road side had recorded in the league over Celtic in twenty attempts, a record that stretched back four years.

Larsson came in for criticism for his performance and was blamed for the pass that had allowed Charnley the opportunity to shoot, although Larsson later blamed Jackson.

Darren Jackson: 'Henrik said that it wasn't a bad pass and that it was my fault for not coming to the ball. He was wrong. It was a bad pass, and I would have transferred him right after that game! I knew nothing about Henrik before he arrived, and we could have got off to a better start. Henrik passed straight to Chic for the winning goal, and I lost on my return to Easter Road. I got pelters from the Hibs fans, but I loved it. I scored a goal, but it was ruled out for offside. It was a dreadful start.'

Malky Mackay: 'We were all under severe pressure. We were entrusted with the task of keeping the history of the club intact. Jock Brown had a chat with the players on the way ahead for the club. Then we appointed a new manager. When Wim came in it was a case of "Wim who?"

'We lost to Hibs, and I scored that day when I grabbed the equaliser. I just remember playing on with a bandage. It would have been nice if my goal had contributed to us getting something out of the game, but sadly it wasn't to be.'

Jansen accepted that Hibs were worthy of the victory and once again stated his desire to bring in new faces to help his side. He, MacLeod and Hay knew that it was impossible for their side to win the league with the players they had at their disposal. Celtic were fragile and short of quality. Paul Lambert continued to be spoken of as a priority signing, but there was resistance from within the camp to give the coach the man he wanted.

Davie Hay: 'Jonathan Gould arrived, and that was down mainly, I think, to Jock. A central defender was badly needed, and Wim had a couple of ideas. But, for different reasons, no deals could be concluded. I suggested Marc Rieper to him, and Wim nodded his head in approval.

'Paul Lambert was another one we wanted to bring in. However, I think there was a clause in his Borussia Dortmund contract that meant if he was transferred before a certain date then Motherwell were due some financial compensation, although I'm not entirely sure about that. We felt Paul was worth waiting for, although we did scout a couple of other potential targets, such as Ipswich's Jim Magilton.'

To get the Hibs defeat out of their system, Celtic needed a game that would guarantee them a win, and they were relieved to see the fixture calendar come up with a Coca-Cola Cup tie away to Berwick Rangers the following Saturday afternoon. Berwick switched the match to Tynecastle, but their Coke dream went flat early on, and they never recovered as Celtic easily won the game 7–0. It was Blinker's first game, and he made a fine impression but was quick to point out in the post-match interviews that he was not the 'new' Di Canio and was his own man. The Dutchman grabbed his side's third goal. Jackson opened the scoring, and Larsson, Wieghorst and Thom took the margin to five by the half-time whistle. After the break, sub Donnelly chipped in with a double to complete a healthy scoreline, albeit against part-time opposition.

The loss to Hibs seemed to be a distant memory by the time Celtic played in the league again two weeks later. Dunfermline were the visitors to Parkhead, and three points should have been a formality. The lead was taken in the 38th minute through Thom after Hamish French was penalised by referee Martin Clark for bringing down Larsson. But Celtic were still fragile, and their supporters were yet to be convinced by the Dutchman and the squad he was assembling. And their doubts were proved correct when Dunfermline exposed the weaknesses in the home side and David Bingham levelled. Then, with 14 minutes to go, Mackay fouled Allan Moore, and French scored with ease past Gould from the penalty spot.

The defeat left Celtic with no points from their opening two games, and there was serious concern that their title bid was already finished. On the evidence of their league games, the team looked as much of a shambles on the park as the club had off it during pre-season in their search to find a new head coach. The fans turned on Jansen, and those who had questioned his appointment in the first place seemed to have had a good point. Even after only two league games, a lot of the Celtic fans wanted the Dutchman dismissed. Jansen would later reveal that he too thought about quitting at that time.

Reservations were also expressed in the dressing-room about Jansen's ability to do the job, and the players asked for a meeting to discuss the tactics he was employing. The players were not comfortable with a couple of things, and the new manager agreed to play a system that they were more accustomed to.

Tom Boyd: 'We lost our first two games and were rapidly falling behind. I suppose, in many ways, it was to be expected, as we had lost Paul McStay to injury, and Paolo Di Canio and Jorge Cadete had made it clear that they had no intention of playing for the club again. Those players had yet to be replaced. However, across the road at Ibrox, Rangers were building from a position of strength.

'There was turmoil around the club after we lost to Dunfermline. And there was pressure on us from the fans. In footballing terms, it was a disaster. I went home after the Dunfermline game and felt we were definitely going to struggle to win the league. If truth be told, I thought Rangers were strong, strong favourites, perhaps as big a certainty as they'd been at any other time during their nine-in-a-row achievement. It was a hard thing for me to admit, but that was the way I felt.'

Darren Jackson: 'We lost at home to Dunfermline to go bottom of the table. The fans were baying for blood. We had a meeting after the game, and a few home truths were spoken. Wim pulled us all in and asked what was going on.

'Every player had his own opinion on what the problem was and some felt that it was down to the tactics being wrong. I believed we were lacking a "togetherness". A lot of foreigners were brought in, and we were strangers. We needed to bond. To put it bluntly, we needed to copy what Rangers had had across the road for a decade. When I was on Scotland duty, I'd see Ally McCoist, Stuart McCall, Andy Goram and Gordon Durie always going around together. I wouldn't say that they were a clique; they were more like brothers. We needed some of that spirit to be able to achieve what we needed to.

'The foreigners and Wim needed to know exactly what was at stake. They needed more education on how important the season was – what stopping 'ten' was all about. With all due respect to the foreigners, I don't think they knew just how big the Old Firm were. They had no idea what the club meant to hundreds of thousands of people all around the world and just how desperate other teams were to beat us. I think Paul Le Guen also found that to his cost when he took over at Rangers. If you underestimate the size of the club, you are in trouble.'

Craig Burley: 'I didn't want to fail at Celtic. The fee Celtic paid for me wasn't a concern, but fucking up was. I wanted to produce a high level of consistency over the season. My level of fitness was really poor at the start. Because the English season started later, I was over a week behind my new teammates. I was pitched right in for a pre-season friendly at home to Parma. I was shittin' myself, because I wasn't fit. Thankfully, I played fine and got through it. The Parma boys turned up with the beach shorts on and that suited me.

'It then started to go wrong in the first two games of the season. My main memory of the Dunfermline game is running out wide to collect the ball trackside to take a throw near the end of the match when we were losing. A fan leaned over and shouted, "Why don't you just fuck off back to Chelsea." I wished I could have. I'd have gone back in a minute. I didn't want to be at Celtic. From then on, I didn't take another throw-in – I left it to the full-backs! Paul Lambert and I used to joke we'd try to get through a game without taking a throw-in.

'The reaction of that fan showed the intensity of the situation – what that season was all about. At Chelsea, we'd win a couple of games and then lose a couple, and it was sort of accepted. In Glasgow? No. No way. You had to win every game. I had to get to grips with that. It was finger out time, because we were in the shit after two games. The fans on the radio phone-ins that night wanted Wim sacked. Nobody would have given us a chance of winning the league at that point, and that was fair enough. We didn't look good enough and didn't look like we would gel as a team.

'I think eight new signings arrived that summer, and it was as if they'd signed on the Thursday, trained on the Friday and been told to stop ten in a row on the Saturday. We had a Dutch manager nobody had heard of and a commentator as general manager. And we had 50,000 unhappy fans. Stop Rangers winning the league? Yeah, no problem! Looking back on it now, it was crazy stuff . . .'

Jonathan Gould also thought that the situation was crazy – but he was delighted about it. He could not believe his luck that he was getting a move to Celtic after being frozen out by Bradford. And he was determined not to be a back-up. He had his sights on becoming number one, and it didn't take long for that to happen.

Jonathan Gould: 'I had been told by Bradford that I was free to leave if I could find myself a club. I was right on the phone to Ronnie Moore at Rotherham and someone involved with Scarborough. Both clubs declined to take me, as they felt I was not what they were looking for. I was down, wondering what the future held for me. Then, out of the blue, the Scottish agent, Murdo Mackay, phoned to say that Celtic were looking for a keeper and there might be something there for me. I didn't waste a second and got right on the phone to my dad. Through his relationship with Craig Brown,

Dad knew Jock Brown. I asked him to make the call to find out if there was anything concrete in it.

'Dad spoke to Jock and called back to say that there was a possibility something might happen. Jock was going to speak to Wim and Murdo [MacLeod] to get their thoughts. Dad told me to keep my mobile phone handy. The thumbs up for the deal could happen at any minute, as Celtic needed to sign a keeper that day to beat the European signing deadline. I was quite excited but not holding out too much hope.

'I had to train with the Bradford youth team that day and spoke to Chris Hutchins to ask if I could take my mobile to training, as there was an important phone call coming through. He said it was no problem but asked if I could take the warm-up. There I was, trying to put the kids through their paces, holding a mobile phone. Now, think about it, back then mobiles weren't the dinky little ones you get these days. No, this phone was the size of a large brick and weighed just as much!

'Sure enough, the phone rang, and it was Jock. The conversation was brief, and all he asked was if I'd be able to handle the pressure of playing in an Old Firm game. My response was positive – as if I was going to say anything else, right enough.

'He was happy enough and told me that he'd agreed terms with my dad on a one-year contract. I had to get to Parkhead by 5 p.m. to register for Europe. I went to see Bradford boss Chris Kamara and asked him if I was still getting a free. He said that I was, and I asked to be released immediately. He told me he couldn't do it that day but changed his mind once I told him it was Celtic and that there was a European deadline involved. Chris looked absolutely shocked by what I'd told him and nearly choked on his toast! Chris said, "God, it's going to look great for me when I tell the chairman I'm releasing you and that you are away to sign for a club the size of Celtic!" He then wished me all the best.

'I jumped in my little Fiat Punto with my wife and put the foot down to get to Parkhead as quickly as possible. I still remember the feeling I had when I came off the M74 and was just a couple of miles from Parkhead. I was nervous but also really excited. I just wanted to get my contract signed to make sure I didn't miss out on this brilliant opportunity. I met Jock at the front door, the contract was signed and I was registered in time for the UEFA Cup. I didn't meet Wim until after I had signed. Wim obviously didn't know me, but I had worked with Murdo MacLeod for a Scotland B game against Switzerland in 1993, and I had a couple of very good training sessions. Murdo must have remembered me from then.

'I was signed as the third-choice keeper – cover for Gordon Marshall and Stewart Kerr – and was on about £1,000 per week. It wasn't the megabucks that some of my teammates would have been on, but I earned £700 per week at Bradford. However, it wasn't about the money. It was about trying to make the most of the unexpected opportunity by forcing my way into the Celtic first team. I arrived at Celtic with no fear, as I had absolutely nothing to lose. The club hadn't paid a penny, and Wim probably didn't expect much from me. The supporters had no idea who I was, so all I could do was work my way up.

'We had lost the opening league game to Hibs, and Wim decided to make a change. I got the nod for the Berwick game, and then I was involved in the UEFA Cup tie against FC Tirol. It was all a bit sudden. I expected to be at the club for five or six weeks before I'd be in with a serious chance.

'The game in Austria was my European debut, and I played a decent game. At the end of the match, Alan Stubbs and Malky Mackay came to give me a hug, which meant so much to me. I probably needed some assurance that my teammates thought I was up to the job of playing for Celtic, and I felt I received it that night from my two central defenders. It was now a case of continuing to work hard and building on the opportunity given to me.

'However, things weren't quite right after we had lost our first two league games. The players called a meeting and asked Wim to attend. We wanted to straighten out a few things and talk about how we were playing. Wim came along and took on board what we were saying. From what I can remember, nothing really changed in terms of tactics and formation, as we more or less played the same way the next game. All I do remember is that the likes of Stéphane Mahé and Henrik Larsson were much clearer about what their roles were on the pitch, and that helped the team.'

For all the panic, Jansen was not taken aback with the way the season had started. It was something he expected, and he had a plan to deal with it, although he did contemplate quitting before deciding to make a go of it. But he was clearly frustrated about not getting various transfer targets he had asked the club to chase on his behalf. The split between Jansen and Brown had started, and it was to get wider and wider with every passing day. MacLeod and Hay were firmly behind Jansen and were against Brown and McCann. A 'them and us' mentality had quickly been established. Big time. And there was no going back. The distance between them was only to widen and something would, eventually, have to give.

Wim Jansen: 'We lost our first two league games, which was not a major surprise to me. You need time to get things right, and it was unrealistic to expect everything to fall into place after two games. But I had a plan in my head and knew I was doing the right thing. We had some good individuals, but we didn't have a good team. I had to get the quality players in for the right positions, Henrik Larsson being an example of that. I knew Henrik would do very well for Celtic.

'We would have stood a better chance of winning games if we had not sold our goal scorers. I wanted to keep Paolo Di Canio and Jorge Cadete. I wanted to bring back Pierre van Hooijdonk. For a variety of reasons, my judgement was not backed, and they were sold and not brought back. We lost more than sixty goals from the three of them. It's hard enough to rebuild a team without having to contend with losing your best players. I spoke to Paolo, but he had problems with his contract, and it was a situation I couldn't resolve, even though I wanted him to stay. I never got to meet Jorge Cadete, yet I would have liked the opportunity to meet him to see if I could have brought him round to my way of thinking.

'The importance of what the season meant to Celtic Football

Club and their people was with me from the first moment. I wanted to stop "ten". Or the way I refer to it is that I wanted us to win one in a row.'

Jansen continued to hand transfer targets to Brown. The search for a striker was the priority, and Celtic were linked with a £1.5-million move for Sporting Lisbon striker Paulo Alves. A £4-million transfer to Celtic of Brazilian World Cup star Bebeto was also the subject of speculation. And Rieper was the man Jansen wanted to plug the leaky defence, but Celtic received some bad news when West Ham boss Harry Redknapp insisted that he would not sell the player because he needed the Dane and the transfer offer of just over £1 million was not enough to bring in a quality replacement. However, there was some positive news on the field, and the Hoops received a boost when they managed to keep a clean sheet in a competitive game.

The Coca-Cola Cup was something Celtic wanted to win, and they were handed a tricky tie, away to St Johnstone. The match was even tougher than anticipated, and it took an extra-time penalty from Donnelly to clinch a place in the quarter-final draw. Phil Scott hit Gould's left-hand post for Saints in the first half as Paul Sturrock's side tried to take full advantage of the lack of confidence in the Hoops' ranks. The game was played at a frantic pace, and both sides created chances, although neither keeper was overworked.

Hugh Dallas then sent Saints sub John O'Neil packing with a red card at the start of extra time for aiming a kick at Malky Mackay. Celtic were awarded a penalty seconds before half-time of the extra period when Stéphane Mahé fired a ball into the box that skidded up and onto the arm of Callum Davidson. Donnelly kept his cool to place his strike past Alan Main. Saints assistant boss John Blackley was sent to the stand by Dallas for protesting, and with seconds to go Roddy Grant was given his second yellow for deliberate handball, reducing Saints to nine men.

It was the kind of result and boost Celtic required. But not everyone was happy.

Jackie McNamara: 'I played right-back in the first two games, and I was my usual self, playing the way I had under Tommy Burns, going forward on the overlap and trying to help out Simon and the other strikers. But I was left out of the game at St Johnstone, replaced by Davie Hannah at right-back. I went to see Wim to ask him why I had been dropped. His explanation was quite simple – he wanted the full-backs to stay put and be part of a proper back four. He didn't want us to attack or to come out. I said to him that he should have told me this, and I would have taken his instructions on board. He said that he had told me. Murdo was also in the office and agreed with Wim. But, to be honest, I can't remember him telling me.'

A cup run provided a much-needed confidence boost, but the priority was to get points on the board in the league, and their next chance to register a victory came at McDiarmid Park, away to St Johnstone on 23 August. Celtic also needed to win to avoid their worst-ever start to a league campaign in the club's 109-year history. It was a nervy start by the visiting side, and they were relieved to see a George O'Boyle effort disallowed for offside. Gould also pulled off a stunning stop to deny Callum Davidson a goal in what was a pivotal moment, not just in that game but, perhaps, in the whole season.

Jansen's men gradually worked their way into the game, and Mackay and Burley both hit the woodwork. Alan Main was eventually beaten in the 44th minute when Donnelly sent over a perfect cross for Larsson. The Swedish striker dived full-length to get his head on it, and the ball flew into the net.

It was exactly what Celtic needed, and they grew in confidence. All of a sudden, there was a belief about the team, and they deserved to score again against Paul Sturrock's side, this time in the 64th minute. Wieghorst gathered a rushed Stewart McCluskey clearance and quickly passed to Jackson. Jackson took a touch, looked up and then curled a 25-yard effort high into the top left-hand corner of the net. It was a finish of the highest quality. Finally, a win had been secured, and Celtic were off the bottom of the table. The relief was clear to see.

Jonathan Gould: 'I made a crucial save against St Johnstone. We won that game 2–0 to stop the rot of league defeats. Had we lost, it would have been the worst start to a league campaign in the history of Celtic. George O'Boyle had a chance to score when he caught a cross sweetly on the volley. His connection was perfect, and I flew to my right-hand side to push it away. It was a pure reflex save. Had George mis-hit it, I'm sure it would have gone in.'

four

Europe – A Turning Point

The league was always going to be the priority for Celtic, but they still wanted a decent run in Europe. Their first Euro match was also their first competitive match of the season, and it came against Welsh minnows Inter CableTel on 23 July in the UEFA Cup.

Celtic's part-time opponents offered little resistance, and the 3–0 first-leg victory gave the Hoops their biggest away win in Europe in 14 years. Andy Thom scored from the spot in the fourth minute, Tommy Johnson scored sixty seconds before half-time and Morten Wieghorst added the third in the eighty-first minute. There was never any danger of Wim Jansen's men losing the game. Gordon Marshall started the season with a clean sheet and Darren Jackson – at that point the only Jansen signing to play – got off to a winning start in his debut.

Former Scotland keeper George Wood was in charge of CableTel, and he knew that his side was in for a tough time at Cardiff Arms Park, the ground where Jock Stein had died 12 years earlier (a minute's silence was observed before kick-off). But the second leg was even tougher for Woods and his players. At Parkhead, a week later, they lost 5–0. Thom (penalty), Jackson, Johnson, Hannah and Chris Hay were the scorers in a pleasing 8–0 aggregate win.

After the predictably comfortable stroll over CableTel, FC Tirol were next to face Celtic on the European stage. The Austrian side were nothing great, but Celtic were capable of crashing to a defeat against the weakest of opposition at that stage. Again, the first leg was away from home. Celtic went into their usual pre-match huddle, but within minutes it was more of a muddle, as the players were all over the place, playing like a collection of individuals rather than a unit. The Austrians were an ordinary side made to look special by a lacklustre Celtic, and they wasted several chances as they cut open the Hoops defence on too many occasions. Jonathan Gould then parried a Francis Severeyns shot into the path of Christian Mayrleb, and he blasted home from close range.

There was defensive disarray yet again as Malky Mackay and Stéphane Mahé were caught ball watching, allowing Mayrleb to nip in and clip the ball over Gould to give his side a two-goal advantage. Mayrleb was then denied a hat-trick after Gould pulled off a stunning stop.

Celtic were a mess at the back and lacked imagination and penetration in midfield. But Gould was in terrific form and prevented his side from an embarrassing level of defeat. Then, out of nowhere, Celtic gave themselves a lifeline when Alan Stubbs scored in the 80th minute. Henrik Larsson was fouled 30 yards from goal by Aly Yilmaz. Stubbs stood over the ball and then unleashed a piledriver that flew past Stanislav Tchertchesov with the aid of a deflection for a goal to keep the Celts in the tie. Somehow, even after a poor performance, Jansen's men had given themselves a good chance of progressing in Europe. But Jansen knew it would be foolish to paper over the cracks and prioritised the signing of a top-drawer centre-half to shore up the dodgy defence. If he didn't, goals would be leaked regularly, and the opposition wouldn't need to work hard to get them.

An unforgettable 90 minutes lay ahead in the return game in front of a crowd of 47,017. Donnelly scored in the 34th minute to put Celtic in the lead, which was pretty much against the run of play after Mayrleb had come close on a couple of occasions. Belgian midfielder Francis Severeyns also wasted a fine chance to give Tirol the lead. Donnelly made them pay when he volleyed home a Morten Wieghorst cross. That goal should have settled Jansen's men, but Mayrleb equalised five minutes before half-time. In what was a roller-coaster game, Thom restored Celtic's lead on the night with a low drive from 20 yards just seconds before half-time. However, frailties were in evidence yet again, and Larsson scored his first goal in Europe at Parkhead by heading past his own keeper from Mayrleb's cross. It was 2–2 at the break, and Celtic knew that they needed to score two in the second half to go through.

McNamara came on for O'Donnell, and the switch made a difference. McNamara twice threatened the Tirol goal, but it was his mate Donnelly who broke down the Austrian defence yet again. In the 68th minute, Pridlo tripped Larsson, and the Scotland striker tucked the penalty kick away with confidence. Less than two minutes later, Burley's deflected shot looped over the head of the Tirol keeper to give the home team the advantage they craved.

However, Celtic hit the self-destruct button again when Tirol pulled one back. Gernot Krinner was left unmarked inside the box and headed home. Celtic needed another goal to progress, and Wieghorst provided it when Donnelly nodded a Stéphane Mahé cross into his path and the Dane buried it from eight yards. The roof nearly blew off the new Parkhead stand when Wieghorst's shot nestled in the back of the net. But even though only three minutes remained, there was still a chance that Celtic would lose another goal, such was the home team's sloppy defending. But there was no cause for concern, as Larsson set up Burley for another goal, the midfielder battering the ball into the net to give Celtic an incredible 6–3 win on the night and an aggregate advantage of 7–5 in what was one of the most entertaining and dramatic 90 minutes ever witnessed at Parkhead.

The joy of winning was soured when it was revealed that Darren Jackson had pulled out of the game just hours before kick-off, suffering from a migraine. However, tests showed that it was much more serious than a common headache. Jackson thought the diagnosis was going to ruin his football career, but the implications were much more serious. Jackson, in fact, faced a brain operation.

Darren Jackson: 'I had settled in well at Celtic. In fact, I thought that I was flying. I played in a pre-season game at home to Roma, and even though I didn't play particularly well I worked my backside off, and the fans gave me a great reception when I was subbed in the second half. I then scored on my home competitive debut against Inter CableTel – not the greatest of opposition, but it was important to get that first goal. We played against St Johnstone and won 2–0 at Perth. Henrik scored the first, and I got the other one. From my point of view, it was a great goal. I was delighted with it. I had started to form a decent partnership with Henrik and felt there was going to be plenty of mileage in it.

'That was on the Saturday, and we were in the following morning to train. As usual, a few fans were there to get autographs and photographs from the players, and they were praising me for my start to the season. Our next game was on the Tuesday night in the second leg of the game against Tirol, and it couldn't come quickly enough for me. We stayed at Seamill on the Monday night, and I woke up with a thumping headache. I went to see Brian Scott, and he gave me a couple of painkillers. I took them and went for a sleep. I had my lunch and felt not too bad. Wim named the team, and I was in it. On the team bus on the way to the game, I was up the back enjoying some banter with the lads, but the headache came on really strong again. My head was pounding. I thought it was going to burst. I spoke to Brian Scott again, and he phoned Parkhead to alert the club doctor, Jack Mulhearn.

'As soon as we arrived, I was taken into the physio's room, and all the lights were turned off. I was told to close my eyes and relax. About an hour before kick-off, Wim came in and asked if I could play. My mind was racing at 100 miles an hour. My brain told me that I wasn't ready to play and that I would be in danger of letting the team down if I did. My heart told me to go out there, because if I pulled out of the game, I might not get back in for a while. Thankfully, my head ruled my heart, and I told Wim I wasn't fit to play.

'I knew I had made the right decision, but when word reached the dressing-room a few of the boys thought that I had bottled it – thought my arse had gone. Looking back, I can sort of understand why they'd think that, but it just wasn't true.

'I stayed to watch the game, and it was some night. We were in, then we were out, back in again and so on. It was an incredible European tie.

'Dr Mulhearn had guests from Rosshall Hospital at the game that night, and he took the precaution of booking a brain scan for me, just in case. I went home, had a good sleep and then drove in to training the next morning. I still had a headache, and Brian Scott said that it was best for me to go to the hospital for a scan. I agreed and thought nothing of it. At that point, I wasn't worried in the slightest – I had no concerns.

'I went home, and Brian phoned me at nine that night. I think a board meeting had been called, as the medical staff had been informed that the scan had shown a dark spot on my brain. It was in an operable place. The board met to decide who was going to tell me. Brian didn't alert me to this. I was just told that I had to go back for another scan. I still wasn't worried. I went back to the hospital the next morning, and Brian and Jock Brown went with me. I sat in the office with the surgeon, Dr Philip Barlow, and he told me that the results were not great for my career. He said that I needed to go in for an operation, as there was a dark spot and too much water on my brain. Jock and Scotty looked at each other and were happy that the news wasn't as bad as what they had been told the previous day.

'I was still gutted. Totally heartbroken. I never gave the operation a second thought. The only thing that was on my mind was that my career was over. Here I was, at 31, having waited all my life to get to one of the biggest clubs in the world, and it was being taken away from me after just over one month. I had to go through a strict medical when I signed, and it took all day. Nothing was left to chance. They found a hole in the pupil of my left eye and a hole in my heart. I never knew I had either. Thankfully, it didn't stop me from signing. Then this happened.

'I phoned my then girlfriend Arlene and met her in Glasgow city centre. I broke my heart crying. We walked around for ages in a daze. I couldn't stop crying. And just to top off the worst day of my life, my car had been towed away and taken to the pound. I'd not put enough money in the meter. I picked up my car and went to Parkhead to watch a reserve game. I sat in the Sky box, and the tears rolled down my cheeks.

'It then got to the stage that I was told the club would honour my contract in full. My career appeared to be well and truly over. I went back to the hospital again, and Dr Barlow had gone to the trouble of getting a second opinion. We were all in his office again. He announced that there was not as much pressure on my brain as first thought and that I might be able to play football again. Jock looked Dr Barlow in the eye and asked him, "If it was your son, would you let him play again?"

'"Yes," was the reply.

'I can't put into words how I felt. My world was turned upside down again.

'I still had to undergo an operation, which Dr Barlow had pioneered. He drilled a hole in my head and lasered a new passageway between the two valves to release the pressure. The operation was a success. The problem had been with me since birth. Nobody knows when it might resurface, if ever again. If I hadn't been taken in for a brain scan, the pressure could have built up and my head could have swollen to almost double its size, and there would have been no guarantees it would have returned to normal.

'It was a dramatic and stressful period in my life. I was headline news, but, to be honest, I think it was overdramatised by the media. My story was on telly, radio and the front pages of the newspapers.

'Dr Barlow was sensational for me, but Celtic Football Club were equally fantastic. I couldn't have been treated better and had things handled in a more professional manner had I been at Real Madrid or Barcelona. The goodwill I received from people was incredible. One of the first faxes came from Brian Laudrup and the Rangers squad. I know you will never take away the intense rivalry that exists between the clubs, but when it comes to the crunch there is a bond. Rangers fans and Celtic fans sent cards. It all made me feel very humble. My dad has kept all my cards and messages.

'I was released from hospital on the day of Princess Diana's funeral, 6 September 1997. I wasn't allowed to drive for six months, but I was back in at Celtic Park on the Monday morning. Jackie McNamara and Gordon Marshall took turns to drive me into work, which was really kind of them. That was the start of a nine-week training period before I was considered ready to rejoin the first-team squad at Barrowfield.

'That first session seems like yesterday, I remember it so clearly. And my first goal that day was a header. I never thought twice about it. The ball came across, and I dived to head it into the net. I was so happy. I felt a fair bit of relief. I then progressed to playing in reserve games. I felt it was important to play to improve my fitness and sharpness. My first reserve game was away to Ross County. County gave me a great reception and presented me with a gift. Tommy Johnson scored a hat-trick. I didn't get on the scoresheet, but it was great to be back.'

The draw for the next round of the UEFA Cup paired Celtic with Liverpool, a real glamour tie that was given maximum coverage by the Scottish media. The first leg was to be played at Parkhead on 16 September. Celtic had notched a couple of much-needed wins going into the match. However, there was still a fear that they could be on the receiving end of a good thrashing if the Reds turned up and played to their full potential.

The Hoops defence was still a cause for concern, and it was no surprise to see the English side take the lead after just six minutes. German striker Karl-Heinz Riedle pounced on a loose ball in the middle of the park and found Michael Owen with a sublime pass. The England striker kept his composure to fire past Gould with a lethal finish for his first-ever European goal. It was a sign that Celtic's formation of three at the back was going to struggle, but Jansen took David Hannah out of his back-line and moved him into the middle of the park. Stéphane Mahé retreated to join Stubbs and Tom Boyd.

Liverpool were expected to run riot and score two or three more, but Celtic gradually got into the game, and Burley, McNamara and Donnelly were all in top form. Having survived several goalmouth scares, the home side were pleased to get to the interval trailing by just one goal. They turned things around and after the break equalised through McNamara. He played a fine one-two with Burley and unleashed an unstoppable left-foot volley past David James. The goal was deserved, as it came during a period of the match when Celtic were dominating. The home fans were right behind their favourites and willing them on. Donnelly responded with a rasping shot that crashed off the underside of the crossbar. Then, in the 73rd minute, Italian referee Cesari Graziano awarded a penalty to Celtic when James brought down Larsson. Donnelly defied his young years to blast the ball into the roof of the net. Celtic Park erupted, the fans thinking their team was on the verge of a memorable victory.

Celtic tried to play out time and kept possession well. Liverpool didn't seem to be too unhappy with a 2–1 defeat, which boss Roy Evans no doubt felt his side would be able to overturn in the second leg. However, Steve McManaman had other ideas, and with just 60 seconds left he scored one of the finest goals ever seen at Celtic Park. He collected the ball 20 yards inside his own half and just ran with it. And ran with it. And ran with it. Celtic players tried desperately to tackle him, but McManaman's quick feet and breathtaking skill kept taking him closer and closer to Gould's goal. He then found himself in a position to shoot, and he curled a magnificent shot past the outstretched right hand of the Celtic keeper. The 3,000 Liverpool fans went crazy, and even McManaman looked a bit dumbstruck, as he hadn't kicked the ball all night.

The match finished 2–2, which was harsh on Celtic after the way they had bounced back to control the game after a torrid opening

20 minutes. But the home fans were happy that their side had put on a decent show, as they had arrived at Parkhead that night fearing the worst.

Regi Blinker: 'That was shaping up to be my most satisfying game of the season in a Celtic jersey. I played well that night and felt I was at the heart of the tempo. Then I went in for a slide tackle and my shoulder popped out. I had to be carried off. I received loud applause from the Celtic supporters. I think they knew how well I was doing. I never got back on that night. That was a personal tragedy, as my game was gathering momentum, and I felt I would have been able to go on a run of good form.'

Craig Burley: 'The Liverpool game gave us belief. Let's be honest, it wasn't a great Liverpool side we were up against, but they were more than decent. They pounded us in the first 15 minutes, but we fought back and took the lead. I think we had put so much into the game that we had nothing left to give in the last five minutes. I felt like I was towing a caravan, wearing a pair of wellies as I tried to get around the pitch.'

Morten Wieghorst: 'I've watched that game a few times on tape and always question myself as to why I didn't just pull McManaman's jersey when he picked up the ball on the halfway line. It was a crazy run from McManaman, I think he went past five or six of our players. I was just too knackered to do much about it. Some of the boys still ask me why I didn't take him out of the game. It was a really exciting night and a great game of football. The atmosphere was terrific, and both sets of fans singing "You'll Never Walk Alone" was one of the best moments I ever had at Celtic Park.'

Jackie McNamara: 'I came on as a sub against Tirol and played right-midfield. I played fine and then got the nod to start the game as right-wingback at home to Liverpool. I was delighted to be given a start in such a big game but not too chuffed at having to do the "graveyard shift" and cover the full length of the park myself! Wim had obviously checked Liverpool out and realised he had to switch from his preferred back four to a back three to have men close to Michael Owen in an attempt to combat his pace.

'Liverpool controlled the early stages, and it was credit to us for getting back into the game and going 2–1 ahead. I scored the equaliser with a left-foot shot and was delighted. I think that goal was a turning point for me. I enjoyed that game, and my performance gave me a lot of confidence. It also gave the team a lift, and we believed we could do something that season. We also started to believe in Wim.'

Celtic's excellent performance in the first leg gave them confidence for the return match at Anfield, a fortnight later. When the draw had paired both great clubs together, Liverpool had been strong favourites to go through, but the Celts were growing in confidence, and there was a belief they could see off the challenge of Michael Owen, Robbie Fowler, Steve McManaman and Co.

Celtic arrived for the game minus Boyd, Thom, O'Donnell and Blinker. In fact, the Celts were so short of players that they listed only five substitutes, even though UEFA permitted seven on the bench. Rico Annoni was given his first start in the Jansen regime, Burley was captain, and Hannah was asked to man-mark McManaman.

It was a pulsating game, with both sides having a go, although the onus was more on Celtic, as they had to get a goal to have any chance of qualifying for the next round. Donnelly had the chance to score, but his lob flew over the crossbar after James fumbled a cross. Larsson and Wieghorst also went close. Liverpool moved up the gears a few times, and Owen went racing through but couldn't hit the target. McManaman then tested Gould. In the second half, Patrik Berger and Paul Ince both came close to opening the scoring. And Donnelly cleared a Riedle header off the line.

It was a spirited performance by Celtic, but the last-gasp goal from McManaman in Glasgow two weeks earlier proved to be crucial. Celtic were, in many ways, unfortunate at Anfield, but there was a feeling that they could have been a touch more cavalier in the final 15 minutes in search of the goal they needed. Instead, the game finished 0–0, and Celtic's run in Europe ended before Christmas yet again. But they walked off the pitch with their heads held high and applause ringing in their ears from their travelling fans and the Liverpool supporters in the Kop.

Celtic gained a lot from the 'Battle of Britain' tie. They found new respect and confidence, which they carried into their league programme, and they went on to record five straight wins as they tried to claw their way back to Rangers. Donnelly and McNamara left boyhood behind in the tie, and they never looked back. They went on to form a fantastic partnership down the right-hand side and gave many displays that season that made the pair of them major contenders for the player of the year gongs.

Hoops skipper Boyd felt the result could have been even better for Celtic had Jansen been a touch bolder in the closing minutes of the match.

Tom Boyd: 'I felt that we should have been a bit more direct against Liverpool. We could have thrown a couple of the big guys forward and launched a few balls at them. It might well have got us the goal we needed to put us through. But Wim stayed with the same system and players, and we were knocked out. It was a prime example of him not changing his philosophy on the game.'

Jansen defended his tactics and explained: 'For me that game was very important, as it showed we were able to compete at a high level. We showed we had quality, and I believe it gave us confidence and belief, as we almost beat Liverpool in the tie. I don't agree that I was negative at the end and could have tried to put more pressure on Liverpool in the closing stages.

'Look at my team? Show me the player who was going to go up front and cause Liverpool problems. We had to play to our strengths, and my idea on football is that if you believe in something from the first minute, then the same should apply to the last minute. If I had the right alternative, then I would have looked at changing things. But we did not have a target man. I wanted a target man in the team and had looked at trying to bring that type of player in, but we didn't have the money to bring in the right one. If I had someone such as Mark Viduka, then I could have changed it, but we didn't have that type.'

Jackson was able to make his way to Merseyside, driven by Tommy Johnson, to watch the game, and being at Anfield made him all the hungrier to return to top-team action as quickly as possible.

Darren Jackson: 'That season was also a difficult time for Tommy. He also missed a lot of games, and we spent a lot of time together. We travelled down to Anfield for the UEFA Cup game against Liverpool and sat behind our dugout. I was heartbroken to miss it. That kind of fixture and atmosphere is what football is all about. I had never questioned my determination to make sure I played for Celtic again, but being at Anfield for that game cemented my determination and drive.'

Simon Donnelly: 'It wasn't something I was laughing about at the time, but I now have a joke with Darren that his head injury created a gap for me to play up front alongside Henrik. I enjoyed my spell with Henrik, and it is a definite highlight of my career to have played with such a talented footballer. I think I was down to play in midfield the night of the Tirol game at Parkhead and was then moved up front to play in Darren's role. I went on to start the next ten or twelve games in that position and thoroughly enjoyed it.

'The games we played in Europe helped shape our whole season. We scored six against Tirol and had to fight back a couple of times in the tie. That showed we had determination and courage. We also had to play Liverpool, and they were probably expected to beat us comfortably over the two legs. But we dug in, played some great football and should have beaten them at Parkhead. I think we came off the pitch that night believing we might just have a chance of doing something in the league.

'Personally, the European games were really enjoyable for me. I scored a volley against Tirol and a penalty. That gave me so much confidence. I then scored against Liverpool and was really pleased for Jackie to get one that night, too.'

Although Celtic didn't get past Liverpool, they gained credibility for the way they performed, and the bonus of not being involved in midweek UEFA Cup action was that they were able to fully concentrate on trying to win the domestic trophies.

five

A Winning Streak

After that dramatic win at home to FC Tirol and the news of Darren Jackson's brain injury, Celtic didn't play a domestic fixture until 10 September, a break for international football being the reason for the lack of activity on the home front. During that period, Celtic appointed Eric Black as head of youth development.

Motherwell were the visitors to Parkhead on Coca-Cola Cup duty, the first of back-to-back fixtures against the Lanarkshire side. This was a match that secured Celtic a semi-final slot in the League Cup and showed signs that the Parkhead club, under the leadership of their Dutch manager, were beginning to get things right, on the park at least. The football was impressive from start to finish. All that was missing was a few more goals, but Celtic felt that if they continued to play with such energy and freedom, a hefty defeat would be inflicted on an opponent before long.

Simon Donnelly, Henrik Larsson, Phil O'Donnell and Andreas Thom all went close in the opening exchanges. Then Larsson scored the only goal of the game in the 27th minute. It came at a time when Motherwell were reduced to ten men, as Greig Denham was off the park with a head knock. Blinker released Stéphane Mahé, and the Frenchman's cross was perfect for Larsson as he arrived at the back post to head past the helpless Stevie Woods.

Chance after chance came and went, but the home side were unable to increase their advantage. On another day, it could have been double figures. Hoops goalkeeper Jonathan Gould was a spectator.

Well were reduced to ten men in injury time when Ian Ross received his marching orders for a second foul on Jackie McNamara, but by that time Celtic had settled for the narrow win that would take them into the last four of the competition.

In the build-up to the game, more new signings had been linked with the club. Barcelona's out-of-favour striker Juan Antonio Pizzi had been mentioned as the solution to the striker crisis in a £5-million transfer from the Nou Camp. But as progress to move the deal forward stalled, David Zitelli was also mentioned, and there was more chance of that £2.5-million transfer from French side Strasbourg becoming a reality. That week, the club also announced plans to build a new training centre and museum, although not the one that was opened in Lennoxtown in November 2007.

One move that finally came off was Marc Rieper's £1.5-million transfer from West Ham. The powerful Danish defender made his debut on 13 September, in an away fixture at Motherwell in the league. Rieper turned in a commanding performance, looking every inch an international defender, and it was easy to see why Jansen had chased him for almost two months.

There was a contrast in fortunes for the Danish stopper's new defensive partner, Alan Stubbs. Signed the previous season by Tommy Burns for £3.5 million from Bolton, the Scouser arrived with an excellent reputation but had struggled to justify the huge outlay on him in his first 12 months.

That afternoon at Fir Park, Stubbs was well short with a passback for Jonathan Gould, and Tommy Coyne nipped in to give his side a third-minute lead. In what was a fiery contest, Celtic equalised through Craig Burley in the 56th minute. But Alex McLeish's side were quickly back in the lead when Coyne managed to escape the attentions of Stubbs to score. The Lanarkshire side were then down to ten men after Greig Denham was sent off by ref Mike

McCurry after an incident with Larsson. Jackie McNamara came on for Thom and once again made a positive impact. Burley scored his second to make it 2–2, and nine minutes from time Donnelly netted when he headed home a McNamara cross.

Sure, the defence was still far from watertight, but this game told Jansen that his players had it in them to recover from setbacks and certainly had plenty to offer, middle to front.

Marc Rieper: 'There was no doubt that Rangers were the team to catch. Celtic had played the better football in many of the games in previous years but couldn't win the important ones. Silly mistakes had proved costly for the team.

'I found the prospect of going to Celtic an interesting challenge. I was at West Ham and felt the time was right for a change. I wanted to play for a top club that would be fighting for prizes, and that opportunity arose for me with Celtic. Negotiations started before the competitive season got underway, and by the time everything was finalised we were into September.

'There was a big improvement to be made in the Celtic team, and I wanted to help. Celtic were a massive club, but they had been underachieving. I suspect the nine-in-a-row challenge really preyed on the minds of some of the players, the home-grown guys, such as Tom Boyd and Tosh McKinlay, the guys with Celtic in their blood. It must have been difficult for them, but it wasn't such a problem for me and the other foreign guys in the squad and on the coaching staff, as we could go home and switch off if we wanted to. We could escape from the pressure, as we weren't surrounded by friends and family wanting to constantly talk about the importance of winning the league.

'It was clear Alan Stubbs had a big role to play at Celtic. He was and still is a very good player. Back then, he needed someone dominant beside him, to do the dirty work, if you like. That allowed him to do what he was good at and use his attributes.'

Malky Mackay: 'When Marc signed, I knew my chances of a regular game were going to be limited, but I made a point of using his presence to my benefit. He was a top defender, a Denmark internationalist, and I could only learn from him. He kept things simple and concentrated on defending, doing everything possible to make sure the opposition didn't score. It was also an education watching Alan Stubbs. Alan is a good friend and played very well that season.

'It was also good for me to be up against Henrik Larsson in training every day. Wim would play a lot of full-scale practice games, and I often had the task of trying to mark Henrik. His running off the ball, the angles he created to receive a pass, not to mention his ability to put the ball in the net made him a top-class centre-forward, yet I think he arrived at our place as a left winger.

'Training with Marc, Alan and Henrik helped my career. When I left Celtic, I had good times at Norwich, West Ham and Watford, and there is no doubt that my time at Celtic with some great players and great coaches helped my career to develop and allowed me to have eight or nine years at a high level down south.'

Aberdeen travelled down from the north to face a resurgent Celtic team. The Hoops were confident after their 2–2 midweek draw against Liverpool in the UEFA Cup, and the Dons were expected to be lambs to the slaughter in this contest. And for the first time in what was to become a regular occurrence during his seven-year stay in Glasgow's East End, it was the Henrik Larsson show.

Fully recovered from his debut, Larsson started to show why Jansen had been so keen to sign him from Feyenoord. He was taking control of games and becoming the central figure in the good things that the team were putting together. Thom also had an industrious game and was unfortunate not to score twice in the early stages. But Roy Aitken's men couldn't hold out for long, and the deadlock was broken in the 26th minute. Donnelly took two Dons defenders out of the game with a lovely piece of skill and then swept in a cracking ball from the wide right area. Larsson was his intended target, and the Swede managed to guide home a fine shot, low past Jim Leighton.

Then, seven minutes from the interval, Donnelly was decked at the edge of the box and Larsson was just too quick for everyone. His slick free-kick sped into the top right-hand corner of the net, giving Leighton no chance. More goals could have been added, but Celtic were wasteful in front of goal. However, it was still a terrific afternoon's work from Jansen's men. The fans left Parkhead raving about the side and genuinely believed that at last their team could pose a threat to Rangers for that season's silverware.

The players could have been forgiven for hiding earlier in the season, as things had looked bleak, but now the games couldn't come quickly enough for Jansen's men. For example, Jackie McNamara was so keen to be involved that he played much of the season through the pain barrier.

Jackie McNamara: 'I got a bang on my knee against Aberdeen. That was the start of my tendonitis. It was painful and got worse as the season went on. I started to limp a lot, and then it wasn't long before I couldn't do anything for four or five days after a game. I'd train on the Friday and that would be my only session before a match day. In the closing stages of the season, I wasn't doing any training. All I was doing was playing games and receiving treatment. I was still in a lot of pain on a match day and had to go through fitness tests before a lot of games.'

The bank balance was £3 million better off that week when the long-running saga involving Jorge Cadete finally came to an end, and he joined Spanish Primera Liga side Celta Vigo. Jansen wanted the money spent as quickly as possible on a quality replacement, and Jock Brown vowed to 'spice up the attack' with the purchase of a goal-machine. Inter Milan's striker Kanu was the latest big name to be linked with Celtic. Jansen admitted that he wanted to sign the former Ajax striker, but the move for the Nigerian wasn't financially viable. McCann then tried to swell the coffers by a further £2 million by asking Monaco to pay that amount for John Collins. The French league side had signed the player on a Bosman, but McCann felt that his club were entitled to a transfer fee. The Celtic powerbroker vowed to get tough with the SFA to help the Hoops win their case, but it collapsed, and they did not receive a penny for the midfielder.

Next, Celtic were back on the road, this time with a tricky trip to Tannadice to face Dundee United on 27 September. The Parkhead men took the lead in the 29th minute when Steven Pressley was short with a headed passback to Sieb Dykstra. Larsson nipped in and supplied Donnelly with a perfect pass. Donnelly knew the Dutch keeper was off his line and cleverly lobbed the ball over him from 15 yards out. Celtic then piled on the pressure, and Maurice Malpas headed a McNamara effort off the line. Thom limped off in the 42nd minute, and it took his replacement, O'Donnell, just 60 seconds to get his name on the scoresheet. McNamara's cross was sweetly met by the former Motherwell midfielder, and he cracked home a left-foot shot past Dykstra.

Celtic had to work hard to keep their lead intact, and they survived a few scares as Gary McSwegan and Robbie Winters came close. Tommy McLean's side deservedly scored in the 61st minute when Rieper fouled Mark Perry 22 yards out. Magnus Sköldmark tapped the ball to Kjell Olofsson, and he rattled it past Gould.

United kept at it, and their passing game was pleasing on the eye, but they lacked a killer instinct in front of goal. Celtic held on and were delighted to take the three points. Stubbs had been outstanding at the heart of the defence. The Hoops supporters also delayed a trackside television interview with Jansen as they belted out the Dutchman's name. It was the first time since his appointment as head coach that the fans had passionately shown their appreciation of his efforts and let him know that they believed he could lead them all the way to a title triumph.

There was dramatic news from Ibrox on 2 October when Walter Smith announced at the Rangers AGM that he would step down as manager at the end of the season. He had met with club owner David Murray and both had agreed that it was the correct decision. Did that announcement unsettle Rangers and give an advantage to Celtic?

Murdo MacLeod: 'When it was announced that Walter was leaving at the end of the season, I felt it was a positive thing for Rangers. They could use it as a spur to drive them on to even more success that season. I could just imagine the likes of Ally McCoist, Andy Goram, Ian Durrant, Brian Laudrup and Stuart McCall saying, "Let's do it for Walter."

'We knew many of the Ibrox stalwarts would follow him out of the door. It had been a successful decade for Rangers, but there was no doubt that the new manager would let a few of them go and spend the huge transfer kitty given to him by David Murray. The players who were not part of the long-term future were told in advance that their time was coming to an end, and they would have wanted to go out with a bang, leaving the place with "ten" in the bag. With the benefit of hindsight, Rangers might argue that it harmed them, because they did not win the title. However, in short, I don't think it gave us any advantage whatsoever. To be honest, what happened across the city was of no major importance to us. Yes, we took notice, but we were starting to hit a bit of form during that period and felt we were capable of doing things on our own.'

During that period at Ibrox, Gazza also threatened to quit, and Richard Gough returned to the club after a short spell in America with Kansas City Wizards.

Kilmarnock were the next visitors to Parkhead on 4 October. Celtic were now starting to play entertaining football and also looked more solid at the back. Their consistency meant that they were once again safe bets for the fixed-odds coupon. But Dragoje Leković, the Kilmarnock keeper, proved difficult to beat in the opening exchanges, and he prevented Burley and Donnelly from scoring. However, he was then beaten in the 18th minute when Thom's cross was volleyed home by Henrik Larsson. The second arrived in the thirty-second minute when the McNamara–Donnelly partnership again combined well, and their one-two resulted in the striker firing home from twelve yards.

Donnelly was involved in the next goal, and this time it was a one-two with Morten Wieghorst. The big Dane found himself inside the Killie box and rattled home a 12-yard shot. And seven minutes before the interval, Celtic increased their lead further.

Martin Baker fouled McNamara, and the kick was taken quickly by Thom to allow Larsson to head home from close range.

Celtic didn't ease off after the break, and Leković had to pull off saves from Mahé, Donnelly, Larsson, Burley and McNamara, but the scoreline remained the same. Jansen was happy with the performance but criticised his players' finishing in front of goal in the second half. However, the first-half performance had been the most satisfying for Jansen and his players since the new manager had taken over.

With Stubbs on form, he became the subject of interest from Sheffield Wednesday. If such an opportunity had arisen during his first season, he would have been keen to find out more, but he was settled now and enjoying his football, and he believed that the title was on its way to Parkhead. After personal problems in his first season, Stubbs was playing superbly, and a lot of the credit for that was put down to him having Rieper as his partner.

Alan Stubbs: 'It helped to have Marc Rieper alongside me. He was a Denmark internationalist and had an excellent pedigree. It's not easy to put my finger on why he was good for me, but I think he gave me more reassurance as a defender. He made sure that first and foremost we defended. It wasn't trying to play, play, play all the time, something I was guilty of. It was about stopping the opposition from scoring. That was always the priority. Marc definitely made us a stronger defensive unit.

'We needed to be strong at the back, but we did struggle a wee bit in the first couple of games. In fact, the whole team struggled. We took a few knocks and bumps during the summer, and the widespread opinion of people outside of Celtic appeared to be that it was a formality that Rangers would win ten in a row. Between Tommy losing his job and the first three or four weeks of the season, hardly a day went by when there wasn't a negative thing to say or write about the club. We had enough on our minds trying to win games without the constant negativity. Every game was a must-win 90 minutes, and the pressure was horrible.

'When I signed for Celtic, I didn't realise the size of the club.

They have a huge fan base all over the world. Tommy showed me the stadium during signing talks, and it had that wow factor. I was in awe. My respect for Celtic and its supporters grew the longer I was there. It was a privilege to play for them.

'A lot of things weren't right for me in my first year at Celtic, and on a couple of occasions I came close to leaving. Mandy had two miscarriages during our first six months in Glasgow, and that made life very difficult for us. We were both very down about losing our babies. We discussed the situation and decided that it was best I spoke to Tommy and told him that I wanted to move back down south. Tommy was taken aback when I told him. He had paid a lot of money to get me, and here I was after a few months asking to walk out on the club. It wasn't what he needed to hear. At a time like that, when the club was trying to stop nine in a row, he needed committed players. But family had to come first for me.

'Tommy listened and then asked what he could do to help the situation. I told him it was more Mandy than me, and there might be nothing he could do. He then asked if I would just give it until the end of the season, and then he would leave it all up to me. I couldn't refuse his request. The club were also great, and they deserve credit. They had made a massive financial investment in me, and they wanted to do everything possible to make sure they got the best value for their outlay. That's the way it should be. It makes sense all round.

'To be honest, the only reason I stayed was because of Tommy. He took on board the problems Mandy had and was great with me and totally understanding. He made every effort to make us as comfortable as possible. Tommy's wife, Rosemary, also went out of her way to spend time with Mandy. We lived not too far away from one another in Newton Mearns, and she'd give Mandy a phone and go shopping with her or go for a coffee and a chat. That was a big help, because I think Mandy sometimes felt isolated and confined to the house. But, in time, she began to like Glasgow more and more. She made friends and got to know the neighbours. In the end, it was actually a wrench for both of us and our two children, Heather and Sam, to leave Glasgow. The kids had Scottish accents. It was only the pull of playing for Everton that made me move. Otherwise, I'd have stayed at Celtic. I have many happy memories and plenty of positive thoughts about playing for Celtic and living in Glasgow. I left in the summer of 2001, and it was a great way for me to go – a Treble-winning campaign in 2001 in Martin O'Neill's first season at the club. What a high.'

Jansen couldn't have been happier with the contribution made by the Englishman and had absolute faith in his ability to do the job.

Wim Jansen: 'Alan Stubbs was a player I inherited, and he was also very important. He was a good defender, and you didn't need to give him too much instruction. He knew what to do. Alan knew what was right and what was wrong. It was a good combination to have Marc Rieper alongside him. Marc would attack the ball, and Alan would break out of defence and help set up attacks. He could hit the ball forty yards no problem and would nine times out of ten find one of his own players. That was not so easy to do, especially when you have the pressure of 50,000 watching and there is so much at stake. The easy thing to do would be pass it five yards to a teammate, but Alan was happy to take responsibility and stand up and be counted.'

Trips to Tynecastle are never easy, and that was the way it turned out on 18 October. Celtic went into the game three points behind the Jambos and knew a defeat would put a serious dent in any title challenge. The game was always going to require a blend of skill, sweat and snarl, and Celtic demonstrated all three in a bad-tempered clash in which referee John Rowbotham booked three players from Hearts and four from Celtic.

The Hoops took the lead through Rieper – that all-important first goal. And after just 21 minutes, they doubled their advantage. Stefano Salvatori took Craig Burley out of play, and the midfielder looked to the referee for a free-kick. However, the advantage rule was correctly applied by Rowbotham, and he allowed Regi Blinker to race towards the Hearts penalty area. Blinker was supported by Larsson, and the Dutchman crossed for his former Feyenoord teammate to drill low past Gilles Rousset.

But Hearts weren't title contenders at that stage by accident. Manager Jim Jefferies made sure that his players never gave up, and his team pulled a goal back in the 65th minute through Colin Cameron when his shot from 12 yards deflected off Stubbs and beyond Gould. The little midfielder then almost equalised when his 20-yard shot was brilliantly saved by Gould. And the keeper was on top form again to deny Paul Ritchie with just seconds left to give Celtic three crucial points.

Jonathan Gould: 'I was pleased to pull off those saves. Hearts were right in it at that stage, and we couldn't afford to give them any extra encouragement by not beating them.

'Peter Latchford was my goalkeeping coach that season, and he was terrific. He had played more than 300 games for Celtic and knew the score. He also knew exactly what I needed and when I needed it. Some people might ridicule the job of a goalkeeping coach and say that it's the easiest job in football, but there is pressure for your goalie to succeed. If you take the job seriously, then it is one of the most important jobs at a football club.

'Peter came up to me at half-time and told me to be on my toes. "This game isn't over for you," he said. "You've got at least two big saves coming up in the next forty-five minutes." He was right. At other times, he'd just pull me aside in the dressing-room with a few minutes to go before kick-off and tell me to be aware from the off, as I would have a save to make in the first ten minutes because the opposition would come out flying. Nine times out of ten he was right.'

Celtic were seldom out of the headlines during this period, and there was speculation surrounding Jansen when Feyenoord claimed they'd consider having him back as coach. He was also in the papers pleading with the money men to clinch a deal for one of the many names he'd given them to solve the team's problem in front of goal. Jackson returned to training that week, and Tommy Johnson played a reserve game and stated that he felt he was good enough to play in the first team every week and score goals, therefore saving the club a fortune in the transfer market. Jansen wasn't of the same opinion.

It was important that Celtic build on the impressive win at Tynecastle. And they did. They followed it up by beating St Johnstone on 25 October – a victory that was to take them to the top of the table for the first time that season after Rangers had lost the same afternoon away to Dundee United, Steven Pressley scoring the winner for the Arabs from the penalty spot. Being in pole position must have been unexpected, considering the team's dismal start to the season. The last time Celtic had been at the top of the table was a year earlier, but the side managed by Burns had only stayed there for one game.

Celtic started the St Johnstone game nervously and were fortunate not to go behind after Leigh Jenkinson and Attila Sekerlioglu came close for the Perth side. But the Hoops got their act together and took the lead in the 31st minute. Nick Dasovic was short with a headed passback to Alan Main, and the ever-alert Larsson nipped in to punish the Canadian midfielder and score.

Paul Sturrock's side conceded another goal four minutes later when Mahé was brought down inside the box by John McQuillan. Referee Tom Brown pointed to the spot, and Donnelly made no mistake as he sent Main the wrong way. Main was man of the match that day as he pulled off a few top saves, denying Burley and the impressive Blinker. McNamara also rattled a shot off the post. George O'Boyle had Saints' only effort on target in the game in the 80th minute, but a super diving save from Gould made sure the Northern Irishman didn't get on the scoresheet.

The win took Celtic's unbeaten run to 13 games and brought a pleasing smile of satisfaction to the face of Jansen in the post-match press conference, but he made a point of being cautious and warned that there was still a long way to go. Indeed there was.

Blinker scored his first league goal of the season in the 2–0 away win at Dunfermline on 1 November. The Dutch winger netted in the 67th minute after his shot was deflected by Greg Shields into the net. Larsson secured the points four minutes from time when he scored with a lovely solo effort after leaving three Dunfermline defenders trailing as he strode into the box and then rolled the ball past Ian Westwater. At that point, Pars gaffer Bert Paton had four strikers on the pitch in search of an equaliser, which was always going to leave gaps at the back.

The margin of victory would have been bigger but for Westwater. The Pars keeper had a fine game and made good saves from McNamara and Larsson when the score was 0–0. Pars had hoped to do the double on Celtic after their 2–1 win at Parkhead earlier in the season and had gone out with a bold 4–3–3 formation. Andy Smith, Hamish French and Allan Moore all forced Gould into action with important saves.

The victory gave Celtic their eighth league win on the trot, demonstrating that they were real championship contenders after their dreadful start to the campaign. Their next league game was against Rangers, when their title credentials would really be put to the test. However, before they even got to Ibrox the following weekend, two major incidents with serious ramifications took place, and after a period of calm the club was back in turmoil. First, in-fighting on the training ground between the squad came to the boil; second, in-fighting between the management department and their superiors (Brown and McCann) came to a head. Despite this, Jansen repeated that he was committed to Celtic and was going nowhere after having been linked with Feyenoord.

six

Internal War

In the build-up to an Old Firm game, preparation is vital. This means good training sessions, tactical discussion between the coaches and the players, and every new player being left in no doubt as to what it means to beat your main rivals. A Glasgow derby during the 1997–98 season also had added significance in that Celtic were desperately trying to stop Rangers from winning the league, and three points from the game at Ibrox would have helped make that happen. But the self-destruct button was pressed at Celtic Park that week, not once but twice.

The first explosion to hit the headlines was Davie Hay's dismissal from his role as assistant general manager on 3 November. The fireworks had started early for the Hoops. Hay was unable to work any longer with his immediate gaffer, Jock Brown. It had got to the stage that the pair couldn't even exchange a 'Good morning'. Hay thought that he was being underpaid by the club and was getting nowhere in his negotiations with the board for a pay rise. Hay was of the opinion that Brown could have helped his case and fought to get his number two a decent wage increase. They were also at odds over football matters. By that stage, an obvious and uneasy split had developed between the first-team coaching staff and Brown and the people in his 'camp'. Hay was on the side of Jansen and his men.

A parting of the ways was inevitable, and Hay was shown the door five days before the visit to Ibrox. Hay had been back at Parkhead for four years after being brought to the club by former boss Tommy Burns. He had lasted just four months in his new job under Brown.

Celtic put out a four-line statement to thank Hay for his services. Jock Brown was quoted in the press release as saying: 'I can confirm Davie Hay has left the football club. We will be making no further comment on the matter.'

Unfortunately, the case between Hay and Celtic became messy – very messy – and ran for months and months – all the way to court as Hay claimed for unfair dismissal. It kept Celtic on the front and back pages with both parties having a go at each other over things that should have remained in-house.

Davie Hay: 'The signings arrived, and, after a dodgy start, the team started to take a bit of shape. The new boys settled well, and Wim was also starting to find his feet. The same couldn't be said for me – I was not a happy man. I felt I was due a pay rise for becoming assistant general manager and the extra responsibility that came with the post. I had several meetings with a member of the Parkhead board, but we couldn't agree on a figure. It started to eat away at me and made me more and more agitated. I felt I was being underpaid and wasn't enjoying going to work.

'It got to the point that there was a total breakdown in communication, which was also the case with my relationship with Jock Brown. This was quite surprising when you think that Jock had been my lawyer. I don't want to knock Jock Brown too much, as we were both at fault. For the good of the football club, we should have had a closer working relationship. Perhaps I felt Jock could have been more supportive, but we weren't seeing eye to eye on football matters, either. There was animosity between us, and our dealings often became aggressive. Voices were raised, tempers flared. It wasn't pleasant. It was just never my style to bite my tongue, although I always had Celtic at heart.

'Wim and Murdo also had a breakdown with Jock. I was firmly

in Wim and Murdo's camp, and only a few weeks into the season a "them and us" scenario had already developed. Something had to give, as there was a nasty atmosphere about our working environment.

'I left Jock with no option, and it eventually came to the crunch. He told me that he could not allow the situation to continue and that my services would no longer be required. Naturally, Fergus McCann backed his man [Brown].

'It was a bit of a tragedy and one of the lowest points of my football career. I'd been in football for a long time and had been previously sacked as Celtic manager back in 1987. I knew that football was a brutal business, but this was me finding that out for myself yet again. As I walked out of the front door after being dismissed, I felt cheated and angry. I had given many years of service as a player, manager and chief scout, and here I was on my way out.

'I decided to take legal action against Celtic on the grounds of unfair dismissal. Just before we went to court, a compromise agreement was offered, and I decided to knock it back. I was stubborn. In hindsight, I should have accepted that offer, and I regret that I didn't. Bloody stubbornness! I felt I had to go all the way and couldn't back down. I lost the case.

'I never looked for the sympathy vote afterwards, although I did receive lots of letters of support from Celtic supporters and other well-wishers. My biggest regret was that I didn't get the chance to work with Wim and Murdo for a longer period. It was a good backroom team, and we all wanted to develop it even more.

'As soon as I met Wim, I liked him. He was a nice man but also a very knowledgeable football man. Of course, after we lost the opening two league games of the season, away to Hibs and at home to Dunfermline, people questioned whether or not he was the right guy to lead Celtic to success. It was only natural to ask those questions. Credit to him for turning things around, putting all the behind-the-scenes animosity to one side and concentrating on winning football games.'

Jansen would have preferred Hay be allowed to stay on.

Wim Jansen: 'I was angry when David lost his job. He helped make the team, and I liked working with him. If you have good people, then you keep them at the club. You try to make them happy. You listen to them and try to come to an arrangement. That did not happen with David. He should have been there the day we won the league. His role in the success of that season can't be understated. He helped to build the team by identifying good players. It wasn't good for the football staff that we lost him. But, then, what was best for the football staff didn't always seem to be the most important thing in the minds of others in powerful positions at Celtic.'

Murdo MacLeod: 'We used to sit for hours and hours after training and talk about football. It was a great education for me. We'd go into fine detail about the strengths and weaknesses of our own players and the opposition players. When Davie Hay was at the club, he would join us, and we used to have a real blether. We'd have a cup of tea in Wim's office. We'd study the opposition, and Wim went with my opinions during the early stages of his time in office. We'd also look at potential signing targets and the condition of our squad and see who we might need to bring in. It was a case of bouncing different ideas off each other. You can't beat sessions like that.

'I missed Davie. The whole football department missed Davie. You keep guys like that. You don't fall out with them. He had worked wonders for the club in the transfer market and should have been given a 'hero-gram' instead of the sack. I felt sick when he lost his job, as he was the man who had made it possible for me to return to Celtic by offering me a position on the coaching staff.'

While there was war behind the scenes at management level, there was also an almighty bust-up brewing on the training field. For a variety of reasons, some of the players were simply not seeing eye to eye. The tension resulted in Tosh McKinlay head-butting Henrik Larsson 48 hours before the Old Firm clash. Again, Celtic appeared on the front and back pages.

A couple of players were of the opinion that it was inevitable that something was going to happen as the season heated up. If it hadn't been Tosh having a go at Henrik, another pair would have been involved in a bust-up. Too many of the players were harbouring simmering resentments. Some thought that Wim was not handling the squad properly and could have treated the fringe players better. They seemed to think that he showed favouritism towards the first-team regulars, including giving them every 50–50 decision during practice matches in training. Some first-team players took delight in some of their teammates not getting much of a look-in, almost as if they were superior to them, and this rightly caused severe resentment. Other players felt that there was a 'them and us' mentality developing between a few of the foreign lads and the home-grown players, which also caused problems. As a result, a bust-up was expected. The players just weren't expecting it to happen at that time, so close to such a vital game.

Ultimately, it was fortunate that there was only one incident that day. Immediately after the head-butt, other players threatened to get involved, in part to give support to Tosh or Henrik, but also to settle their own differences. There was almost a good old-fashioned free-for-all.

Murdo MacLeod: 'Perhaps Tosh's frustration got the better of him, and I think him not being in the first team played a part in the incident with Henrik. I was only two or three yards away from it, and Tosh gave Henrik a helluva smash. We pulled Tosh away and sent him away from Barrowfield. Tosh tackled hard in training, but the head-butt was so out of character.

'I felt for Henrik. There's no doubt he lost his confidence after the incident, and it took him a while to recover, to trust the training ground again and be comfortable there. It also knocked the squad for six. We were all shocked by it.

'I met Jock Brown later that day, and he asked me what I thought the solution was. He told me that Tosh could be sacked for the incident and that this might be a good thing, as it would save the club money. I was not in favour of that. I never at any point wanted

Tosh to be sacked. Jock Brown brought out a book the following year, and I'm told that in it he stated that I wanted Tosh to be sacked for head-butting Henrik. Absolute rubbish. And I phoned Tosh to tell him that. Quite simply, in my opinion Jock wanted some form of revenge for what I had said about him in an interview with the *Sunday Mail* a few weeks after my time at Celtic came to an end. For me, that tells you a lot about him.

'I don't know if Tosh and Henrik ever shook hands or if Tosh ever apologised. Wim and I certainly never insisted on them shaking hands, as we felt it was better for them to sort it in their own way and in their own time. I've never asked Henrik or Tosh what happened after that.'

Brown held a meeting with Jansen and MacLeod to get their version of events from the training ground that day. He was left in no doubt that McKinlay was the guilty party. Brown also spoke to Larsson about it. Brown came to the conclusion that action had to be taken against the Scotland defender and met the player to tell him he would be fined. To his credit, McKinlay never disputed any of the claims made against him and accepted his punishment. He met with Larsson to apologise a few days later. He also asked captain Tom Boyd to call a meeting to give him the opportunity to stand up in the dressing-room and apologise to the squad.

Jackie McNamara: 'People who don't know Henrik might think that he is a quiet guy with a deep voice and that he is perhaps arrogant. I don't think that's him. He can be hard to read, but he knows what he wants. I've a lot of time for Henrik. I like him as a person, and his record as a footballer speaks for itself.

'I sensed something was brewing that day, probably had been for a while, and I don't just mean with Tosh. I think a few of the lads felt that they were really on the outside and not a proper part of the manager's set-up. Naturally, that caused a bit of resentment and friction. The fact that there wasn't a lot of communication between the coaching staff and the players also didn't help. A few of us felt that something was going to happen one day in training. We just weren't sure when and with whom. It turned out that it was between

Tosh and Henrik. Tosh headered Henrik. I'll never forget the thud it made as his head made contact. What a noise! It would have knocked me out. But Henrik stayed on his feet. However, it helped bring us all closer together. A few things between the players were aired and sorted. And a few things between the management and the players were thrown into the open and sorted.

'We then had to play Rangers two days later, and the club was in the headlines yet again for negative reasons. We lost, and my memory from that day was Richard Gough's celebration after he scored a goal. A few of us thought that he gestured that Rangers were going to do ten in a row. I tucked that away, hoping to prove him wrong at the end of the season. It was another wee spur, if you like.'

Tom Boyd: 'Wim was very hands on every day and took every training session. His main focus was on the first XI, and most of his work was always with them. If you were not in the first team, then you felt like an outsider. That approach created animosity between the players. I didn't agree with the way Wim went about his business at that time, but I could see where he was coming from.

'He also hated changing his team and his formation. We got him to switch from 4–3–3 to 4–4–2 for, I think, the 2–1 home defeat to Dunfermline. Of course, that went pear-shaped and normal service resumed after that.

'Regardless of our result on a match day, Wim was never one for deep discussion after the game. He would always wait until a Monday morning. I'm not sure why he went about his business that way. Maybe it was because his English wasn't very good, and he preferred time to gather his thoughts. And he never, ever, swore. Come to think of it, I don't think he ever raised his voice.'

Tommy Johnson: 'We had a great team spirit, but a kind of rift had developed between some of the foreign lads and some of the others in the squad. I'm not exactly sure why. There wasn't a particular incident that sparked a divide. It was one of these things that the players knew was going on, but it was allowed to fester. It had to come to a head at some point, as we knew things couldn't continue as they were. The incident between Tosh and Henrik was the turning point. That incident wasn't how we imagined we'd get things sorted, but ironically it did bring the squad closer together. There was no squad meeting or anything – it just sort of happened. The rift disappeared, and we became a solid unit after that.'

Immediately after the training session that became known as the 'Battle of Barrowfield', Larsson boarded a plane back to Sweden to attend a family funeral. It was feared that he wouldn't return, as he would not be able to work beside McKinlay. But, after things calmed down, Larsson, his face still swollen, returned from his homeland in time to be considered for selection for the game against Walter Smith's side.

So, things were sorted? It didn't look that way in the game as Celtic turned in a well-below-par performance.

seven

Losing to Rangers

Celtic went into the first Old Firm game of the season on 8 November in a chaotic state after Tosh McKinlay's head-butt and Davie Hay's sacking. Larsson played, but, predictably, there was no place for the Scottish defender in the squad.

Whether the events at Celtic had anything to do with it or not, there appeared to be even more determination about the Rangers team. They had brought back Richard Gough from Kansas City Wizards to help them attempt to clinch ten in a row. It was also Walter Smith's first of his final run of Old Firm games after announcing he'd be stepping down as manager at the end of the season.

Rangers dominated the early stages, and a Gough header rebounded off Old Firm debutant Jonathan Gould's right-hand post. There was also an early blow for Celtic when Alan Stubbs was subbed for Rico Annoni after Marco Negri's elbow caught the Scouser in the eye.

For three seasons during the reign of Tommy Burns, Andy Goram had made the life of the then Celtic gaffer a misery, pulling off save after save. He was at it again in this game, and when Larsson's header was superbly saved by the Gers keeper Wim Jansen must have felt the way Burns had. Minutes later, following a Simon

Donnelly cross, the Swede was again denied by the brilliance of the Scotland number one, who managed to keep out another headed effort.

Marc Rieper had a fine game for Celtic that afternoon but could do nothing to prevent the only goal of the game. After an early spell of pressure from Celtic, Rangers replied in style and took the lead in the 29th minute. Brian Laudrup raced away from Stéphane Mahé, and his cross was like an arrow towards Gough's foot. The veteran stopper showed the composure of a prolific marksman to guide the ball sweetly into the net past Gould. Gould then made good saves from Alex Cleland and Paul Gascoigne to keep Celtic in with a chance of not leaving empty handed. But that notion all but disappeared in the 81st minute when Mahé was red carded by referee Kenny Clark for a lunge on Laudrup. It was his second booking, following an earlier one for clattering Negri. Rangers took the points, and the victory meant that Ibrox boss Smith had lost just five of the twenty-five league clashes with Celtic during his time in charge.

Stéphane Mahé: 'Ah, Old Firm games. What was it about me and those games? They are supposed to be the best occasions you can experience as an Old Firm player. You are supposed to revel in the atmosphere, feel the need to win the game and underline your supremacy, thrive on the chance to be kings of Glasgow for another week.

'But every time I played in one, I seemed to see a red card. At least it feels that way. I had some great Old Firm games – the 5–1 win when Jozef Vengloš was manager certainly sticks out as the best ever – but I also had some ones I'd rather forget about for ever.

'My first one was like that. At first, I was buzzing with the atmosphere, lapping it up. Then we lost a goal, and I got sent off for two challenges. Laudrup was the man that hurt me most, because he was my direct opponent when we lost that day. I don't remember how I felt as I walked off the park or sat in the dressing-room at the end of the game. The one thing that does stick out, though, and one that typifies the Celtic side of that era, was the attitude of my teammates afterwards. They were down. We'd just lost the first Old Firm game of the season, and it was like a hammer blow to our league chances. One game doesn't win the league, it's done over the course of a season, but psychologically Rangers had hit us badly.

'That was bad enough, but I was sitting there having left the side with ten men, feeling even worse. Yet, no one pointed the finger of blame at me, there were no arguments – only an arm around me to help me keep going. And that spirit was borne out in our next game against Rangers. We didn't win the game, but we played right to the final minute and equalised. We showed we weren't going to give up without a fight.'

It was another painful Ibrox memory for Stubbs.

Alan Stubbs: 'When I signed, I didn't fully appreciate what nine in a row was all about. I'll never forget my first Old Firm game at Ibrox the season before. There was a big crowd, 90 per cent of them Rangers fans, and there was a hostile atmosphere. I was spat on by several Rangers fans as I made my way down the tunnel for the warm-up and when we ran out for the start of the game. I thought, "Fucking hell. What have I done?" When you went to retrieve the ball during the warm-up, the Rangers fans would invite you over to get it from them and then keep it. They'd verbally slaughter you and then throw the ball in the other direction.

'I found the abuse ferocious and personal. To be spat at in any walk of life is disrespectful. I hated that. It was horrible. But it shows that an Old Firm match is more than just a game in Scotland. After playing in Scotland for five years, I can respect that way of thinking now. I'm proud to say that I was a part of Scottish football when there was so much at stake between the Old Firm clubs and that I played my part in helping to stop Rangers create their own piece of history.

'The religious element of playing in Scotland is something I will never forget. At times, the whole religious thing and the way some people used it in their lives disillusioned me. I grew up as an Everton supporter, and we had a rivalry with Liverpool. But there was always a respect there. We would walk down the street together on the way to the derby match. Some people would sit together. It wasn't that way with many of the Old Firm fans. Not being from Scotland, I found the whole Catholic and Protestant thing very hard to come to terms with. But I did enjoy playing in the Old Firm games.

'The thing I found hardest was trying to stay calm the night before the match and in the final few moments before kick-off. There was also intense media coverage for five or six days in the build-up to the game. The newspapers couldn't get enough of it, and sometimes there would be eight or nine pages on the game in one day. There had to be a back-page story on the match, and it was even better if there was also a front-page story on an Old Firm player. I used to try my best to be courteous to the media and give as many interviews as possible. But there was that fear factor after the interview about how your words would be interpreted and what the headline might be. We used to have a laugh in the dressing-room about it, and there was always a sigh of relief when you read the stuff and didn't have a problem with what had been written.'

Jonathan Gould: 'I was sore to lose the first Old Firm game. We badly wanted to win it. My memory from the game is Richard Gough running away to celebrate his goal with both hands in the air and his ten fingers spread. I'm not sure what kind of signal he was trying to send out, but Rangers must have gone home that night and been pretty confident they were going to win the league again. The outcome of Old Firm games usually have a huge bearing on the destination of the title, and you never like to lose one. Yet we only took four points from twelve in the league against Rangers that season.

'What we lacked in points against them we made up for in harmony. Of course, we had one or two incidents on the training field, but that happens at every club five or six times a season – at least. It's a good thing to get things off your chest. The worst thing is to keep your problems and grievances boiling inside, as they eventually spill over.

'We had an excellent team spirit, and we all gelled very quickly. Wim brought in team players, guys willing to get stuck in. We had no prima donnas, not that we would have entertained them if we did have. There was also a nice touch of shaking hands with everyone, something I'd not had at previous clubs. Every guy in the dressing-room shook my hand when I signed and wished me all the best. I made sure I shook every new player by the hand after that. It was a small thing, but important, nonetheless.

'From the outset, I was very naive as to the importance of the ten-in-a-row thing. The foreign guys, such as Regi, Marc, Henrik and Stéphane, would have been the same, I'm sure. I reckon it was maybe a good thing, as we didn't have any excess baggage to carry around. Yes, we lost the first Old Firm game, but we had enough belief to think that we'd be able to bounce back. However, it was vital to beat them in the next Old Firm match or, at the very least, not lose it.'

The bright spot for Celtic in a horrendous week was that Paul Lambert signed for the club in a £1.7-million move from Borussia Dortmund. From the outset, he had been identified as a priority signing by Jansen and his backroom team, but there appeared to be some reluctance on the part of Jock Brown to push the deal through. It was the belief of people on the coaching staff that Brown did not want Lambert.

Lambert enjoyed his life in Dortmund. He was adored by the supporters, and respected and rated by his teammates and management. He had won the Champions League with the German outfit in May 1997 when they'd defeated Juventus. Dortmund wanted to offer him a lucrative new contract. Off the park, though, Lambert had his personal problems. His young son, Christopher, wasn't in the best of health, and Lambert agreed with his wife Monica that a return to Scotland was the best option. Only the Old Firm could afford his transfer fee and were big enough to tempt him back. Rangers were sounded out but declined to follow up on the tip-off. It was different with their rivals. They wanted him, but Lambert's agent at that time,

Gordon Smith, wasn't happy with the way Celtic were trying to conduct business.

Gordon Smith: 'It was made clear to me by Wim Jansen, Murdo MacLeod and Davie Hay that they wanted to sign Paul. I had established a transfer fee with Dortmund that would release Paul. Because of the circumstances surrounding Paul's reason for wanting to leave Germany, Dortmund put a very fair price on him. It was also non-negotiable. I informed Celtic of the price and expected the deal to be done quite quickly. But Jock Brown was stalling. I don't know why.

'I was aware there might be a problem at Celtic's end and approached Dortmund to ask if there had been any contact. Dortmund weren't pleased with Celtic and the way they had tried to conduct their business. I was told by Dortmund that Celtic had made a derisory offer. I thought at that point they might pull the plug on any proposed deal, but their respect for Paul and his family meant they didn't rule out doing business.'

Realising the deal could collapse, Jansen made a personal plea to Lambert after a Scotland international match at Celtic Park. They had a private meeting in the Parkhead boot room, but it wasn't totally satisfactory and still left the deal hanging in the balance. It all hinged on Brown, a scenario the Dutchman would have preferred to have avoided.

Wim Jansen: 'The chase to get Paul was quite complicated. I knew his qualities from seeing him play and from some videotapes. He was in Glasgow for a Scotland game at Celtic Park, and we managed to get a few words with him to explain how much we wanted him to leave Borussia Dortmund and join Celtic. He was left in no doubt from that meeting that we had lots of confidence in him. It was a meeting that helped to clinch the transfer. Davie Hay and Andy Ritchie were both very important in getting the transfer to happen.'

Paul Lambert: 'I told Wim that day at Parkhead that I didn't really want to come. I was of the belief that people at the top of the club didn't want me, and there was no way I was going to leave

Dortmund, a club that couldn't do enough for me, to go to a club where people in the boardroom thought I shouldn't be wearing the club jersey. Wim asked me to give him one more chance to sort out the deal. I knew he really wanted me but had my doubts the deal would happen. My other option was to stay with Dortmund. My son was still having convulsions, so the best option was to return to Scotland. I left it with Wim to try to move it on.'

It was made clear to Brown how badly Lambert was wanted. Not completing the transfer wasn't an option for the general manager. The deal eventually did go through on 5 November after the transfer fee was agreed, despite Dortmund's best efforts to get Lambert to change his mind. Lambert's last game was a Champions League match at home to Parma, and the crowd gave him an unforgettable send-off.

Gordon Smith: 'Paul had to sign some forms after the game to finalise his release and allow him to move to Celtic. We were in the office of the Dortmund sporting director, and he produced the necessary documentation. Emotions were still running high in the office, as it was only an hour after the fans had said goodbye to Paul. They had given him a fantastic farewell. I was really touched by it.

'Michael Meier produced a pen and offered it to Paul to sign the papers. Paul reached out, but at the last second the pen was pulled away. The Dortmund sporting director told Paul that he was making a big mistake and that there was still time to make a U-turn on his decision. "You are a hero here, Paul. Stay and enjoy the rest of the season with us. Don't go. Really, why are you going back to Scotland?"

'Paul explained that it was a decision based on what was best for his family. The pleas from Dortmund were genuine, and I remember thinking to myself at the time that I would have not bothered signing the papers and would have opted to stay put.'

Wim Jansen: 'In my way of thinking, Paul Lambert was the most important part of the jigsaw. I wanted him in from the start, but it was not possible. But he eventually came to us, and I knew it was better late than never. Paul brought the perfect balance to the team.

'He was also my coach on the pitch. I spoke a lot to him after every game. We would also both come in most Sunday mornings, and we would sit and chat about the team and the opponents. Paul was a big, big help on the pitch.'

Paul Lambert: 'Whether Jock Brown wanted someone else instead of me has never been tested in a court of law. However, my own view is that he would have preferred to have had someone else. For some strange reason, he didn't want me. I said as much in my book, because if you write a book you have to give an honest account of the things that have happened to you. People might not necessarily agree with what you say, and it might upset them, but all you can do is give an honest assessment. I have bumped into Jock a couple of times in recent years, and I have said hello. I don't hold grudges. Life is too short.'

eight

Keeping the Title Hopes Alive

A home game against Motherwell on 16 November was Celtic's next fixture. This clash would usually have signalled three points in the bag, but the match ended in a surprise defeat. Celtic pounded the Well goal and came close to breaking the deadlock on several occasions. Stevie Woods pulled off a great save to deny Alan Stubbs, and then Simo Valakari cleared an effort off the line from the same player. Henrik Larsson had a goal disallowed for offside and saw a header crash off the crossbar. Stephen Craigan also cleared a Regi Blinker effort off the line.

Blinker was then red carded by referee Willie Young for elbowing Kevin Christie. Owen Coyle put Motherwell ahead, and they looked good for the three points, as they defended well and used the man advantage to great effect. Young then disallowed a Craig Burley effort, and Alex McLeish's side scored again with seconds remaining when Coyle sent sub Mickey Weir clear and he slotted the ball past Jonathan Gould. It was a poor result and a disastrous home debut for Paul Lambert.

After the defeat, observers were predictably emphasising that Celtic needed to bring in a proven goal scorer.

Darren Jackson: 'My fight to make a top-team comeback continued, and I was invited by Craig Brown to join the Scotland squad for a friendly against France in St Etienne. I wasn't chosen with a view to playing. It was just a gesture from Craig to give me a change of scenery, and I was grateful to him. That said, I was feeling good at that time and enjoyed the couple of training sessions. Craig gave an interview to the media and praised me on the way I had fought back from the operation and the way I had worked hard to regain my fitness. He also said I could have played in the game for him, such was my attitude and desire. We lost the match 2–1.

'The impression I got from Wim when I returned to Celtic from international duty was that he wasn't too happy with me and did not appreciate Craig's comments. Celtic played Motherwell at home that day, and we lost 2–0. I wasn't in the squad. But I was named as a sub for our game against Rangers at Parkhead.'

Defeat wasn't on Celtic's agenda when Rangers came to Parkhead on 19 November. This midweek clash delivered everything you expect from an Old Firm game – except a winning goal. Celtic started the game at a furious pace, and Paul Lambert came close with a drive just inches wide of Andy Goram's right-hand post. But Rangers weren't for sitting back, and Jonas Thern released Paul Gascoigne, whose surging run created space for Marco Negri. But the Italian shot wildly over the crossbar from just 16 yards when he had plenty of time to pick his spot. Negri then forced Gould into a save in the 31st minute.

After surviving the early pressure, Celtic looked set to take the lead through Simon Donnelly on the stroke of half-time, but Stuart McCall slid in with a brilliant last-gasp tackle to prevent the Scotland player from getting a close-range shot in on Goram.

Gazza was sent packing in the 58th minute by referee John Rowbotham after the whistler felt the midfielder was guilty of an illegal use of the arm in the face of Morten Wieghorst after the pair had tussled. This should have been a signal for Celtic to dominate, but it was Rangers who took the lead in the 71st minute. After a few misses, Negri eventually found the net. He played a one-two with Gordon Durie and had time to smash a low shot past Gould from a fairly tight angle to send the 3,000 Gers fans inside Parkhead into a frenzy.

It looked as though the Celts were set for a defeat, but Alan Stubbs had something totally different in mind. In injury time, Celtic forced a corner kick, Goram misjudged the flight and the ball ended up at the edge of the box. Jackie McNamara was there to collect it, and his cross to the back post was met by Stubbs. The Scouse defender showed magnificent spring to rise above every other player and send a header past Goram.

The result meant Celtic hadn't defeated Rangers in ten league clashes. It was a spirited fightback, but the performance was still not enough to suggest there was the class and the self-belief in the team to ensure they had enough to end their fiercest rivals' domination.

Alan Stubbs: 'I'm not just saying this because it was my goal, but I think that was a big turning point. Had we lost, I think we'd have had only a slim, slim chance of winning the title.

'Andy Goram had one of his usual top-class games against us that evening, and when I played against him in my first season at Celtic he was often the difference between the teams. He was outstanding, and his reflex saves sometimes defied belief. He used to make a lot of us feel totally deflated, and we often had to ask ourselves if we'd ever score past him.

'I managed to do so in that game, and we left the field feeling like we'd won the game. Rangers must have felt like they'd lost. Had I not scored, we were looking at three defeats in a row and the possibility of our league season being over in November. Don't get me wrong. I'm not saying it was a defining moment, but it definitely had a bearing on the destination of the title.'

Darren Jackson: 'I was overjoyed. It was great to be back. I remember the Celtic fans singing "Walk On" as we came out for the second half, and it sounded to me as though it was the loudest rendition ever. More than likely it wasn't, but that's how it felt. I then came on as a sub, and the cheers I received from the Celtic fans were deafening. It felt like the crowd was the loudest I'd ever heard it. Of course, it wasn't. But that was the emotional state I was in.

'Gazza received a red card that night for slapping Morten Wieghorst, and Rangers took the lead when Marco Negri scored with a shot across Jonathan Gould. To be fair to Gouldie, it was down to his weak side – which could have been any side, to be honest! Alan Stubbs levelled the score in the final moments of the game, and I ran into the net to retrieve the ball. But my studs tangled in the net, and I fell on my backside. It appeared on *Soccer AM* on the Saturday morning in one of those "embarrassing moments" clips!

'On a more serious note, Alan's goal was a huge psychological boost. If we had lost that night, I think we would not have recovered to go on and win the league.

'I was glad to be back, and the lads in the squad were pleased for me. The same could not be said for everyone, though! My brother-in-law Jim is a big Rangers fan and he sat in with the Rangers fans that night. He gave me absolute pelters. He sat next to Ian Durrant.'

On 22 November, Dundee United came to Celtic Park for what was a dress rehearsal for the Coca-Cola Cup final eight days later. However, given the choice of sacrificing one for the other, Wim Jansen would have taken the three points from the league fixture before any silverware.

Andy Thom was given a rare start, having been on the bench for every game since 4 October. And the German responded positively with a fine display. In the first half, Blinker almost made it 1–0 for Celtic, and Gary McSwegan forced Gould into a brave save at the other end. Then, 11 minutes before half-time, the Hoops were awarded a penalty by referee Hugh Dallas after David Hannah was bundled over by Erik Pedersen as he tried to get on the end of a lovely Thom cross from the right. Thom took the kick and steered it low to Sieb Dykstra's left-hand corner.

Dykstra was poor in the 63rd minute when he spilled a powerless McNamara shot, and Larsson was there to roll it over the line to make it 2–0. Celtic were now in cruise control. They scored again in the 68th minute when Steven Pressley lost possession to Wieghorst and he fed Thom. The striker made no mistake and expertly shot across Dykstra into the right-hand corner of the net. Then, 13 minutes from time, Simon Donnelly sent Larsson clear, and the Swede made no mistake when he chipped Dykstra for his 12th goal of the season to make it 4–0.

It was a fine day for Celtic, and Thom was given a standing ovation when he was subbed eight minutes from time for Tosh McKinlay. However, there were no such plaudits from the stand for Blinker. He was booed by the Celtic fans as he continued to struggle to make an impact at the club.

nine

Coca-Cola Cup Triumph

Cup football is about booking your place in the next round regardless of how poorly you perform. And that was the case for Celtic when a Craig Burley strike handed the Parkhead men a 1–0 victory over Dunfermline on 14 October to book their Coca-Cola Cup final slot.

It wasn't pretty to watch; in fact, it was a hard slog for the travelling supporters to watch their heroes go through the motions. But did any of them care as they left celebrating the vital win? Not a chance. If watching their side lift silverware meant sitting through some games in which they weren't entertained with free-flowing football and pretty passing moves, they were willing to settle for that in the short term. Success, more than anything else, is what the Celtic supporters wanted, and they seemed set to get their way in the Coca-Cola Cup.

Perhaps the importance of the semi-final was the reason that Wim Jansen's players did not quite hit top form. With just over 20 minutes remaining, Celtic needed a player to rise above the mediocrity and grab the tie by the scruff of the neck. They found exactly what they were looking for in Burley. Brought in to be the difference in the middle of the park, the Scotland midfielder certainly didn't let Jansen down when he needed him most.

A great run from Jackie McNamara down the right created panic in the Fifers' defence, and his pass found Henrik Larsson, who laid the ball into the path of Burley to strike a powerful shot low into the net from 22 yards. As much as the game was forgettable, nobody could begrudge Celtic the victory and a contest against Dundee United for the right to take home the trophy.

Ibrox wasn't a happy cup venue for Tommy Burns during his time as Celtic manager. He lost the 1994 Coca-Cola Cup final to First Division side Raith Rovers on a penalty shoot-out and then the Tennent's Scottish Cup semi-final to Falkirk, who were also a league below the Hoops, three years later. But they were back at the home of Rangers on 30 November, this time to play against United. On this occasion, there was no upset, and the Hoops ran out comfortable 3–0 winners. Marc Rieper opened the scoring after he powerfully headed home a Morten Wieghorst cross. That was in the twentieth minute, and just three minutes later the lead doubled when Mark Perry was slack with a pass and Larsson intercepted. As he ran in on Sieb Dykstra's goal, he had options on either side but chose to shoot from 20 yards, and the ball deflected off Maurice Malpas and into the back of the net. Regi Blinker and Andy Thom also had chances to score but missed.

The destination of the trophy was left in no doubt when Burley put his side three ahead in the fifty-eighth minute. Blinker drove in a cross, and Burley was brave enough to steam in and bullet a header past the helpless Dykstra. It was a disappointing display from United, as they delivered very little in the way of a threat to Jonathan Gould, but Celtic's fine performance can't be overlooked. It brought Jansen his first trophy as manager and started to dispel any doubts some people might have had about his ability to steer Celtic to a successful campaign. It was also the first time Celtic had lifted this particular prize in 15 years.

The players enjoyed their moments of adulation but couldn't believe that Jock Brown tried to hijack one of their moments of glory. As the jubilant Celtic fans waited outside Parkhead for the team bus to return from Ibrox, Jansen had to tell the general manager to hand the trophy to Tom Boyd.

This was not the first time Brown had tried to interfere in team matters, much to the annoyance of the Dutch coach. At the start of Jansen's reign, Brown had come into the manager's office after games to chat to Jansen and his opposite numbers. Jansen felt Brown had no right to be in the inner sanctum and that the manager's office was strictly off limits to non-football people.

A few players were also not happy with Brown's influence at the start of the campaign. On the way to games, he would turn up in the official team shell suit and invite himself up to the back of the bus to chew the fat with the players. The players were not happy and let it be known that Brown had no place in their pack.

By that stage of the season, the relationship between Jansen and Brown was over. The Dutchman wanted nothing more to do with him. Interfering with team matters, the delay in securing Paul Lambert's signature and finally the sacking of David Hay was too much for Jansen. Their relationship was beyond repair and could never be recovered.

But none of this could cloud the joy the players felt as they secured their first trophy of the season. And no one was happier that day than Italian defender Rico Annoni, who celebrated the cup win by wearing a green, white and gold wig as he lapped up the success.

Rico Annoni: 'The city of Glasgow and the supporters of Celtic made me feel very welcome. I would do little things to try to give something back and show my appreciation. I started to wear one green boot and one white boot. And I wore a curly wig when we celebrated winning the Coca-Cola Cup. Small gestures from me, but I think the fans were pleased to see me make an effort to bond with them and let my personality shine through. At most of the clubs I played for, I had a strong relationship with the supporters. When I left Roma to join Celtic, I hired an aircraft to fly over the Olympic Stadium and display the message "Thanks Roma fans for your support". I had the same feelings for the Celtic supporters.'

Regi Blinker: 'It was a nice feeling to win this prize. We were all different characters, but strong characters. The Celtic team of 1997–98 reminded me of the Feyenoord team I played for in 1993. There was a great bond and a desire to do well for the teammate standing beside you.

'Wim was also just about the same manager for Celtic as he was that year with Feyenoord. His vision and his approach hadn't changed. He was always a boss who liked to explain things in a simple way. He didn't like to complicate the game of football. I think he had also mellowed by the time he got to Celtic. At Feyenoord, he would raise his voice and be confrontational if he felt it necessary. At Celtic, he was calm and never shouted at the players. His man-management was good. He would say to me in a quiet moment before a game, "Regi, if you want to take a player on, then do it. I can't think of a defender in Europe who'd be able to stop you." Out on the pitch, I'd go for it. And if I did beat the defender, I'd think, "There you go. Wim's right." He was also hard on me when it was necessary. He was always telling me to be on the touchline, facing into the game when I received a pass. "Never receive the ball out wide with your back to goal," he'd say. "Face the game. Face the game."'

Marc Rieper: 'We knew the League Cup was a small piece of silverware, but it was a marker that we had something to offer that season. We had won a domestic prize, and now we were going after the big prize. We had a determination to stop Rangers winning another title. I scored a goal, and I enjoyed the moment. I also thought Morten Wieghorst was exceptional that day.'

Morten Wieghorst, who was man of the match in the cup-final win, was equally complimentary about his fellow countryman: 'Marc was a great signing. Before joining the club, he phoned me to ask about Celtic. I think his mind was already made up, but he just wanted a little bit of reassurance. Mind you, he knew a lot about Celtic and the challenge that was ahead of him, and he was right up for it. I don't think I could have got him to change his mind about coming even if I had tried. He was a no-nonsense defender, exactly what we needed. The Celtic fans liked his style, and he soon became a firm favourite. His goal sent us on our way to win the cup that day.'

Jackie McNamara: 'It was brilliant to win the Coca-Cola Cup. I'd never won anything, and it was a great feeling. To go to Ibrox and win a trophy was special. Morten and Marc played so well that day.

'I got drug tested after the game and couldn't produce a sample at first. It took ages, so the team bus left without me, and I missed going back to the Celtic Park and being greeted by the fans. I was raging. In the end, I got a taxi back to Parkhead from Ibrox.

'The team had a great social life that season. We'd eat and drink together at least once a week, and we'd go karting quite often. I remember one day we were in T.G.I. Friday's for a few cocktails, and I was on the strawberry daiquiris. Craig Burley was up to his usual pranks and put his false teeth in my glass. I didn't know until I felt his falsers hit off my own teeth. It was disgusting. I lifted his teeth out of the glass and pretended to throw them away. The players and the bar staff spent half an hour looking for them. Burley was shouting, "I'm naked without my teeth. I'm naked. I'm away home." I had put them in my pocket and gave them back to him once I'd had a good laugh watching him squirm.'

Jonathan Gould: 'After we won the Coca-Cola Cup, Jock Brown gave me a new contract. I made sure that it included a clause stating that if we won the league, I was due another pay rise and a new deal. I sort of forgot all about it, and it wasn't until a couple of months into the season that I reminded Jock about it.'

Davie Hay: 'I felt the big turning point was winning the Coca-Cola Cup in November. That proved to Wim and the squad that they could win silverware. The players also gelled well off the park and credit to Craig Burley, Alan Stubbs and Tommy Johnson for organising events to bring the players closer together, which definitely helped on match days. Good team spirit can sometimes be the difference between success and failure.'

The club were happy to have won the tournament, but one player who walked away from Ibrox that day with questions to ask himself was Paul Lambert. He was dropped to the bench by Jansen after failing to come close to the kind of form that had persuaded Celtic to pay nearly £2 million for him. But, being an honest pro, there were no tantrums from Lambert. He knew that he didn't deserve to be in the team and that he had to recapture his form quickly. In the event, it took him a while.

Paul Lambert: 'For two months, I couldn't kick my own backside, let alone a football. I couldn't get going, couldn't pass to myself, let alone a teammate. I just couldn't get Borussia Dortmund out of my head. I'd go home and speak to Monica about it. It was a strange feeling to be playing for such a big club, in such an important season, but not being able to get into it.

'Thinking about it now, I suppose it was a natural reaction. Dortmund became such a big part of my life, and I'd won the Champions League with them less than six months earlier, but I had to leave because my young son Christopher wasn't keeping well. It wasn't like I didn't like playing for them or they didn't want me to be there. They understood my reasons for wanting to return to Scotland, and the club and fans gave me a wonderful send-off. I played against Parma in the Champions League, and the supporters stayed behind for an hour to say goodbye. It nearly brought a tear to my eye. I also walked out on the club after we had qualified for the later stages of the tournament. We got to the semi-finals again that season.

'There was also talk of me going to Juventus. An agent spoke to me on behalf of Mr Moggi, club president, shortly after we defeated Juventus in the Champions League final and asked if I'd be interested in moving to Turin. I'm not sure, but maybe it was because Didier Deschamps was moving and they were looking for a replacement. It was flattering, but I was happy to stay with Dortmund. Dortmund are a massive club, absolutely massive. I played in front of around 65,000 every week, and now they have an 83,000-capacity stadium.'

Alan Stubbs was delighted to get his hands on his first piece of silverware after having moved to Celtic 16 months earlier. He too had suffered from family problems when he moved to Glasgow, which didn't help him find his true form. In a bid to help, Tommy Burns had decided that it was a good idea to make him captain. Stubbs was honoured but had his reservations. Some senior players in the Celtic dressing-room felt that it wasn't right that a new player should be given the armband so quickly. But Stubbs knew that he couldn't knock back the offer, as it might have been construed as a sign of weakness.

Alan Stubbs: 'Tommy appointed me as captain for a spell, and it was a surprise. It gave me more responsibility and also meant that I had to keep my eye on the ball at all times. I think I sort of took away games for granted when I first came to Scotland, thinking that every fixture against a "wee" club would be a formality. It wasn't. To get a victory, you had to be 100 per cent mentally prepared. But our preparations weren't always ideal, and when you entered an away dressing-room you couldn't wait to get the job done and get right back on the team bus. The away changing-rooms at Dundee and Dunfermline stick in my mind for some reason. They weren't particularly nice facilities. I think the toilet cubicle at Dundee was in the dressing-room with only a partition separating it from the changing area. It was a real eye-opener. On more than a few occasions, I thought to myself, "What kind of ground is this?"

'Teams were also desperate to beat us. When I was at Bolton, I was sort of used to being the underdog, and we had some memorable battles with the likes of Arsenal and Liverpool in the cup competitions. But this was different. Every side gave their lot to beat us. Some players would be Celtic fans and ask for a jersey after the game, and others wanted to rip it off your back during the game because you played for the Catholic team in Scotland. I just couldn't get my head around it. It was a whole new concept for me and the non-Scottish lads at the club. I hadn't known religion to play a part in football before I arrived in Scotland to play for Celtic.

'But the only thing that was on my mind that day was to enjoy winning the cup. We had waited a long time to be known as "winners", and this was a small, but vital, step in the right direction. Had we lost to United, we would have been on a downer, and our supporters would have felt like chucking it. Thankfully, it was all positive.'

ten

Celebrating Success

The month of December was always going to be huge for Celtic, and the five league games they were due to play in that thirty-one-day period would give a clearer indication of their title credentials. But there was also business still to be done off the park, and the chase for Harald Brattbakk came closer to its conclusion. Other clubs were interested in the Norwegian striker, and he had the option of joining Portuguese giants Benfica, but Parkhead seemed to be his preferred destination. Davie Hay was sure of Brattbakk's credentials and claimed in a newspaper article that the player had the quality to score the goals to take Celtic towards the title.

Fergus McCann worked hard to finalise the deal, and as he was doing so it became public knowledge that he would walk away with an estimated £30-million profit when he quit Parkhead after his five-year stint at the helm, which would be some time during the summer of 1999.

The first port of call in Celtic's hectic December league schedule was away to Bobby Williamson's Kilmarnock on 6 December. Henrik Larsson, Craig Burley and Simon Donnelly all tested Killie keeper Dragoje Leković and were distraught to find no way past him for the entire 90 minutes as the game ended in a disappointing 0–0 draw for Celtic. In a game full of penalty claims and fearless tackling, it was entertaining stuff and a tough one for referee Mike McCurry to handle. In the end, he turned down three pleas for spot-kicks from the home side after Jérôme Vareille, Pat Nevin and Paul Wright all asked the question of the whistler and on every occasion were denied. McCurry could have also red carded Tom Boyd when he looked to be ready for a second yellow after fouling Vareille. Overall, Celtic may well have felt relieved to leave Ayrshire with a point, as they were under the cosh for long spells, and the Killie central midfielders Mark Reilly and Gary Holt had a strong grip on the proceedings.

The 0–0 scoreline meant they trailed league leaders Hearts by a massive seven points and got the vital month off to a dreadful start. The positive from that 24-hour period was that a deal to sign Brattbakk was finally agreed. Due to the two- or three-month chase to land him, his reputation soared, and he arrived as the man expected to solve Celtic's goal-scoring problems. It was a touch unfair on Brattbakk, and time would show that he didn't have as much talent as had been suggested. More than 40 members of the media were at Glasgow Airport as he landed to begin his new Hoops career.

Harald Brattbakk: 'Celtic first expressed an interest around September or October time. I had been doing well in the Champions League and had attracted attention from a few clubs. I was keen to explore any options, because I felt like a change of club and moving to play in a bigger league. I spoke to Rosenborg and explained my feelings, and told them I wanted to challenge myself to see how well I could perform in a league abroad. They understood my situation and agreed to keep me informed of any interest.

'Then I heard Celtic were asking about me. The two clubs were in talks and eventually agreed a transfer fee. I was given permission to fly to Scotland to discuss personal terms and to see the stadium and the city. Before my arrival in Glasgow, all I knew about Celtic was that they were a huge club and had a famous rivalry with Rangers. But I didn't quite realise what football meant to the people of Scotland and the media until I touched down in the country.

'On arrival, there were TV crews, newspapers, cameramen, radio microphones – everyone wanted a piece of me to find out my feelings and thoughts about Celtic. I had never experienced anything like it in Norway. I also think that I surprised them a little bit with my appearance. I don't think that they expected this skinny guy with glasses to be the new Celtic striker. I think they thought, "This guy doesn't look like a footballer." But that's just me – that's my appearance.'

On Tuesday, 9 December, Celtic faced a potential banana skin at Pittodrie. But they coped with the pressure to come away with one of their best results of the season.

Darren Jackson scored many goals in his career, but his strike that winter night is one he'll never forget. In his journey to Parkhead via clubs such as Meadowbank Thistle, Newcastle United and Dundee United, the Scotland striker had been involved in quite a few memorable moments. The strike in the match against Aberdeen wasn't a contender for goal of the season, but it meant everything to Jackson. His cool, confident finish in the 73rd minute made sure of another win for Celtic and also announced his return to health after a lengthy spell in rehabilitation following his brain surgery. And no one could blame him for celebrating his goal with such passion, because it marked the resurrection of his career and fired out a warning to new £2-million striker Harald Brattbakk that he had competition for a starting slot.

Henrik Larsson netted the opening goal, against the run of play, just a few minutes before the interval. Aberdeen had the better chances, both Billy Dodds and Stephen Glass forcing good saves from Jonathan Gould, but when Larsson is in your team there is always the chance that he'll find the back of the net just when you need it most. Stéphane Mahé's low cross was knocked out by Jim Leighton, but only to Larsson, who steered his shot powerfully into the net.

However, the night belonged to Jackson. His last start for Celtic had been against St Johnstone almost four months earlier. And his return to fitness was perfectly timed, as Celtic desperately needed a fresh face to help turn results around. Prior to the win at Pittodrie, they had dropped ten points in their previous five matches. The victory brought them closer to Rangers and league leaders Hearts, while Aberdeen were left rooted at the foot of the table.

Darren Jackson: 'My first goal after the operation came at Aberdeen in a 2–0 win. Regi Blinker hit a shot, and Jim Leighton couldn't hold it. I followed in to get the rebound and slammed it home. It felt great, although it gave me no pleasure to do that to my great friend, Jim Leighton. I ran over to the huge travelling support and launched myself into them. Thankfully, the ref didn't book me. He had grasped the situation. As I ran away from the celebrations, I screamed at the top of my voice, "I'm back."

'I was also happy for Jack Mulhearn, Brian Scott and Jock Brown. When I made my comeback, I gave each of them a bottle of champagne as a small token of my appreciation for their help. But I told them only to open it when I scored a goal for Celtic. To be honest, I thought it would end up being a vintage bottle!'

Hearts were expected to put up a strong challenge when they came along the M8 to the East End of Glasgow on 13 December, and a victory for them would have more or less killed off Jansen and his players' challenge for the league crown. But Hearts were a disappointment and didn't force Gould into a single save all afternoon. The Hoops totally dominated the game, and it was a surprise that they only won by a single goal. The only consolation for Hearts was that they remained top of the league that night, something Jim Jefferies was delighted about.

Jambos keeper Gilles Rousset was in exceptional form, and he denied certain goals for Blinker, McNamara and Larsson with top-drawer saves. Paul Lambert had a storming game for his side that afternoon, pulling the strings in the middle of the park and starting to show the kind of form that had persuaded Celtic to bring him back from Germany.

Brattbakk came on just before the hour mark to make his long-awaited debut. He had a couple of chances but never really troubled Rousset. Still, he and his teammates were given a standing ovation by the Hoops fans at full-time, although the adulation was most directed at Craig Burley. The midfielder had emerged as the goal hero when he'd scored with a cracking drive in the 79th minute after persistent play from Larsson to hold off the challenge of Allan McManus and get the ball across the box. The three points were much needed, and it was doubly satisfying for Celtic when the news filtered through that Rangers had dropped two points away to Dunfermline, a surprise result for all concerned.

It had turned out to be an excellent day for Celtic, but there was one player who wasn't exactly smiling from ear to ear.

Darren Jackson: 'I was on a high after scoring at Aberdeen and took my place for granted against Hearts. I was floating after that game and fully expected to line up from the start for the visit of Hearts to Parkhead. But I was brought back down to earth with a huge bump by Wim. Talk about being deflated. He called me in to see him in his office on the Friday to tell me that he was leaving me out of the team. Jackie McNamara would be taking my place on the right-hand side of midfield. It was a real kick in the teeth, and I was absolutely raging. I decided it was best to get out of Wim's office as quickly as possible.

'I came on as a sub, and I was still angry from the day before. I wasn't properly focused and just ran around not concentrating properly on the job I should have been doing for the team. My only thought was to kick any Hearts player who came within striking distance. But we won the game 1–0, and it was a huge result. Hearts were very much in the title race that season, and it was a vital three points.

'I could not see where Wim was coming from at the time, but looking back on it now I realise that he was perhaps right to leave me out. I had been through an awful lot in the previous three or four months, and playing on the Wednesday at Aberdeen and four days later might have been slightly too much for me. He perhaps thought that I would make a greater impact coming off the bench.

'However, my loss was to be Jackie McNamara's and Celtic's gain. Jackie was brilliant that day, and I think playing out there was a real turning point in his season. It was also great for Celtic, as he went on to play a significant role in our title success.

'When I got into my car after the Hearts game, I turned on my mobile phone and had a few voicemails waiting. Some were to say that they thought Wim had been wrong to leave me out and that I would bounce back. But the one that sticks in my memory most came from Gazza, my friend from our days together at Newcastle United. Referring to my shout at Aberdeen of "I'm back", Gazza's message was short and to the point: "Aye, too right you're back – back on the fucking bench!" It made me laugh.'

Craig Burley: 'I felt I was starting to make a good impression when the goals went in. I never thought for a minute that I'd score so many, as I was never a box-to-box player. The goals were a bonus. That said, I hated the right-wingback role wee Broony used to make me play for Scotland. That really pissed me off. Because of that role, the Celtic fans probably thought that they were getting that kind of player. However, that wasn't the real me. Things took a positive turn after a couple of months, and although the fans never chanted my name I felt that they were warming to me. They were too busy chanting "Rico, Rico" after he tried one of his 40-yard overhead kicks!

'The winning goal against Hearts was important. It came quite late on, and we needed the three points. Henrik set it up brilliantly for me. I was now really enjoying my football, and the family had settled. We'd lived at my grandparents' wee house in Cumnock at first, and that took its toll on us. But we were now in our own home and feeling good about life. On the park, I was also the fittest I'd ever been. Yet, ironically, I was drinking more than I ever had.'

Part of the success that Rangers had enjoyed over the previous nine years had been put down to their team spirit – they were more like brothers than teammates. During an interview in the middle of their nine-in-a-row run, Ibrox captain Richard Gough said, 'The team that drinks together, wins together.' It was a reference to the long, boozy days out that he and his teammates enjoyed a few times a month.

When Alan Stubbs signed for Celtic, he couldn't believe the lack of bonding sessions between the players. He could count on one hand the golf days or nights out that the team had during the 1996–97 season. Stubbs told himself that if he was going to stay with Celtic and enjoy success in 1997–98, the lack of socialising between the guys would have to be addressed. Burley was only too happy to help out with the arrangements, and the squad spent most Tuesday and Saturday evenings together. December is traditionally party time, and the team enjoyed their nights out during that period as much as anyone.

Alan Stubbs: 'We had a togetherness under Wim. Sometimes you can have very good individuals but not have a very good team. We were victims of that in my first season at Celtic. I think Wim signed "team" players, and we all shared a willingness to roll up our sleeves. We also enjoyed some good nights out as a squad, and we'd have dinner and a few drinks twice a week. It was a big surprise if we didn't go out together, especially after we won a game. The most important thing of all was that it gave us a release away from the intense pressure of the whole ten-in-a-row thing. It was good to get away from that for a night.'

Craig Burley: 'Do I miss playing football? No, not one little bit. Do I miss the lads and the dressing-room? Yes. I loved the boys in the Celtic dressing-room. We were together all the time. At Chelsea, we'd have one night out a year, not because we didn't get on, but mainly because some guys lived more than 90 minutes away from where we'd want to go. So, there wasn't much socialising as a group.

'It was totally different at Parkhead. As soon as the words "night" and "out" were mentioned, the hands couldn't go up quickly enough. The Saturday nights would roll into Sunday lunchtime, and the Tuesday nights would roll into Wednesday lunchtime. They were serious sessions. We saw the Rangers lads out quite a lot, and they weren't used to seeing the Celtic players on the town. I think they respected our camaraderie.

'Wim knew we liked a night out, but he didn't know the half of it. If he had, I think he would have had a seizure. Murdo was more aware and tried to manage it by having a quiet word here and there. That season we did everything you'd tell a young professional not to nowadays. We spent a year bevvying our way to the title!

'And it wasn't just the Scottish lads and Stubbsy and Tommy Johnson who liked a night out. The Scandinavian boys made the most of it. Rieps loved a night out, and so did Morten and Henrik. Morten was like the "Hollow Man" – he could drink for hours and you'd never notice. The Scandinavians were just more discreet than the likes of me, Stubbsy, Simon and Jackie. Darren came out all the time as well, but he was a two-can Dan.

'I sometimes wonder where I got the energy to play 50 competitive games that season. We had quite a small squad, and the pressure, mentally and physically, got to us sometimes. I think I must have been fuelled by bevvy.'

Murdo Macleod: 'The players enjoyed going out for a few drinks. Wim never had a problem with that. He was all in favour of it. However, he made it clear that he wanted his players to be known for being the best team in the league and not the best drinkers. Their nights out were good for team bonding, and guys such as Marc Rieper, Stéphane Mahé, Henrik Larsson and Regi Blinker got to know each other, as they didn't have a clue about one another as players or as people. Wim and I kept our distance from the socialising, though. It wasn't our place to be out with them. Anyway, we saw them often enough at training!'

Wim Jansen: 'I deliberately kept my distance from the players. It was not so important for me to be involved with the players away from the practice pitch. It was much more important for me to have their attention and respect in the dressing-room than on the golf course. That's not to say I didn't want them to socialise together and become friends instead of just a group of people working in the same building. But I couldn't be seen to force them to go for dinner or to have a golf day. It had to happen naturally. It had to come from them. I couldn't force the issue.

'But they did get it together, and they had some good organisers.

Wim Jansen and Murdo
MacLeod quickly forged
a trusting relationship.

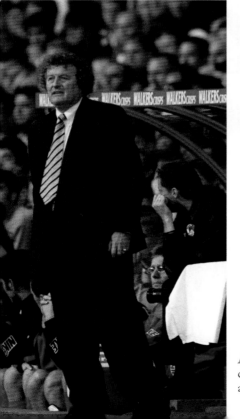

Wim Jansen gets Henrik Larsson prepared for
his ill-fated debut at Easter Road.

An anxious Wim Jansen can only look on
during Celtic's incredible UEFA Cup tie
against FC Tirol at Parkhead.

Stéphané Mahe gets to grips with Michael Owen, but the young Liverpool striker had the last laugh with a goal in the first half of the 'Battle of Britain'.

Jackie McNamara is congratulated by Morten Wieghorst, Henrik Larsson and Simon Donnelly after his UEFA Cup goal against Liverpool.

Simon Donnelly slots home a penalty as Celtic turn the screw on Liverpool at Parkhead.

Jackie McNamara wheels away in delight after netting against Liverpool in the UEFA Cup.

Henrik Larsson
shows the black eye
he was left with
after his infamous
training-ground
bust-up with
Tosh McKinlay.

Tom Boyd celebrates Celtic's
1–0 Coca-Cola Cup semi-final
win over Dunfermline.

Wim Jansen looks at Murdo
MacLeod for inspiration as
Richard Gough seals a 1–0
win for Rangers at Ibrox.

Andy Goram can only watch as
Alan Stubbs' dramatic late header hands
Celtic a title lifeline at Parkhead.

It's party time at Ibrox as the Celtic players celebrate their Coca-Cola Cup triumph against Dundee United.

Jonathan Gould went from reserve football at Bradford to lifting the Coca-Cola Cup with Celtic

Darren Jackson is engulfed by the jubilant Celtic fans as he celebrates his return from serious illness with a goal at Pittodrie.

Craig Burley slides home the opener as Celtic stun their Old Firm rivals in the Ne'erday derby.

INSET: Henrik Larsson is first to congratulate Craig Burley after he opened the scoring against Rangers at Celtic Park.

Paul Lambert's stunning strike seals a 2–0 win over Rangers at Parkhead.

Dunfermline's Craig Faulconbridge keeps the championship champagne on ice as his dramatic leveller stuns Celtic at East End Park.

INSET: Harald Brattbakk eases the title nerves as his goal seals a 2–0 win over St Johnstone on title-winning day.

It's party time at Parkhead as Malky Mackay leads the singalong.

Ian Stubbs gives Darren Jackson a lift as the title celebrations continue.

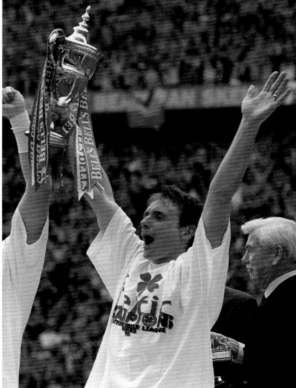

Stand up for the champions as Tom Boyd salutes the huge home support.

Phil O'Donnell played a major part in Celtic's title success and will be sorely missed by family, friends, fans and teammates. Here he is celebrating with son Christopher. (Courtesy of Eileen O'Donnell)

Rico Annoni hails the jubilant Celtic fans.

Celtic players celebrate their title win, but the party quickly turned sour as news of Wim Jansen's departure was made public.

Fergus McCann and Jock Brown's style of management upset the players and coaching staff during a turbulent season off the pitch.

I think Craig Burley and Alan Stubbs would push for the players to get together for a social day. I was happy to see them enjoy being together, because what I learned during my own playing career was that for a team to succeed and be successful the group has to be like brothers.

'I knew they were having fun and liked to have some beers. That is normal. But I never wanted to see them on a night out, never wanted to be with them. My former coach at Feyenoord, Vujadin Boškov, always said that it was better for the coach not to see his players in "action" off the field. If you get involved in that, then it is only natural you would look to see who liked to drink alcohol the most and how much they would take in an evening. You can guess about some things, but on certain things it is maybe better to not know the 100 per cent truth.'

Hibs were the visitors to Celtic Park on 20 December – a day Andy Thom was linked with a move back to Germany to play for Werder Bremen – and there was plenty of festive cheer around Parkhead by full-time. The Hibs defence played the part of Santa Claus by gifting their opponents several chances. Stuck at the bottom of the table, Jim Duffy's side defended poorly during the 5–0 defeat. They'd gone 13 games without a win.

Burley – now looking a bargain at £2.5 million from Chelsea – opened the scoring in the 23rd minute. Wieghorst and Larsson put their side three ahead before the interval. Larsson got his second after the break, and Burley completed the rout to give Jansen's men their sixth clean sheet on the trot.

Celtic's trip to Perth on 27 December to play St Johnstone was their third that season. Having won 1–0 and 2–0 in those earlier matches, there was an understandable degree of optimism as they headed up the A9 during the busy festive period. But they ended up well and truly stuffed by Paul Sturrock's men. George O'Boyle gave his side the lead in the 72nd minute and what was ultimately a crucial three points for the McDiarmid Park club in their fight for Premier League survival. Allan Preston swung over a corner into the heart of the six-yard box, and it came through a crowd of players to O'Boyle. He prodded it towards goal, and McNamara couldn't prevent the ball from crossing the line. It was a deserved win for the Saints, as they pressurised Gould time and time again. Celtic never competed properly, and it was only after they fell behind that they showed any urgency. Urged on from the touchline by Jansen, Brattbakk, Burley and McNamara all had decent efforts but nothing seriously troubled Alan Main.

Gould had enjoyed three clean sheets against the Saints but knew that he was fortunate not to have conceded a couple. There appeared to be a personal battle going on between him and O'Boyle. The Northern Ireland striker had had several chances to score in the previous clashes but had been either off target or Gould had denied him. It was different on this occasion, and no one could begrudge O'Boyle his goal.

Jonathan Gould: 'I think George O'Boyle probably had more chances to score against me than any other striker in the league that season. He must have had eight or nine really good chances. He scored the winner against us, and it was a terrible result. We had been on a decent run, and it was the first goal we had conceded since Marco Negri had scored at Parkhead. I really thought I had a chance of going on to keep seven or eight clean sheets. O'Boyle made sure that didn't happen.'

Jansen was bitterly disappointed with the application of his players and left them in no doubt at full-time that that kind of display just wasn't acceptable. Celtic's next game was at home to Rangers, and it was a game they had to win to prevent them falling further behind in the title race.

eleven

Ne'erday Victory

Perhaps the most significant turning point of the league season came on 2 January when Rangers visited Parkhead. Walter Smith's team were four points ahead of Celtic going into the game, and victory would have just about secured them the title. Celtic knew that defeat was not an option.

In terms of possession, Rangers started the game the better, and Brian Laudrup had the upper hand on Rico Annoni, although the Italian defender recovered to keep the Dane at bay. Rangers had plenty of possession, but they couldn't create clear-cut chances for their prolific striker Marco Negri to trouble Jonathan Gould.

Towards the end of the half, however, Celtic started to have more and more of the ball, their midfield of Paul Lambert and Craig Burley taking a grip on the proceedings. Tom Boyd also played brilliantly down the left-hand side – so much so that Smith took off Rino Gattuso and brought on Gordon Durie to try to combat the Hoops captain.

The score was level at half-time thanks to the brilliance of Andy Goram. But the Rangers keeper was totally helpless when Celtic took the lead in the 66th minute through Burley with an unstoppable right-foot shot after he was set up by a lovely pass from Jackie McNamara. It was a deserved lead, although Rangers looked dangerous when Paul Gascoigne came off the bench to replace Jörg Albertz after 72 minutes.

However, it looked more likely that Celtic would increase their lead, and Harald Brattbakk came close on a couple of occasions to scoring on his Old Firm debut. Henrik Larsson also hit the post, and Goram produced a top save from Darren Jackson. The second goal came four minutes from time, and it was a screamer from Lambert. He let fly with his right foot from around 20 yards, and the ball flew into the top left-hand corner of Goram's net. It was the kind of goal players dream about but seldom see become a reality. It was Lambert's first for Celtic and one that secured the victory. It was the first time in a decade that the Hoops had won the New Year fixture and their first league win over Rangers since May 1995.

Jansen had always hoped that his players had it in them to win the title without being sure that they could do it. He changed his mind at the final whistle that day and felt the championship was going to end up at Celtic Park.

Wim Jansen: 'The moment I truly believed we were going to win the league was the day we defeated Rangers 2–0. We beat them by playing soccer, and that 90 minutes gave me so much satisfaction. We showed our quality all over the pitch, and it was maybe the finest game we played that season. The players were under intense pressure to win and had to show they were capable of overcoming the hurdle of beating Rangers. Had we not won, Rangers would have been in a very strong position to win the league, and we would have struggled to catch them.'

Paul Lambert: 'I quickly found out that we had to win every game. Defeat just wasn't an option. But you really felt it in an Old Firm game. Andy Goram had been having a great match, and, as usual, it was going to take something special to beat him. We were one up through Craig's goal, and then I smashed that strike in from the edge of the box. It was one of those strikes that if I had to hit it another 100 times, probably only a handful, at most, would go in. I loved it. It was a special moment in my career.

'Dortmund is a one-team city, which means that everybody loves you. In Glasgow, it is a goldfish bowl, and you have to get used to that. I think I also still thought that because my dad watched Rangers I had to be a Rangers man. But I started to train with St Mirren when I was 12 and signed for them when I was 13. I had no allegiance to Rangers. I was committed to St Mirren. If I wasn't playing football, I'd watch the St Mirren first team or reserves. Even still, I had doubts that I was going to be accepted by some supporters, as I thought that they might doubt my commitment to their club. However, I never felt I had to prove myself as a footballer.'

Craig Burley: 'Simon Donnelly's dad said to me that you were never fully accepted as a Celtic player until you had scored against Rangers, and I wondered if that was true. When I did score against them, I was put through by a lovely little reverse ball from Jackie. Goram was on form, and it had to be well struck to beat him. The feeling of scoring in that game is hard to describe. Amazing, just amazing, was how I felt for the 20 seconds after I'd scored. Lambo then made it two with a brilliant shot, and there was a release of pressure after that, as we knew we had won. And we thoroughly deserved the victory.'

Jackie McNamara: 'I felt strong in that game against Rangers and confident that we were going to win. I set up Craig for his goal and was pleased with my reverse pass. I was in the players' lounge after the game beside Richard Gough, and the highlights of the match came on the telly. When my pass for the goal was shown, Gough said, "I knew you were going to do that. Just knew you'd go for that reverse pass." I'm like, "Yeah, Richard. Sure you did! Why did you not intercept it then?"

'Overall, I thought Rangers were bad losers that day. I think that in most of the Old Firm games we lost, we lost with dignity. But Rangers had a patronising attitude towards us that day. It was like they felt that they were still far superior to us and were in no doubt that we wouldn't threaten their ten-in-a-row bid. Again, it was another wee spur for me. The result was so important, and we knew we had to win. There was the fear factor of letting a lot of people down if we lost the game.'

Tom Boyd: 'We went into the Ne'erday fixture knowing it was ten years since we had defeated them and that we had to take three points to have a serious chance of winning the league. We dominated the game. In fact, I think we were outstanding. Andy Goram pulled off a few great saves but could do nothing to keep out the strikes from Craig Burley and Paul Lambert. We also defended bravely and superbly that day, and it was one of my favourite games of the season. On a personal level, I felt it was one of my best performances of the campaign. I played at left-back and enjoyed going forward on the overlap. Rino Gattuso played at right-back that day, and I think I gave him a bit of a headache.

'I played in every position in the back four that season. I was at right-back and central defence. Alan Stubbs was often the spare man, and Wim liked Marc Rieper to pick up the striker, especially if he was a target man. I sometimes played as a sweeper with three markers in front of me. I enjoyed that role – saved me bombing up and down!'

Rico Annoni: 'I enjoyed playing against Brian Laudrup. I also played against his brother, Michael, in my first Serie A game. I played for Como and was young and inexperienced. Michael played for Juventus. I took his legs away from him inside the first 15 minutes.

'I was able to handle Brian more legitimately. I always felt quite comfortable against him. I felt I played my part that day against Rangers. The big games seemed to bring the best out in me. They made me very excited. I also played well at Anfield against Liverpool in the UEFA Cup. I had to give close attention to Steve McManaman and Robbie Fowler. The Rangers games were even more special.'

Jonathan Gould had a couple of saves to make that afternoon, yet he shouldn't have been anywhere near the stadium. He had a serious eye infection, which had virtually blinded him. For fear of losing his place in the team if he declared the full extent of the problem, the keeper chose to do a sneaky one and organise private treatment in an attempt to ease the pain and give him some level of vision.

Jonathan Gould: 'Nothing less than a win would have been good enough that day. We were in front of our fans, and we owed them the chance to see a victory over Rangers. To do it in such style, with two candidates for goal of the season, made it even sweeter. Paul and Craig scored belters and deserved to enjoy their moments when they raced away to receive the plaudits of the Celtic fans.

'It was the only win we tasted against Rangers that season, yet I shouldn't have played in the game. I had a really bad eye infection and never let on just how serious it was. I had been carrying it for about a week and had gone to see a specialist to get medication to clear it up. I made the appointment on my own – never told a soul at Celtic. I didn't want them to know in case it cost me my place in the team. To be honest, I could hardly see and shouldn't have left my house, never mind played in an Old Firm game of such importance. Thankfully, I didn't have too much to do – the boys protected me well. For once!

'I couldn't have asked for better defenders than Alan, Marc and Tom to play behind. Marc would attack the ball and attack the striker if necessary. Alan would bring the ball down and play a pass, link the game from the back. They were a great blend. Tom had great pace and could cover them from the full-back areas if required. Marc and Alan would not stop moaning during a game, and I sometimes wondered if they had a competition to see who could shout the loudest and piss the most teammates off.

'Marc was especially good at moaning, but he was also a top, top defender. A giant and powerful man, he wouldn't surrender anything on the pitch. I think he was the unsung hero of the Celtic team that season. He certainly made my job much easier than it might have been.'

After a couple of appearances coming off the bench, Brattbakk made his first start that day following his transfer from Rosenborg. He almost scored a double, but just never quite managed it. The 'nearly' tag followed Harald around for the rest of the season.

Harald Brattbakk: 'When I signed, I sensed the huge level of expectation from the first moment. I felt it on myself, felt it on the team. I knew we were expected to win every game. It was a lot of pressure, but it was similar at Rosenborg.

'I received quite a bit of criticism for my performances in the early stages, and the negative stuff that was written and said about me did bother me. I wanted to play. I was desperate to impress, but I have to admit it did not go too well at the start. Scottish football is definitely more physical than in Norway, and teams would try to unsettle me on the pitch by being more physical to stop me performing.

'I came on as a sub in a few games, and then Wim told me I was starting against Rangers in the New Year game. I was nervous, I suppose. We won the game, which was an important part of winning the championship.

'The team was in good shape and results were good, but it wasn't quite falling into place for me. I played every week for Rosenborg, and if I went two or three games without scoring, it was never a major problem. At Celtic, it was different – totally different. After I had gone three games without scoring, people wanted a new striker brought in. That kind of thinking was new to me and didn't help me to relax and settle into my new environment.'

Simon Donnelly had been a regular in the Celtic team for almost four years but had rarely tasted victory in an Old Firm game. He watched it eat away and take its toll on senior Parkhead figures, such as Paul McStay, Peter Grant and boss Tommy Burns. With that in mind, Donnelly probably enjoyed the win as much as any other player, as it was a sort of payback for the heartache and punishment his former teammates and manager had endured during their barren Old Firm spell.

Simon Donnelly: 'From the beginning of that season, Rangers had continuity, and we were starting from scratch. In fact, we were probably starting from a minus position. They had some kind of hold over us, as we seemed to batter them game after game and not score. It got to us. I've no doubt about that. I think it was evident

in the likes of Paul McStay and Peter Grant. They were desperate
to be in a title-winning side during the period when Rangers
dominated. Both of them carried the weight of the club on their
shoulders. It wasn't fair on them, but being such great Celtic men
they wouldn't have had it any other way.

'Rangers were a force, and that New Year win was so important.
That day, Rangers failed to respond to the challenge we put in front
of them. They were no longer able to get away from us. Finally, we
were on the verge of catching them, and I felt confident we would
overtake them by the end of the season.'

No matter how good and important a result is, it isn't always to the
full satisfaction of every player. Regi Blinker badly wanted to be a hero
in an Old Firm game and would love to have sampled the feelings
Burley and Lambert had that day. But, by his own admission, his
performances against Rangers in a Celtic jersey were disappointing.
It's something that still rankles with him to this day.

Regi Blinker: 'During my three years with Celtic, I don't think
that I ever made an impression in a game against Rangers. I was
either injured or on the bench. When I did play, I wasn't involved
as much as I should have been. They were the games of the year,
and the situation still gets to me when I think about it. I think
of Alan Stubbs scoring against them – Paul Lambert and Craig
Burley scoring against them. I wanted to savour those moments
for myself.

'My first season just didn't go to plan. The fans weren't convinced
about me, and the media gave me a few beatings. In fact, I recall one
headline that had me down as 'Regi Stinker'. That hurt – of course
it did. However, thinking about it now, it was probably right.

'Because of the situation, I was often tense, and my confidence
took a battering. When you are a wide player, you have to have self-
belief, and mine was temporarily gone. Thankfully, I could switch
off when I got home at night. I didn't take it away with me from
the pitch. That would have driven me crazy.

'Wim tried his best for me, and he gave an interview to the
Scottish newspapers, asking people to give me a break. Perhaps

because of things like that, one or two of the lads thought Wim showed favouritism towards me. David Hannah used to wind me up and say that Wim was my dad. He also used to say that to Henrik.'

Craig Burley: 'The boys felt really sorry for Regi. He tried his best and worked hard. He had talent, but it never worked out for him. We tried to put an arm around him, as he took more than his fair share of stick from the media and the fans.'

It was up to Celtic to kick on after the Old Firm victory, and they arrived at Motherwell on 10 January for their next game upbeat and in good form. However, 90 minutes later they had doubts as to whether they really had it in them to win the title. Former Celtic striker Willie Falconer played for Alex McLeish's side that day, and he broke the deadlock in the 54th minute. Gould and his defenders hesitated when it came to dealing with Lee McCulloch's corner kick, and Falconer rose unmarked to power home a header.

This wasn't in Celtic's plan, but they responded well and had a good go at their opponents. It was going to take something special to beat on-form Motherwell keeper Stevie Woods and that moment of magic arrived when Lambert cracked a rasper of a shot home from 30 yards, every bit as good as his strike against Rangers the previous week. Larsson then tumbled inside the box after a challenge from Brian Martin. It looked a dubious penalty, but referee Martin Clark wouldn't listen to any of the incensed Motherwell players' complaints.

Larsson would have taken it, but he had picked up a knock in the incident with Martin, and it was left to sub Darren Jackson. On for Brattbakk in the sixty-first minute, the former Hibs striker had the chance to put Celtic into the lead eight minutes later when he stepped up to take the spot-kick. Jackson agonisingly knocked the ball wide, but it would have been harsh on Motherwell had they taken nothing from the game after putting so much into the 90 minutes.

Darren Jackson: 'We played Motherwell at Fir Park and went there on a high after defeating Rangers 2–0. The game finished

1–1, and I missed a penalty. Charlie Nicholas gave me stick on the telly and said I should never have taken the kick. It was a muddy day, but I accept that it was a poor kick. When the ref awarded it to us, I ran to retrieve the ball, and my intention was to hand it to one of my teammates. But nobody came forward to take the ball from me. I had to hit it.'

The Tennent's Scottish Cup provided Celtic with a distraction away from the title race. Having won the Coca-Cola Cup, the Hoops fancied a bit of success in this competition and the chance of completing the Treble. Greenock Morton came to Parkhead for the third-round tie on 24 January. Brattbakk opened the scoring in the sixth minute when he coolly finished after being set up by a defence-splitting pass from Stubbs. There was a feeling amongst observers that the floodgates would open and it could end up a cricket score against Billy Stark's side, but Ton keeper John Hillcoat was in excellent form. He saved from McNamara and Burley. Burley and Larsson then had efforts cleared off the line.

With the clock ticking and Morton not out, there was a sigh of relief six minutes from the end when Larsson and Burley combined at the edge of the penalty area to set up Jackson. The substitute – who had replaced Brattbakk nine minutes earlier – managed to stick out a foot to ram the ball high past Hillcoat from twelve yards. Jackson was tripped for a penalty in the final minute, and Larsson was given the chance to score. However, he blasted the ball well over Hillcoat's crossbar. The performance was average, but all that mattered was that Celtic were in the draw for the next round.

Midweek games in the middle of winter were never welcomed by players. The conditions were generally poor, and a journey to Tannadice on Tuesday, 27 January was always going to be a hazardous trip with the potential for Celtic to drop points.

Their fears were totally founded, as United took the lead in the 24th minute through Kjell Olofsson when he got in front of Lambert to flick the ball past Gould for a cool finish. Celtic immediately went in search of an equaliser and had United pinned back for the rest of the first half.

After the restart, it was once again Celtic making all the play, but United were looking dangerous on the counterattack. McNamara failed to appear for the second half, and Donnelly took over on the right-hand side. Jackson also took over from Brattbakk, and Jansen was rewarded when the pair combined, along with Lambert, to hit the equaliser just when it appeared as though they were running out of ideas.

With 14 minutes remaining, Jansen's men were staring down the barrel of a defeat, which would have been a serious blow to their championship hopes. Also, Celtic were looking at an away record of one win in five since they had lifted the Coca-Cola Cup. But they got the victory, and it took them to within three points of league leaders Rangers.

Goals from Donnelly and Burley secured the win – one that United must have felt was totally unjust. In the 76th minute, Jackson produced the deftest of touches on the edge of the area to tee up Lambert, but his shot was blocked by United keeper Sieb Dykstra. However, Donnelly was on hand to send an angled shot into the back of the net. It was the lifeline Celtic needed, and with just three minutes left Larsson sent Donnelly dashing to the byline. The cutback found Burley, and his shot deflected off Magnus Sköldmark, wrong-footing Dykstra, who could do nothing to stop the ball ending up in the back of the net.

Simon Donnelly: 'Some games are easy to remember, and that was one of them. We had dropped points in the previous league game, and we looked like dropping all three in that one, too. I think the bookies would have given long odds on us winning the title if we hadn't fought back to win that night.

'I came off the park feeling I had made a worthwhile contribution. I felt good about myself. I couldn't help but think about Tommy Burns after that game. Tommy had broadened my horizons as a footballer and had taught me how to play as an attacking wide midfielder. I had thought that I was an out-and-out striker, because that's where I had played for my school team and for my first wee while in the Celtic first team. But Tommy and Billy Stark would take me for extra sessions in the afternoon to try to educate me. They'd ask me to play a bit deeper and to be more aware of what was going around me. Basically, I had to learn to appreciate the game and value teamwork.

'I became much more involved in games and started to help my teammates score goals. When I was in possession, I'd look up to find the right pass or look for a run from a teammate. I set up quite a few goals in the 1997–98 season, and I took enormous satisfaction from doing that, just like I did when Craig scored the winner against United.

'I also worked with psychologist Tom Lucas, which was a big help. He helped you to reach your peak fitness as well as working on the mental aspects of your game. I got more from the physical side of things, going swimming to build up my strength and stamina. It brought an extra edge to my game. Tom also provided you with personal stats on your performance. How many passes you made and your shots on goal. It was helpful to see the strengths in my game and the areas I needed to work on. Nowadays, the stats are supplied to all managers to look over, but that wasn't the case back then, so it was great to have Tom analysing my performance.'

Darren Jackson: 'That Tannadice win was a huge victory. Things weren't really going our way, and I came off the bench and thought that it would be best to stir things up. Sieb Dykstra was in goal for United and wasting time at every opportunity. I threw the ball at him like a missile on one occasion and told him to get on with taking the goalkick. He wasn't happy and threatened to batter fuck out of me. I kicked everything in sight, unsettled United and played my part as we won 2–1.'

Aberdeen were the next side to try to stop Celtic, but they failed. On Monday, 2 February, Celtic defeated them 3–1. It takes character to win a championship, and Celtic showed it that night when they came from behind to win and avoid a disastrous setback. Early on in the match, Brian O'Neil set up David Rowson, and his shot deflected off Stubbs and into the back of the net. But Celtic didn't crumble and started to batter Aberdeen's packed defence in front of 46,000 fans. The Hoops hit the woodwork through McNamara on two occasions, and Jim Leighton was in brilliant form. But there was only so much that the Scotland keeper could do, Wieghorst levelling the score in the 22nd minute.

With McNamara in irresistible form and Burley and Wieghorst taking charge of the midfield, a second goal was always coming. And it duly arrived after just 35 minutes from Larsson. Stubbs fired in a free-kick that was flicked on by Rieper, and the Swede was on hand to climb above his marker and bullet a header into the back of the net.

Celtic were always in the driving seat, but with just one goal in it there was a danger that Aberdeen might snatch an equaliser. Substitute Jackson ensured that this didn't happen, though, when he smashed a Donnelly cross into the roof of the net with just minutes remaining. It allowed the anxious home support to relax and kept the title charge going strong. That night, Celtic moved level with Rangers and Hearts on 48 points.

A match is never over until the final whistle is sounded, and Celtic found that out to their cost on 8 February when they lost an injury-time equaliser to Hearts at Tynecastle. Celtic paid the price for not playing to the death, although the injury time added by referee Bobby Tait did appear to be on the generous side. Seconds away from moving two points clear at the top of the table, Jansen's men eagerly awaited Tait's whistle to bring proceedings in the capital to an end. One goal ahead thanks to McNamara, Celtic appeared to have secured victory over Hearts just twenty-four hours after Rangers had only managed to draw with Dunfermline. It would have been the perfect weekend for Celtic with both title rivals dropping points. However, the unthinkable happened for the Hoops when Hearts bagged an equaliser out of the blue. A deflected shot spun into the path of José Quitongo, who twisted and turned inside the penalty box. The Celtic defenders desperately tried to avoid bringing him down at the risk of giving away a penalty, but Stéphane Mahé made a sliding challenge as Quitongo was about to pull the trigger and unfortunately helped take the ball past the hapless Gould. Jansen simply bowed his head, and Murdo MacLeod turned and slapped the roof of the away dugout in frustration.

Celtic had enough chances to win a couple of matches throughout the 90 minutes. Brattbakk was the biggest culprit for failing to make the most of his opportunities in front of goal.

Jackie McNamara: 'I felt terrible that day. I had a fitness test before the game and didn't think I'd make it. Yet I went on to play well and scored our goal. I also set up a great chance for Harald, but sadly he missed it. Hearts equalised in injury time – by the way, I don't know what kind of watch Bobby Tait used that day – through Quitongo. I received a bottle of champagne from Sky for being man of the match and had to do an interview. Quitongo then got interviewed after me, and I wanted to smash the bottle over his head. His voice really irritated me. I was distraught at not winning that game.'

Darren Jackson: 'We were at Tynecastle and led 1–0. There was around three or four minutes of stoppage time, and Hearts equalised through José Quitongo. Wim started with Harald Brattbakk alongside Henrik, but I thought I merited a starting place with Henrik.

'Wim put me on as a sub, but it was late in the game, and I felt I should have been on earlier. As was often the case with me at that point in the season, I was frustrated. My body language wasn't right, and I was perhaps more intent on booting the opposition than I was on concentrating on playing football.

'To lose the lead when the title race was neck and neck between us, Rangers and Hearts was a huge disappointment. At time-up, our dressing-room was not a place for the faint-hearted. There were heated exchanges all over the place. A few of us booted the walls and bottles of juice in frustration. We had some very opinionated players in our squad, and we all had our say. Wim took it all in, but he was very headstrong, and 99 times out of 100 it was Wim's way.'

Craig Burley: 'When it boiled down to it, we could play football. We knew when to get serious and when it was time to sort out the opposition. Our players were all capable and had talent. We were clever on the pitch and knew what was required. We would also get each other by the scruff of the neck if that was required. I almost broke my toe booting a hamper in frustration after we lost a late goal to Hearts. There would often be disagreements in the dressing-room and on the park.

'Rieps and Gouldy would also go at it big time. Rieps used to hate the fact that Gouldy would never come off his line to take a cross ball, and he would scream at him to do so. Gouldy would just laugh. Rieps used to say to Gouldy that the opposition only had one shot but still managed to score two goals. Training was also competitive, and we would half each other in two. Wim would stop the session and ask us all to calm down. You know, we didn't stop that Rangers team by being talentless pissheads.'

Monday-night football was on the agenda for Celtic again the following week when they had to travel to Dunfermline on 16 February to play a Scottish Cup tie for a place in the quarter-final. As expected, the game was a scrap and rarely pretty. But Jansen's side could have made life much easier had they taken their chances against a stubborn Pars side at East End Park. Both teams had opportunities to take the lead: Celtic were guilty of bad finishing; Dunfermline just couldn't find a way past the in-form Gould.

The match officials also played their part in keeping the score down. Referee Willie Young decided against awarding the visitors a penalty when Brattbakk was brought down inside the box after a rash challenge from Greg Shields. Linesman Jim Dunn then infuriated the Celtic players, Wieghorst in particular, when he flagged for offside as he tapped home a Mahé cross.

Eventually, though, Celtic managed to take the lead, and it came from the most unlikely of sources. Mahé turned Shields inside out in the penalty area before drilling a low shot past Ian Westwater into the far corner. And when Brattbakk netted his second goal for the club, his previous having come in an earlier round of the same competition, Celtic looked to be home and dry. The Norwegian fired a McNamara cross high into the back of the net in the 67th minute.

It should have been game over, but substitute David Bingham ensured an uncomfortable final nine minutes for Jansen's side when he pulled one back for the Pars. However, the Hoops held out to secure a quarter-final tie away to Dundee United.

On 21 February, it was back to league duty when Kilmarnock visited Parkhead. Celtic were intent on notching up victories as quickly as possible, and they got off to a fine start when Brattbakk gave them the lead after ten minutes. McNamara found Larsson, who raced towards goal. Gordon Marshall came out to narrow the angle, and the Swede cleverly played in his strike partner. The man from Norway looked offside as he stroked the ball in from six yards out, but referee Alan Freeland thought differently. Brattbakk hit a post five minutes later, and then Kevin McGowne had to react quickly to clear one of the striker's efforts off the line. But it was 2–0 by half-time after Brattbakk scored at the back post from a Larsson cross.

Celtic had several one-on-one opportunities in the second half, as the Kilmarnock defence seemed unable to cope with their opposition's running and movement off the ball. Brattbakk completed his hat-trick in the 70th minute when he slammed home a Simon Donnelly cutback. And he notched another to round off a memorable day for himself after Burley and Jackson combined to set him up.

It was a comfortable victory but not such a good day for Marshall. He had moved to Rugby Park the previous month in a £100,000 transfer from Celtic, but he had played well and had stopped the score from being even more one-sided.

The win meant that Celtic had secured 14 points out of a possible 18 in the league since the turn of the year. That kind of form suggested that they had a real chance of winning the league.

twelve

Phil O'Donnell

There was a midweek game at home to Dunfermline on Wednesday, 25 February. Celtic comfortably won 5–1 to end a fine 24-hour period for them, as Rangers had dropped points at Kilmarnock. Henrik Larsson opened the scoring after three minutes. Harald Brattbakk doubled the advantage in the 27th minute. There had seemed little danger when Stéphane Mahé had released Brattbakk down the left wing. However, the Norwegian had other ideas, cutting inside before unleashing a breathtaking shot into Ian Westwater's top left-hand corner. It was Brattbakk's seventh goal in three games and made it 3–0 going into the interval. Morten Wieghorst later made it 5–0 with a fine volley. Andy Tod hit a consolation for the Pars, and Tommy Johnson was carried off with knee ligament damage.

The scorer of Celtic's fourth goal that night was Phil O'Donnell.

Phil passed away nearly a decade later on 29 December 2007. He collapsed on the pitch during Motherwell's 5–3 victory over Dundee United at Fir Park. It was a tragedy, and totally unfair on his wife Eileen and their four children, Megan, Christopher, Olivia and Luc. Eileen doesn't deserve to be without her husband, and their kids shouldn't be deprived of their dad.

In different ways, his death touched everyone in football, from his teammates and colleagues at Motherwell to nearly every club in Britain, all of which held a minute's silence or applause in his memory. Football supporters, players and former players from all around Scotland visited Fir Park to leave flowers, football jerseys and memorial cards as a tribute and mark of respect to the former Fir Park skipper. Phil was liked by all.

I was due to meet him on 2 January to listen to his views and memories of playing for Celtic during the 1997–98 season. That arrangement was made on the phone the day before he died, and I was looking forward to it – he was a genuine guy and really good company. We had been trying for weeks to meet up, but the busy Christmas period and work and family commitments had delayed our conversation. A dedicated family man, Phil had been busy buying Christmas presents for the kids or taking Megan to her piano lessons – he spoke proudly of the way she was progressing on the ivories.

I thought that it was important to have a presence from the O'Donnell family in this book. His teammates from 1998 agreed. His close friend and former teammate Simon Donnelly was good enough to approach Eileen on my behalf, and she kindly, and bravely, agreed to contribute, as it was what she wanted and what Phil would have wanted, too.

We met at her home in Hamilton. Despite her obvious grief, Eileen made me feel most welcome, and there was a real warmth about her – she was such a nice person. There was a lovely presence of Phil: photos from his playing days with Motherwell and Celtic and family pictures proudly displayed; and many cards and letters received from people offering their condolences, from the wives of former teammates to a hand-written letter from the prime minister, Gordon Brown. Eileen was touched by all the cards and condolences she received and will forever be grateful for their compassion and understanding in the days and weeks after Phil's sudden death.

Eileen and Phil both attended Holy Cross High School in Hamilton and began dating when Phil was starting out as a young professional at Motherwell. Eileen was commencing a nursery-teaching course at Motherwell college. Their relationship blossomed, and they later married and were blessed with four lovely children. Eileen was at Phil's side as his career developed. She recalled how happy he was playing for Celtic in the 1997–98 season and also how privileged he felt to be a footballer.

Eileen O'Donnell: 'A whole load of family and friends went to the Dunfermline game on the second-last day of the season. My cousins were there – John, Antony, Patrick – and my uncle John Devine, Phil's sisters Monica and Trisha, Phil's dad, Bernard, Willie Bodwick, Jackie Gallagher and Jim Kirwan. I had my camera with me that day. Sadly, it didn't go to plan, and we all had to wait another week to win the league.

'It all worked out the following week against St Johnstone, and we were all so happy. Phil was so proud to have played on such an important day in the history of Celtic. We had a party at our house that night, and I remember Phil rounding us all up to get back to the house to get on with the celebrations.

'The party was great, and we all had a brilliant time. When we got up the following morning, there was a huge bottle of Moët champagne, ornamental size, at our front door. Someone must have taken it from Hamilton Palace and left it at our place. Phil gave it to my cousin John Devine, and it reminds us all of the day that Celtic won the league and of the party we had that night.

'Phil liked to be organised. All the Celtic players and wives went to Loch Lomond to see Oasis. Simon Donnelly was Oasis daft. It was mobbed, with people climbing on other people's shoulders to get a proper look at the stage. People kept trying to steal Paolo Di Canio's hat, and he wasn't too happy about it! Because it was so busy, a lot of us got split up, and Phil was worrying where everyone was, trying to get us all back together for the journey home.

'He just loved playing football. It was a hobby he had the pleasure of doing every day as his job. Yet he struggled every day with his body. It took a fair bit of punishment, what with injuries and operations. Too often he was in plaster or on crutches. He hated the "injury" label that seemed to follow him. But he was never angry about it. His determination was unbelievable. He was knocked down so many times, and he got back up, determined to prove people wrong.

'We had really dark days at Sheffield Wednesday. That was when Phil was at his lowest. He was injured a lot down there, and that was the only time I ever heard him speak about packing in the game. Again, he bounced back.'

Phil also played his part in helping Celtic to end a seven-year trophy famine when they defeated Airdrie 1–0 in the Tennent's Scottish Cup final in 1995. He had moved to Parkhead from Motherwell nine months earlier in a £1.75-million transfer. He was already a hero for the Fir Park faithful after scoring in their 1991 Tennent's Scottish Cup-final win. Then his bond with Celtic began.

Eileen O'Donnell: 'Phil was so happy when Tommy Burns signed him for Celtic. We got married in July 1994, and he signed two months later. When you sign for Celtic, you become a part of a huge family that stretches back for generations. They say you are never forgotten if you have played for Celtic, and that was evident by the number of players and management, past and present, who came to Phil's funeral. The church was just packed. And the people outside. My goodness. Phil would have been so embarrassed at the turnout. But we were touched by the number of mourners from Motherwell and the rest of Scottish football who turned up, and by the people who travelled up from England and who flew in from abroad. It was amazing. The kindness and goodwill shown by everyone was unbelievable.'

Phil's dad Bernard has his son's medals and his Scotland cap on display. Christopher has his jerseys from the Scottish Cup finals with Motherwell and Celtic.

Motherwell was Phil's first and last professional club and gave him and Eileen one of their happiest days.

Eileen O'Donnell: 'Phil really enjoyed the 1991 Scottish Cup final that he won with Motherwell. My dad, Benny, died the Sunday before the final, and we decided not to tell anyone at Fir Park in case they thought that Phil wasn't strong enough to play. It was a shame, because my dad had asked for a ticket for Hampden to watch Phil. He was a Manchester United supporter, but we were chuffed he was coming to see his son-in-law. In the same week, Motherwell manager Tommy McLean's dad also died, which made the final even more emotional, as Motherwell were playing his brother Jim's team, Dundee United.

'That final was one of the most exciting games I've ever been to. Motherwell won 4–3 after extra time, and it was so special for the club. Phil was fortunate enough to score one of the goals. He still has his jersey from that day in a frame alongside his 1995 Scottish Cup final jersey from when Celtic beat Airdrie.

'Phil was so happy for Tommy McLean. He really respected him as a person and as a manager. Tommy could be hard on him, but it was for Phil's own good, I suppose. He was the old-school type, but he had a wee soft spot, too.

'It was a dramatic cup run to get to Hampden. I remember one game went to a penalty shoot-out against Morton. I hid in the toilets, as I was too nervous to watch!

'The kids and I, and our family and friends are all so proud of everything Phil achieved as a footballer and as a person. We miss him.'

The Celtic players and coaching staff from 1998 were equally proud of the part Phil played in their title success and wanted to put on record their memories of their former teammate.

Simon Donnelly: 'It doesn't feel right to be speaking about Phil in this way. He should be here, giving you his own memories from the season. It's so sad.

'Phil was a friend and teammate for thirteen years, from our days at Celtic through to the four years we had together at Sheffield Wednesday. We both had our share of injuries down there, and I hope that I helped Phil get through some dark moments. I know he certainly helped me. Like us all, Phil hated being injured. He just wanted a clear run – wanted to be one of the lucky guys who could play 40 games a season uninterrupted. Yet what he did manage to achieve in the game, 95 per cent of footballers will get nowhere near.

'When he played, he was at his happiest. I know he was proud to have played for Celtic and honoured to have played his part in the 1998 title-winning team. We had a bond, and I'm proud to say that he was my friend. I was so fortunate to spend a lot of time in his company. I only wish he was still here to give me more moments to cherish.'

Darren Jackson: 'People always say nice things about people when they die, but the words and tributes for Phil have been totally accurate. He was the nicest boy, husband, father and friend you could ever meet. I am genuinely proud to have been his friend.'

Jackie McNamara: 'I sat up with Simon Donnelly after Phil's funeral, and we kept asking ourselves, "Why is it always the good guys?" Phil was a genuine guy. A great guy. As a person, Phil could walk into any company and be totally at ease and make others at ease, too. After my mum passed away, Phil and Eileen came on holiday with us to the south of France, and they were a great comfort to me and my family at that time. They always put others before their own well-being. I used to see Phil socially at least three times a year, and I was out with him and Simon for a Christmas night out two weeks before he died. I'm so glad I have that night to remember – to have spent quality time in his company before he passed away. I know his family are very proud of him, and they have every right to be. Eileen, Phil's dad, Bernard, and the rest of the family have conducted themselves with humility and are a credit to Phil. He is sadly missed.'

Wim Jansen: 'I was stunned when Murdo phoned to tell me about Phil's death. My thoughts immediately turned to his wife and four children. My thoughts are still with them.

'Phil was a great team player and a very nice person. He never gave me a moment of bother during my time at Celtic – never once moaned about team selection. He was very mature and understood that managers have to make decisions, ones that might not always be in his favour. He was very unfortunate with injuries, and being sidelined disrupted his game. I wish I could have had Phil O'Donnell permanently available for selection. He was an asset to the team, but I think there would have been so much more to his game had he been able to string together an injury-free run of 25 games or so.

'Whenever he was in my team, I knew I'd be able to count on him to produce a positive performance. He could play a very direct game and was able to penetrate the opposition and make it look effortless. You need to have good ability and good fitness to do that, and Phil had both.'

Alan Stubbs: 'Phil had a big influence in the Celtic dressing-room, but in a quiet way. He wasn't a shouter or a show-off, but he always made sense when he spoke. He had the full respect of the squad.

'He had talent, and he was a perfect professional. He treated his body well, and everything was primed for match day. Yet he struggled to overcome some injuries, and that prevented him from having an even better career with Celtic and Scotland.

'On a night out, he rarely drank alcohol. On the odd occasion that he let himself go a little bit, a different side to Phil would come to the surface. He showed a dry, almost wicked sense of humour and was really good company. It's so sad that such a nice person has been taken away at the age of just 35. My thoughts go out to his wife Eileen and their four children. But they know more than anybody else that Phil was an absolute gentleman, and they have every reason to be proud of what he achieved in his life as a husband, father and footballer.'

Jonathan Gould: 'When I heard what happened to Phil, I was saddened and shocked. I was on the other side of the world, 14,000 miles away in New Zealand, but it struck me like I was still in Scotland. As a footballer, Phil was reliable – probably one of the most reliable I've played with. He was never outspoken in public, but behind closed doors he was a strong influence, and when Phil said something he had the full attention of everyone in the room.

He was the captain of Motherwell and was tipped to go on and be involved at coaching and management level, that's how highly he was rated by qualified people in the game.

'As a person, he was a lovely guy and one of the most dedicated family men I've ever known.'

Rico Annoni: 'Phil was always there to help solve any little problem I might have had during my early days in Glasgow. He was always prepared to assist and make people feel welcome. I can't recall him ever being sad. He always had a smile. That showed he was happy with family life and happy to play for Celtic. I was sad and shocked when I found out that he had died. He was far too young. I was on holiday in Africa when I found out about his death and was unable to attend his funeral. But I will pay my respects to his lovely family and visit his gravestone the next time I am back in the country.'

Harald Brattbakk: 'I was living in Florida for a year, studying to become a commercial pilot. I checked the Internet every day for the football news from Norway and Scotland. That is how I found out that Phil had passed away. It was horrible to discover the awful news. When you hear of things such as that happening to other people, you think, "That's a real shame." But when it is someone you have worked with closely, been friendly with, it is absolutely sickening. Phil was a lovely person, and my thoughts are with his wife and four children. Phil was a total family man, and I'm the same with three young children. My heart goes out to them.'

Murdo MacLeod: 'Life isn't fair when you are taken at just 35. Phil seemed to be enjoying his football again at Motherwell and was doing such a great job, helping to bring on the young players who were enjoying such a super season. He was terrific for Celtic during the 1998 title run-in, and there is no doubt that his energy was what the team needed in the final few weeks of the season. My thoughts are with Phil's family.'

Paul Lambert: 'I knew Phil from our days in the Scotland Under-21 team, and we got on very well. We had kids roughly the same age, and our wives got on well. His death is tragic. He was a massive player for Celtic and was a lovely guy.

'He had a very good sense of humour and loved a laugh and a joke. I remember being in the dressing-room before a home game against Aberdeen. Dr Jo was in charge, and Eric Black and Danny McGrain were also there. Phil was sitting next to Simon Donnelly, and as the starting line-up was being read out they both took a fit of the giggles. I caught them out of the corner of my eye and could see that both of them were away with it. Totally gone. All I could do was stare at the floor and think, "Don't laugh, don't laugh." I managed to hold it together and then went through to the shower area. Both of them were bent over a treatment table, howling with laughter.

'I can't believe Phil has gone, though. It is truly horrific.'

Marc Rieper: 'When I heard about Phil, I was devastated. He was a nice person and was fortunate to have a lovely family. He also cared for the well-being of others. He was never confrontational and preferred to smile. I liked that about him. It is such a shame that he is no longer here. My thoughts are still with Eileen and their children.'

Morten Wieghorst: 'When I think of Phil, my first thought is what a genuine guy he was. Phil was already at Celtic when I signed for the club, and he was the one guy who made me feel really welcome. He looked out for me and made it easy to settle. When you move to a new club, particularly one the size of Celtic, to have a teammate like Phil was priceless. He was a genuine guy and always had a happy face. He was also a fantastic player and one that Wim Jansen knew he could rely on during that season.'

Malky Mackay: 'Phil and I are the same age and grew up playing against each other at schoolboy and youth level. I got to know him more when we were at Celtic, and he was a fine man. He was also lucky enough to be surrounded by his fantastic wife Eileen and their lovely children. I enjoyed being with him. He was so genuine.'

Regi Blinker: 'I have read all the comments about Phil and

how people have described him, and I think they have been spot on – he was an excellent person and professional. He was a quiet man, but he still liked to have an opinion. At one stage, he was my competitor for a place on the left of midfield, but he was still my friend. You could not help but like Phil, and I certainly did.'

Craig Burley: 'Phil came on a two-day bender to Dublin with some of the boys. We arrived on the Saturday night and flew home on the Monday morning. We were due to meet at the hotel bar on the Sunday afternoon and everyone was there on time apart from Phil. There was no sign of him, and no one could raise him. Next thing, Phil appeared with about half a dozen shopping bags. He'd been out buying presents for Eileen and the kids. You'd have thought he'd been away in Australia for a year the amount of stuff he had bought. He then bought more presents at the airport. That was Phil: dedicated to his family.

'When he moved to Sheffield Wednesday, we'd go and visit him and Simon Donnelly. My family would stay at Phil's, and we'd be made really welcome. We'd have a few drinks, and I would surface late morning, my head thumping. By then, Phil would have been up for a few hours, been to mass and have the bacon and eggs on. He was a lovely guy. I miss being able just to pick up the phone and chat to him.'

Tommy Johnson: 'I went on holiday with Phil, Eileen and the kids a few times and enjoyed every second. Phil was great company. When we were at Celtic together, we knew he was a real family man, but when we holidayed, I got to see up close just what a devoted dad and husband he was. He was also one of the lads and enjoyed coming away with us to Dublin for a couple of nights. We'd all be keen to find out where our next pint was coming from, and Phil would be trying to make sure we were eating properly and not drinking on an empty stomach. Phil was just a right good lad. He meant a lot to me.'

Henrik Larsson: 'I find it very difficult to speak about Phil in this way. He should still be here. His loss is a tragedy. Guys like Phil are few and far between. When I arrived at Celtic, he immediately offered his support and guidance, which is what any new player looks for when they arrive in a new city and walk into a new dressing-room. He also spent time telling me about the history of Celtic. I could see the club meant a great deal to him and he was very proud to be a part of it. He was very unlucky with injuries but was still a big influence on the team and in the dressing-room. He would run all day for us and had talent to go with his energy. He was a lovely man and a credit to his family and his profession.'

Tom Boyd: 'I played with Phil in the 1991 Scottish Cup-winning side. Phil was still a young lad but displayed maturity beyond his years to score that afternoon. His goal was a blend of bravery and ability. He has been sadly missed and will continue to be missed. He was a fine person and one of the very few in life that you could honestly say didn't have a bad bone in him. His career was hampered through injury, but when he was available to play, he made a significant contribution and can be ever so proud of the part he played in the 1998 title success.'

Stéphane Mahé: 'I was impressed with Phil the footballer. He was a terrific midfielder, a real talent. But my abiding memories of Phil are of the person. We didn't socialise together a great deal, but he underlined my image of a Scotsman. To be a Scot, you should be kind, welcoming and friendly. Phil had all of those qualities and touched every person he met, including me. I always felt a sense of warmth when I was in a room with him, because even when we didn't speak the same language I knew he wanted to make sure the foreign guys like myself belonged at Celtic. He helped bridge the gap between foreigners and Scotsmen, and I'll never forget him.'

PHILIP O'DONNELL
25 March 1972 – 29 December 2007

thirteen

The Get-out

There was shock on the morning of 22 March when it was revealed that Wim Jansen had a get-out clause in his contract. He had signed a three-year deal when he took over, but both parties had the option of terminating the contract, as long they gave four weeks' notice before the end of the season. Fergus McCann and Jock Brown were not happy with the story being in the public domain and tried to rubbish the claims. However, Jansen spoke to Celtic's official club hotline to confirm that he did have a clause in his deal, although he didn't say whether or not he intended to activate it.

Until the day Jansen actually did confirm that he was leaving, the guessing game as to when he would do so was rife. People reasoned that the most obvious cause for him to quit would be the breakdown between him and Brown. In and around Parkhead, it had been known for months that the pair weren't on talking terms, but there were other signs that they no longer got on, such as them no longer turning up for the pre-match press conferences together. At the start of the season, they'd enter the Celtic media room at the same time and sit side by side at the top table to speak to the television, radio and newspaper reporters. By November, they'd arrive at different times and could barely stand within ten yards of each other. A body-language expert would have had enough material to last the rest of the season.

A few weeks before the get-out story appeared, Brown felt the need to speak at a press conference about their relationship and admitted that they did not see eye to eye. Speaking on 1 February, he said, 'When I came here and searched for a top-class coach, I was looking for someone with the right credentials. I certainly wasn't looking to appoint my best pal. When we went for Wim, I knew I wasn't bringing in a guy whom I would be going for a pint with after work. What was required was a man with a strong will and a single-minded approach. That's exactly what we've got, and I'm delighted about that. It doesn't matter whether we like each other or not. We're not running a popularity contest. Of course we have had different opinions on one or two issues. He expresses his views clearly, and I do likewise. I'm sure the same things happen in your offices and at every other big club in the world. Normally, these differences are private and confidential, but here they've been fed out.'

The players were concerned about the possibility of Jansen leaving and did not want it to happen. After a dodgy start, his personality and ideas had grown on most of them, and they'd come round to his way of thinking.

Craig Burley: 'We were winning games and on course for the title. That papered over the cracks in the relationship between Wim and Jock Brown. There was also a problem with Fergus McCann, but that was to a lesser extent, I believe. The players all knew that Wim couldn't stand Jock. The way Wim was being treated by Jock and the interference in matters of football was haunting him. I think Jock Brown thought he was general manager and chief scout.'

Alan Stubbs: 'It was a big blow to think we were going to lose Wim. I got on very well with him, as I think most of the players did. He was softly spoken and philosophical, a very astute and clever man. It was probably only after he left that we fully appreciated how clever he was.

'That said, I thought some of his training sessions weren't great

– quite boring, to be truthful. But they were put on for a reason. He wanted to find out which players would speak up, find out who were the strong characters and the people he could rely on.

'Players would have bad games, but he never criticised us or pointed the finger in public. He just used to say, "That is football. That is life," and move on to the next game. The angriest he used to get was when he didn't say anything. You could just tell with his hand movements, and he'd occasionally throw something to the ground to show that he was frustrated and miserable.

'For a manager not to shout and bawl is what the foreign lads are used to, but the British players found it a bit of a culture shock. There was no screaming in your face or pinning players against the wall. Wim would pause, then choose his words carefully.

'The players would bollock each other if necessary, and the manager knew that he didn't need to say anything. He liked the fact that the players would voice their opinions and that arguments were heated. He'd step in when he felt the time was right to calm us all down and just remind us who the gaffer actually was.'

Jackie McNamara: 'Wim was a really deep thinker. He was always alert, watching the players, seeing how they reacted to different situations and learning about their characters. Every Friday, he would play a practice game, usually nine v. nine. We could tell by that what the starting line-up for the next day was going to be, apart from one or two positions, as he would play his strongest side in one of the line-ups. It wasn't mix 'n' match. However, he always put me in the weaker team, and then when he named the team on a Saturday I was usually in the starting line-up. Towards the end of the season, I asked him why he did that to me. His explanation was straightforward. He told me that it was because he knew my attitude would remain the same and I'd play as well no matter which side I was on.

'In contrast to that, on one occasion David Hannah wasn't happy with Andy Thom and voiced his anger. Andy had pulled out of the second leg against Liverpool, and David had been asked to play. Our next game was a few days later, and Andy declared himself fit to play at training on the Friday. Andy was put in the "starting" team, and Davie was back in the "other" side. Davie was raging and kicked things in frustration, shouting and bawling. That was the way he reacted to being left out of the team, and Wim did not like to see that attitude.

'One time, I was away on Scotland duty for a game against France in St Etienne. But I was left out when it came to the match and wasn't even on the bench. Billy Dodds was the same. I was raging. My wife Sam was pregnant at the time, and she was having one or two difficulties. I could have been at home with her instead of being in France for nothing. Billy and I found a hospitality room, and we got stuck into the food and drink. I continued drinking when we got on the plane to come home right after the game. I was steaming by the time I arrived at Glasgow Airport at around 2 a.m. Darren Jackson and I had a room at an airport hotel. Sensibly, Darren went for a sleep before we had to go to training at Parkhead. I sat up drinking with Doddsy. I think I had my last whisky and Coke at 7.30 a.m.

'I went to the room to collect my suit carrier before heading for training with Darren. I picked up my suit carrier, tried to place it over my shoulder and toppled over to one side. I was gone. I was like Del Boy in the classic *Only Fools and Horses* sketch when he falls over in the yuppie bar. Darren said, "There must have been some weight in that suit carrier!"

'Darren still wasn't meant to drive after his brain op, but I was in no condition to get behind the wheel, so he drove us to training. We were on the M8 when we went past Ally McCoist, who was being driven into Glasgow by Derek McInnes – Coisty was banned from driving at that time. As we passed their car, I hung out of the window, giving them the finger and shouting abuse. It was all in good fun. I have a lot of time for Coisty. He sees the funny side of things like that.

'When we arrived at the ground, I went in to see Brian Scott, and he took one look at me and shook his head. "There's no way you can train. Go take a shower."

'I insisted that I was fine, and then Wim came in. He could smell the drink, and the way I was staggering about must have been a giveaway!

'"You OK, Jackie?"

'"Fine, gaffer, fine. How are you?"

'"I don't think you should train today, Jackie. Take the day off. Get a good sleep."

'"No, no, gaffer. I'll be fine."

'Of course, I wasn't. I went out onto the pitch and pulled up after running 20 yards. I was out of the game.

'The next day, Wim and I had a quiet word. "You feeling better today, Jackie?" He had a wee smile on his face. I had been totally out of order the day before. But Wim knew, because of things that were going on at that time, that a blowout was exactly what I needed. I was delighted that Wim treated me like an adult. Other managers wouldn't have.'

That, however, wasn't to say that Jansen was a soft touch, and the players all had first-hand experience of him when he was in a no-nonsense mood. He could sense from a mile off when the players were trying to pull a fast one.

Craig Burley: 'I was the stand-in captain when Tom Boyd was injured. We had a break of about ten days between games, and the boys asked me to approach Wim to ask if we could get away for three or four days on a "club trip" to somewhere with a bit of sunshine to do some training and recharge the batteries before the title run-in. I agreed and promised the boys that I'd come back with a result. Murdo knew the plan. Wim was in his office, and I chapped on the door. Murdo was in there with him.

'"Wim, the boys were wondering if we could go away on a club trip to Spain, or somewhere and . . ." He was reading a paper, and his glasses were down at the tip of his nose. He said no without lifting his head out of the paper. I started to ask again, and he just repeated his first answer, still not looking up at me. Murdo grinned. I went back to the dressing-room with my tail between my legs. I said to the boys that I had really tried hard to change his mind and really had him wilting, but after much agonising we had decided that we should stay here. Bullshit. The conversation had lasted less than 30 seconds, and only one man had been in control.

'Yet he wasn't bothered what we called him. He never insisted on being called gaffer or boss. I called him Wim. When I was at Chelsea and Ruud Gullit was the manager, Dennis Wise used to call him "Big Nose". So I suppose Wim got off lightly!'

During his ten months in Scotland, only a handful of people really got to know Jansen away from the football field. People wanted to know more, but there was never any chance of him lowering his protective shield. He never gave a one-to-one interview during his time in this country, and he gave no indication as to what made him tick off the park.

Wim Jansen: 'What was there to know? I take milk and sugar in my coffee, but that is not important. It is not so important what I like to eat or drink. My private life has always remained private. It's the way I like it. It's the way my family like it. The only thing that mattered was Celtic winning the league that season.

'I hardly ever read the newspapers, something that stemmed from my time in Japan when, obviously, I couldn't understand their language. So, not reading the newspapers in Scotland was nothing to do with my opinion of the Scottish media. The only time I got to know what was in the newspapers was when John Clark would have a word with me if he felt I should be informed about any comments made by any of my players or against any of my players.'

Murdo MacLeod was one of the very few people who had any idea of what Jansen was about off the pitch. MacLeod and his family got close to Jansen and his wife, Cobi. Indeed, MacLeod was one of the first to find out that Jansen would be activating his get-out clause.

Murdo MacLeod: 'Wim told me that he was leaving with a few weeks of the season remaining. There was a get-out clause in his contract, and he had decided to activate it. I was taken aback, as I hadn't known that he had such a clause until I'd read it in a newspaper a few weeks earlier. At that time, I'd asked him about it, but he hadn't given me a definitive answer on whether he would use it or not. I was then stunned when he told me that he was not going to stay on as head coach.

'I knew he would be a big loss to the club and to the dressing-room. Wim loved attention to detail, and he hated missing out on any piece of information on the opposition. For example, if a rival team played with a left winger, he would ask Paul Lambert to move 15 yards across to the right-hand side from his central role to offer support to the full-back. That might seem incidental, but it was important, and that kind of small detail impressed coaches in the game. Alex McLeish asked me a few times about Wim and was keen to tap into his knowledge and tactical awareness. Tommy Burns also asked me about Wim to enhance his own coaching.

'As far as I'm concerned, Wim was ten years ahead of any other coach who'd worked in Scotland. He was playing different formations before they became fashionable. Wim was also meticulous in his plans for training. The sessions were always good, although they were simple. Wim didn't believe in overcomplicating things, but he insisted on a high tempo. There wasn't a lot of running, but we had full-scale games at match speed. Wim hated to see players walking and would insist on them passing and moving. Seeing a player walk on the training field was one of the few things that made Wim angry. It was good that we had quite a tight squad and worked with no more than 20 players. We'd split the players into two groups – I'd take one and Wim would take the other. And then we'd switch.

'Wim was very hands on and always wanted to be at training to monitor the players. He would spot quite a lot about the players. He'd say to me after training that he thought a certain player or players weren't too sharp. But he was not a control freak and would allow me my say. I'd be in the dressing-room with the players more often than him on training days and would get a feel for how the players were. I'd go to him and say, "I think so and so should get a day off" or "It might be good to let so and so go away on his own and do an hour of shooting practice", and he would not have a problem going along with my judgement.

'He was also very much in favour of letting players decide if they wanted to play in reserve games. The Scottish mentality was that if you were out injured for five or six weeks, you would play a couple of reserve games before you would be considered for the first team. A lot of players hated playing for the "stiffs", and Wim gave them the option. He knew there was no point in forcing a player to play for the second team. He also hated to see a player getting injured in a reserve game. So, that meant a player really had to produce a high level in training when he returned from injury to catch Wim's eye. Tosh McKinlay and Malky Mackay were great trainers and wouldn't hold back. Yet they rarely played for the first team. I felt for them.'

Danny McGrain was a member of Jansen's backroom staff and said: 'Wim was a great football man. He impressed me. He never raised his voice and kept things simple. He was so calm and so laid back, but the players knew who was boss. When he spoke, the players stopped tying their laces or taking a drink.

'When he comes back to Glasgow, he must try to avoid me, because I love being in his company and tapping into his knowledge. I'm always asking him questions, searching for information, because he is such an intelligent man. He was a breath of fresh air that season.

'He also wanted to see the young players progress, and he joined me one day on the training field when I was trying to get Jamie Smith to lift his head when he had the ball at his feet. I had set out cones and was hoarse shouting at Jamie to look up as he dribbled. I think Jamie also had a sore neck! Wim came out and simplified the whole exercise. He stood at one end of the pitch and Jamie was at the other. Wim had a red marker in one hand and a white one in the other. Jamie had to run towards him with the ball and keep an eye on Wim so that he could shout out the colour of marker Wim was holding aloft. There was a big improvement in Jamie after that.'

Paul Lambert was probably the closest player to Jansen, although their relationship was strictly professional. When most of the staff were taking advantage of a day off, Lambert and Jansen would be at Parkhead, sharing ideas. Lambert enjoyed benefiting from his coach's wisdom.

Paul Lambert: 'Wim was great. At Dortmund, I was given confidence to play against any team and with any individual. There was no inferiority complex out on the pitch. Wim was similar, and I enjoyed working for him. I also enjoyed his company, just sitting for an hour or two listening to his stories and experiences. You know, when you looked at his CV, every player should have wanted to benefit from his knowledge. Johan Cruyff rates Wim as one of the most knowledgeable people he has ever worked with in football. For me, that says it all.

'So, I took in what he said. I wasn't going to be ignorant and not try to learn from him. I loved those mornings in his company, loved his stories from his national team days with Holland and his experiences with teammates and coaches.'

Jansen's situation dominated the thoughts of the players, and whether it was coincidence or not they won only three of their seven remaining league games. Without Jansen actually admitting it to them, the players knew that it would be a major surprise if he stayed on. One or two received subtle hints from the Dutchman as to his intentions.

Morten Wieghorst: 'I was out of contract and went to see Wim about my situation. The content of his reply was quite vague. I can't remember his exact words, but I left the meeting with the feeling, purely from reading between the lines, that he wasn't going to be the manager the following season. I had no complaints about my contract negotiations. The most important thing was to win the league. That was all that mattered. I cherish my league championship medal. It brings back so many happy memories of that season at Celtic and the friends I had. We were a close group of players and would run that extra yard for each other. Most of us still keep in touch, and I think we have friendships that will last.'

Things were also not running smoothly at Ibrox, and Rangers decided to sell Paul Gascoigne to Middlesbrough for £3.5 million. Gazza had problems at the club, and Walter Smith and David Murray felt it would be best to move him on for such a decent transfer fee. However, there was no doubt Gazza still possessed talent as a footballer, and his exit was good news for Celtic, as he was still a potential match winner in any company.

fourteen

The Run-in

Three days after their emphatic victory against Dunfermline, Celtic travelled to Easter Road to face a Hibs side deep in relegation trouble. Eager to avoid two defeats on the trot against the Hibees after their opening-day 2–1 loss, Celts knew that they had to leave the capital city with nothing less than three points if they wanted to maintain their title charge.

On heavy pitches on cold, blustery afternoons, silky soccer is never going to be in evidence, and Celtic knew that the Hibs match would be a roll-the-sleeves-up type of affair. They won the game 1–0 thanks to a goal in the 25th minute from Marc Rieper. Jackie McNamara's corner kick was met by Rieper's head, and, under pressure from Alan Stubbs, Hibs keeper Bryan Gunn failed to hold the ball. It dropped towards the line, and Jimmy Bocco booted clear. But the ball went in Rieper's direction, and he controlled his shot to score from 14 yards out. Alex McLeish and his players were raging with referee Jim McCluskey for not awarding a foul against Stubbs. However, Celtic deserved to win. They controlled the middle of the park, with Craig Burley, Morten Wieghorst and Paul Lambert all in good form.

Barry Lavety had a couple of decent chances and Grant Brebner – on loan from Manchester United – had a reasonable game, but

Hibs didn't do too much to trouble Jonathan Gould. Henrik Larsson played well, and Stéphane Mahé also came close to getting on the scoresheet, but it was only to be a one-goal victory, which, at that stage, was all that mattered.

Celtic had a fortnight's break from league duty after that game. Their next test was the visit of Dundee United to Parkhead. But before the United game, they had a trip planned to let off some steam.

Craig Burley: 'We used to enjoy a couple of days away in Dublin for a drinking session. We'd go a few times a season. We'd fly out on a Saturday night and come back first thing on Monday morning in business class. Wim started to get wind of it, and he'd cancelled training on a Monday morning, because there would be maybe nine or ten of us away. Murdo would get in touch to tell us that Wim thought there was no point putting in training if we were all hung-over.

'That day against Hibs, Stubbsy went down injured with a cut to his head. It looked a bad one, and Brian Scott came on to give him treatment. I went over to check on Stubbsy but mainly to find out if he would be fine to travel to Dublin with us that night. Scotty patched him up, and he made it.

'Scotty loved our squad. He worked at Parkhead for around 25 years and said that we were the group he enjoyed working with the most. He liked listening to the patter, as we all did. I used to want to get into training as quickly as possible to listen to the boys' banter and hear what they had been up to.'

With the Coca-Cola Cup in the bag, a Tennent's Scottish Cup win was required if Celtic were to have a chance of completing a historic Treble. The quarter-final tie was away to Dundee United, a difficult draw. It was played on 8 March, a Sunday afternoon, in front of a live television audience. Harald Brattbakk gave his side a tenth-minute lead when he beat United's offside trap to get on the end of a Henrik Larsson through ball. The giant figure of Sieb Dykstra stood between the Norwegian striker and the goal, but Brattbakk kept his nerve and rounded the Dutch keeper to stroke the ball home. It was a lead Celtic were grateful for, as just 60 seconds earlier Maurice Malpas had struck the Celtic crossbar with a header from an Andy McLaren corner kick.

But United weren't to be denied when Robbie Winters chipped a pass over the head of Marc Rieper towards Kjell Olofsson. The striker caught it perfectly on the volley, and his shot rattled in off Jonathan Gould's crossbar. Olofsson added his second to put the Tangerines into the lead just after half-time, a goal that pleased Tommy McLean, who was now watching from the stand after having been sent packing from the technical area by referee Kenny Clark.

Celtic showed resilience to bounce back and level the game. Simon Donnelly was supplied by Brattbakk and then found Wieghorst, who picked his spot to slot the ball between Dykstra's legs and into the net. The game then looked to be heading for a replay until disaster struck for United defender Erik Pedersen in injury time. Larsson sent a cross ball into the path of Brattbakk, but the striker failed to connect. However, the ball was travelling at pace, and it deflected off Pedersen's knee and past Dykstra from close range. It was a cruel twist for Pedersen, but Celtic could argue that they had worked hard for their slice of good fortune.

Dundee United's subsequent trip to Parkhead on Sunday, 15 March, should have been a comfortable victory for Celtic. The Hoops had already beaten the Arabs four times that season, and United had racked up just seven wins from twenty-eight games – only bottom club Hibs had a more embarrassing record. In front of a noisy home crowd, Celtic controlled the game and had chances to be three up inside the first twenty minutes, but Larsson was denied twice by Dykstra and Brattbakk missed a decent opportunity.

It was left to Donnelly to break the deadlock, his goal coming in the 27th minute. Wieghorst's cross was flicked on by Brattbakk, and Donnelly then curled the ball with his right foot past Dykstra from eight yards.

Celtic continued to batter the United goal with Brattbakk and Larsson coming close. Dykstra then prevented Wieghorst from scoring with a breathtaking save. That was in the seventy-third minute, and just two minutes later United levelled. Craig Easton found Olofsson inside the box, and the powerful striker despatched a low shot past Gould. Considering that Olofsson had netted 19 times so far that season, it was no wonder that Gould looked at his defenders with an angry stare, bewildered as to why they had left the striker unmarked.

Having cut United open so often in the first hour of the game, Celtic were now devoid of ideas, and the game finished 1–1. Jansen's players left the field angry at dropping two points. The Celtic fans left the stadium fearing another title for Rangers.

The next match was one of the most hazardous hurdles in Celtic's run-in, but Jansen's men cleared it as they closed in on the title. Pittodrie is always considered one of the toughest away trips on the fixture list, and with Aberdeen having not lost a goal at home in five matches it was always going to be a massive test for Celtic. Indeed, the last goal conceded by the Dons at Pittodrie had been on 9 December when Darren Jackson had netted.

With both defences so strong, it seemed more than likely that a win for either side would be by the only goal, and so it proved. After almost eight hours without losing a goal at home, Aberdeen finally buckled when Celtic took the lead just before the break. Larsson hit a free-kick wide for Lambert to aim a hopeful cross into the penalty area. John Inglis flicked the ball away at full stretch, and it fell perfectly for Stéphane Mahé; however, before he could shoot, he was upended by a rash David Rowson challenge. Referee John Underhill rightly pointed to the spot, and Burley stepped up to slide the ball low to Jim Leighton's right for his 12th goal of the season. Jackson, on for the ineffective Brattbakk, should have sealed the win when he was sent clear, but his first touch was poor and so was his shot. But it was another win for the Parkhead club, and a massive one at that.

Jonathan Gould: 'I enjoyed that game. It was a narrow victory and one we badly needed. Derek Whyte had a header, and it was going in all the way, right into the top corner of the net. I flew across and managed to get my left hand to it. That was probably my most satisfying save of the season. It was also great to leave Aberdeen with three points tucked away. It was a difficult venue to go to, and their supporters showed animosity towards us. They never hid their feelings and made it clear that they wanted to see every one of us down and out. But we had better players than them, and at that stage of the season there was a real determination not to slip up.'

In terms of the race for the title, there was a titanic battle on the cards at Parkhead when Hearts came to Glasgow's East End on 28 March. With twenty-nine league games played, Celtic were top of the league going into the game and wanted to increase their two-point advantage over the second-placed Jambos. To have a realistic chance of winning the league, Hearts had to improve on their record of just two points from a possible eighteen in meetings against the Old Firm that season. That wasn't the form of champions.

Hearts avoided defeat, coming away from Parkhead with a 0–0 draw, but Celtic knew that if Jim Jefferies and his players were to have been the main threat that season, they would have defeated them on their own ground. The Hoops' fiercest challenge still came from Rangers.

David Weir almost gave Hearts an early lead, but with Lambert in fine form Celtic then took a grip on the game. There was a terrific atmosphere inside the ground, and Stubbs came close to scoring. Lambert then set up Larsson, but he was denied by an outstanding challenge from Paul Ritchie, who had a powerful game at the back for Hearts.

Celtic were dealt a blow when the influential McNamara hobbled off with an ankle injury, and Mahé was also carried off late in the game. With so much at stake, it was inevitable that the game would blow up at some point, and Burley and ex-Celt Stevie Fulton squared up after Stubbs accused Neil McCann of diving.

Wieghorst and Jackson also had chances to score. Jackson then set up Donnelly, and his shot looked a cert to open the scoring, but, from nowhere, the outstretched hand of Gilles Rousset turned it over the bar. At the final whistle, the Celtic players were angry with referee Bobby Tait, who added less than a minute of injury time despite there having been several hold-ups in play to allow players to be treated for injury.

The league title was the priority, but the Scottish Cup ranked right up there, and it became even more important when the semi-final draw paired Celtic with their Old Firm rivals on Sunday, 5 April. As Hampden was still being redeveloped, Parkhead was officially a 'neutral' venue that day, and the stadium was evenly split between both sides.

The match was to be Andy Goram's final Old Firm game at Parkhead, and, in many ways, the man with the creaking knee joints and podgy physique saved his very best for this appearance. He had made Tommy Burns's life a misery with save after save. In fact, Burns had felt compelled to say in one post-match Old Firm press conference that it would be written on his gravestone that 'Andy Goram broke my heart'. Jansen must have felt like Burns after the semi. Celtic dominated the early stages, but the Rangers keeper pulled off three stunning stops to twice deny Larsson and a superb strike from Donnelly.

Rangers were masters at soaking up pressure and then hitting Celtic on the break. McCoist did just that, giving his side a precious lead in the second half, and Jörg Albertz added a killer second. Burley scored in injury time to pull one back, but getting the better of Goram for once was too little, too late for Celtic. Rangers marched into the final for a game against Hearts – which they lost 2–1 in Smith's final game in charge. Being out of the cup meant Celtic only had the league title to concentrate on, but they faced a difficult journey in their next game in pursuit of that special prize.

Celtic had to make their way down the A77 to Ayrshire to play against Kilmarnock on 8 April. It was a wet Wednesday night, and it couldn't have been a game Jansen and his players fancied too much. After losing three days earlier to Rangers in the Scottish Cup, Celtic had to show they had the mental and physical strength to bounce back. This night was all about getting in and out as quickly as possible with the points in the bag.

After a low-key start, Larsson opened the scoring in the 19th minute. It was his first goal since 21 February – ironically, also against Kilmarnock. Larsson found O'Donnell with a sweet pass, and the midfielder managed to dribble past Gus MacPherson. O'Donnell then put in a wonderful cross, which was met sweetly by Larsson, and his header flew into the net past Marshall.

That goal should have helped to settle Celtic down – but it didn't. They continued to show nerves, and Kilmarnock sensed this. That said, Marshall pulled off two brilliant saves just before half-time to deny Donnelly and Wieghorst. Nevertheless, Bobby Williamson's side felt aggrieved to be one down at the break and made sure that they were right back in contention for victory in the fortieth minute when they levelled. Pat Nevin displayed fine skill to get to the byline, and his cross was met by Paul Wright. The striker made a perfect connection with the ball, and his shot looked net bound until Gould managed to stretch out his hand and claw it back out. Unfortunately for the keeper, the ball rolled straight into the path of Alex Burke, and he rattled it home from a tight angle.

Celtic feared that they were about to drop more crucial championship points and knew that they had to show resilience to avoid another setback. O'Donnell forced Marshall into a top-class save, and then in the 55th minute the lead was restored through Donnelly. Gary Holt gifted possession to Burley, and his first-time pass found Jackson. With fine vision and a neat touch, he laid it into the path of Donnelly. Most people would have expected the striker to hit his shot with some power, but he took a touch, dropped a shoulder and then had the audacity to chip the ball over Marshall from just inside the box. It was a goal right out of the top drawer – a marvellous move and a fantastic finish.

Killie kept at it, and Ray Montgomerie almost scored in the closing stages, but Gould denied him with a one-handed save. In the end, Celtic got the job done, and the win put them at the top of the table with 66 points from 31 games.

Simon Donnelly: 'Big Marsh won't thank me for highlighting this, but the goal I scored against him was perhaps my most satisfying of the season. We didn't have a great record at Rugby Park, and the conditions were poor that night. Taking all the circumstances into account, Rangers and Hearts probably expected us to slip up and drop two points, but we dug deep and came away with a vital win. My goal was important. I lifted the ball over Marsh, and it was such a sweet moment.'

Sunday, 12 April was a vital date in the calendar. Another Old Firm game loomed. Celtic went in to the match at the top of the league. However, at the end of the 90 minutes Rangers had overtaken them after a 2–0 win. Walter Smith's men had a superior goal difference, which put them in pole position. It was also to be Smith's last game in charge of the Ibrox club against the Hoops.

Celtic had plenty of possession and threatened Goram's goal several times, but there appeared to be a lack of belief from the players and severe doubts that they could leave Ibrox with a victory. Rangers took the lead in the 24th minute through a cracking long-range effort from Jonas Thern. The talented Swedish midfielder gave a glimpse of why he had been signed on a Bosman from Roma to become the highest-paid player in the country. His 25-yard volley gave Rangers the lead, and they didn't look back on that cold, windy afternoon.

Lambert, Stubbs and Rieper all put Goram under pressure in search of an equaliser, but Celtic just didn't look like they were going to score. The match was over as a contest in the 66th minute when Albertz scored yet another glorious goal for his team. The German midfielder collected a pass from Gordon Durie and pounded his way towards goal. Burley was in pursuit but just couldn't get close enough to mount a serious tackle. Albertz made sure he created an angle for himself on his favoured left foot and drilled a low shot past Gould.

Having been in such a commanding position at the top of the table, Celtic had now surrendered their lead and given Rangers the edge. As the Celtic players trudged off the Ibrox pitch, their body language suggested that the doom and gloom of recent weeks was going to continue and, ultimately, cost them the championship that they were so desperate to win and had been favourites to just three weeks earlier.

In contrast, Rangers had the swagger of champions. With their heads in the air and their chests puffed out, Gough and his teammates had that glint in their eyes that suggested they were about to pull it off and going to make it ten in a row. The battle was now down to the nail-biting stage, and Celtic knew they had to improve dramatically.

Darren Jackson: 'I was invited by FIFA to go over to Paris to play in a game organised to mark the run-up to the 1998 World Cup finals. Craig Brown, I think, had put my name forward to represent Scotland, but Wim told me he wanted me to stay for the Kilmarnock game, and that was fair enough. Gordon Durie took my place in the FIFA game. We beat Kilmarnock, and that was as good a result as we had all season. It was vital.

'I started the game against Rangers at Ibrox, but I had a virus and probably shouldn't have played. Fair play to Wim for selecting me, but I was coughing and spluttering, totally breathless. It was a poor game for me and the team. Rangers were right back at us.'

Marc Rieper: 'I could see why Rangers had won nine titles. They were very well organised and had a strong squad. But I felt they looked a bit tired compared to the previous seasons. I think some of their players were over the hill and just didn't have the same hunger that they'd had previously. They also sold Paul Gascoigne during the season, and there was constant speculation surrounding Brian Laudrup's future.

'I often dined with Brian. We rarely spoke about football when we were out, but when we were on international duty there would be some friendly banter. However, I think he felt we had a strong team that season and maybe the tide was turning in our favour. He could sense the hunger and spirit we had in our dressing-room. I don't think Rangers deserved to beat us in the Scottish Cup game.

They took eight out of twelve points in the league but that could have easily been reversed.

'When I joined Celtic, the bookies had Rangers as strong favourites. In fact, I think one or two might have paid out after we lost our first two games of the season. You can understand why, as Celtic were in a poor state, and there was only a low level of expectation. That all changed during the second half of the season, and we had a feeling we could do it after we beat Rangers at New Year.

'It was very important to tighten up defensively, and the priority had to be about winning and not about playing good football. I think better football was played under Tommy Burns, and we weren't as big a threat going forward as perhaps Celtic teams had been in previous seasons. But we just clicked, and the main objective was to be solid and organised. We had disagreements about the style of football we played. Some players felt we should have been more flamboyant, sticking to the traditions of the club by playing attacking football all the time. I was very opinionated and frank as to the way I felt it should be done. I insisted on us being solid and concentrating on cutting out the loss of silly goals. I had to be very strong about this. It was the best way for us to win the championship.

'Paul Lambert was an important signing. He was a top player and had played on the biggest stages in club football. He was very solid, very professional and very organised – not your typical British style of player from that period.'

On 18 April, Harri Kampman's Motherwell arrived at Parkhead. A victory was a must, but the Lanarkshire side were determined not to be the whipping boys and caused a sensation when they took the lead in the 12th minute, Stevie McMillan's neat volley flying past Gould. Celtic responded well and battered away at Motherwell, forcing their keeper Stevie Woods into some terrific saves. But he was helpless just three minutes later when Burley shot home from ten yards after getting on the end of a lovely O'Donnell pass. Burley then scored again when he was on the end of a Larsson chest down, rifling home a terrific shot. The midfielder was also involved in the third goal, his cross finding Jackson, who nodded the ball across the goalmouth for Donnelly to tap in. In the 62nd minute, Celtic made it 4–1 when Burley was the provider for Donnelly, the striker making no mistake. Burley and Donnelly were outstanding throughout, but there was also a standing ovation for Jackson when he was subbed eight minutes before time. He had played his part in this crucial win, and the applause he received was in total contrast to the previous week when he had been booed by his own fans as he cut a sad figure leaving the field after the defeat to Rangers.

On 25 April, Hibs were the visitors to Celtic Park. Hibs were still fighting relegation, and the three points were supposed to be a formality for Jansen's side, especially as the Edinburgh club had recorded just one victory in the East End of Glasgow in the previous six years. But the Hibees, then managed by Alex McLeish, weren't for making it easy. There was even some fighting talk in the build-up to the game when McLeish asked referee George Simpson not to be intimidated by the home crowd of more than 50,000. He also asked his players to stand on the halfway line and stare out the Celtic players as they went into their huddle. Bit by bit, McLeish's pre-match plans worked. Celtic never really got going, and too many of their influential players were out of touch.

Hibs keeper Bryan Gunn hardly had a save to make, and Donnelly missed a sitter from six yards. Murdo MacLeod and McLeish were sent to the stand in the 73rd minute after a touchline war of words. But the main controversy came five minutes before the end when O'Donnell tumbled inside the box after a challenge from John Hughes. The Hibs players insisted that he had dived and stood over his body as he lay on the deck to let him know how they felt. George Simpson agreed and waved play on. The official was strong that afternoon, and Celtic blew the chance of another victory.

At that stage of the season, a 0–0 draw was not in the script. It meant a nail-biting finish was on the agenda, and it was going to be about which side could hold their nerve better.

Murdo MacLeod: 'I felt totally relaxed about the final month of the season. I was comfortable with the pressure. It was in our own hands, and that was the scenario we wanted. Naturally, there was a lot of tension, and I knew both sides would drop points in the run-in.

'Compared to us, Rangers had no pressure. Rangers were out to change history, and we were out to stop it. If we failed, we would have been remembered as the team that couldn't stop ten in a row – not a pleasant thought, to put it mildly.'

fifteen

A Wasted Opportunity

It's Saturday, 2 May. Rangers are at home to Kilmarnock. A win for Walter Smith's team will put them on seventy-two points with one game to play. Celtic are on seventy points with two games to play. There is nothing Wim Jansen and his players can do. It's totally out of their hands. Some of them have the radio on, tuning in to every kick of the ball. Some have gone shopping. And some of the players have locked themselves away with a do-not-disturb sign on the door.

Things are not going to plan for Rangers. It's the final minutes of the game, and the score is still 0–0. Rangers need to win. Smith, his players and the fans are nervous. The 90 minutes are up, but there is no sign of referee Bobby Tait blowing for full-time. It is 1998, and there is no electronic scoreboard on display from the fourth official to indicate how much time will be added on.

Bobby Williamson's players are under a bit of pressure but coping admirably. Then the unimaginable happens. Killie race up the park, and Ally Mitchell scores the winning goal. The extra minutes should have been time for Rangers to find a winner, but it didn't happen. Smith and his players are distraught.

Celtic only need to win at Dunfermline the following day to be crowned champions. Despite having won just two of their previous five league games, the title is still in their own hands . . .

The Celtic fans had managed to get tickets for every part of East End Park, and their presence dwarfed the home crowd on what was a sunny Sunday afternoon. Demand for tickets was so fierce that Celtic decided to beam the game back to Parkhead so that thousands of supporters could watch the day of drama unfold from the North Stand. The Dunfermline DJ even got in on the act and played Lou Reed's 'Perfect Day' before kick-off. It all got too much for one Celtic fan, and he was ejected from the ground by police fifteen minutes before the match began.

Donnelly was in the action week-in, week-out for Celtic, and he was to play his part in this game. First, he was denied by top goalkeeping from Ian Westwater. Then, in the 35th minute, he finally beat the Pars keeper with a low shot after receiving a superb pass from Larsson. The championship was surely in the bag. Celtic kept at it, looking for a second goal, but nerves were evident in the dugout, in the stands and on the pitch. The tension was unbearable as Dunfermline crept into the game, throwing men forward in an attempt to get something from the match.

And they did when Scott McCulloch lumped a high free-kick deep into the Celtic penalty box and sub Craig Faulconbridge sent a looping header agonisingly over Gould with just seven minutes left. Things nearly got worse when David Bingham almost scored after Gould failed to hold a high ball. Morten Wieghorst then thought he had won the title for Celtic on the final whistle when his header looked goal bound, but McCulloch booted the ball off the line.

When the final whistle sounded, Celtic's Danish midfielder grabbed the ball and booted it out of the ground in frustration. It was unbelievable. The title was being handed to Celtic on a plate and yet questions were still being asked of them. Another weekend of torture lay ahead.

Murdo MacLeod: 'I sat in the house and listened to the Rangers v. Kilmarnock game on radio. With ten minutes to go, the scoreline was 0–0. It was going great. But I couldn't listen. I was too nervous. I moved two rooms away, pretending to myself that I wouldn't be able to hear it. But I still could. Every kick of the ball, every second that ticked away, I was aware of it.

'Bobby Tait was the referee. Bobby now admits himself that he is a Rangers fan and that he should never have been in charge of such a game. It was a scandalous decision by the SFA. I really don't know what they were thinking about by making such an appointment. The score was still 0–0 when the 90 minutes were up, and Bobby played on. But the amount of time he added on backfired on them, as Kilmarnock scored through Ally Mitchell to take the points. I let out a scream when Mitchell put the ball in the net.

'Bobby is now on the after-dinner speaking circuit, and part of his act centres around that day. To be fair to Bobby, he takes the mickey out of himself and says that after Kilmarnock scored he played on for ten more minutes in the hope that Rangers would equalise before Walter Smith eventually shouted to him from the dugout, "Bobby, just blow for full-time. We're never gonna score!"

'I often do the after-dinner stuff with Bobby, and we have a laugh and a joke about it. As far as I'm concerned, Bobby played a major part in opening the door for us to win the title.

'I phoned Wim after the final whistle, and he was aware that Rangers had lost. We were both delighted. We had to play Dunfermline the following day at East End Park, and three points would have won us the title. Simon Donnelly put us in the lead, but Dunfermline were getting back at us, and I remember Wim coming out of the dugout, shouting at the players to move up the pitch, as they were sitting far too deep. Dunfermline had a free-kick, and we were camped on our own 18-yard line. We were punished, as they scored through a header from Faulconbridge. The ball seemed to go in in slow motion.

'We were all desperately disappointed. It was a beautiful, sunny day and just about perfect for winning the title. But failing to win it at East End Park allowed us to go and do it in front of our own fans at Parkhead the following weekend.

'I tried to be upbeat and reminded the players that it was still in our own hands. Tom Boyd approached me and Wim to ask if we could stay at Cameron House the night before the St Johnstone game. We had switched to staying there quite early in the season. It was Wim's decision – just another one of his subtle little changes. The first time we stayed away was before our home game against Inter CableTel in the UEFA Cup, and on that occasion we stuck with tradition, staying in our usual hotel in Seamill. But Wim wasn't satisfied, as the training facility was the front lawn of the hotel, and we had to use a bench as a goal. We knew that it had been good enough for the Lisbon Lions, and Wim respected that, but times had moved on, and he wanted better facilities.'

Simon Donnelly: 'I was driving in East Kilbride and heard the news on the radio about Kilmarnock beating Rangers. I phoned Jackie to speak to him, and we were both really excited about the following day at East End Park. The players and the fans probably thought that day was going to be a formality and that all we had to do was turn up and stick on the jerseys for 90 minutes to win the league.

'I scored our goal and thought that it was going to be the winner that made history. Yes, I was excited. I fancied making a piece of history. Then Dunfermline scored, and Craig Faulconbridge stole my moment of glory. I was gutted – we all were.'

Darren Jackson: 'Our chance to wrap up the title and stop Rangers making history came at Dunfermline. It was a game we were all desperate for. But I had vibes all week that Wim wasn't going to start me. I remember having a bite to eat at Parkhead before we made the bus journey through on the morning of the game, and I said to Alan Stubbs and Malky Mackay that I had absolutely no chance of starting the game and would be lucky to even find a place on the bench. They laughed at my pessimism and told me not to be so silly.

'The next thing I knew, Wim had asked for me to go to the manager's office. Murdo was there, and Wim was behind his desk. Waiting. I knew what was coming. I took a deep breath.

'"Darren, you won't be in the 14 today. Sorry."

'"It's a fucking joke and you know it," I replied. I couldn't hide my emotions. The look on my face must have told the story. There was nothing more to say. I walked out. The boys were buzzing, and my stomach was in knots.

'Looking back, Wim was doing it for the right reasons – of course he was. It must be hard for a manager to tell a player he isn't going to be involved in one of the most important games in the history of the club. Murdo and I were teammates at Hibs, but that didn't get me any preferential treatment, nor was I expecting any.

'I was down. I was disappointed. But I had to keep in decent spirits for the sake of my teammates. There was far too much at stake.

'We had a night out on the Tuesday, and a few of the boys were in a right state. We started at the Amber Regent for dinner and then went to T.G.I. Friday's for cocktails. It probably wasn't the best idea to go out just four days before the league decider, but we decided we needed to let off some steam. We were out quite a lot together that season – Saturday, Tuesday, Saturday, Tuesday – and I believe that helped us bond and ultimately played a significant part in our title success.'

Wim Jansen: 'I had no favourites. I had no players that I liked better than any of the others. I was the boss, and I made the decisions. It is only natural some of the players would not agree with some of my decisions. That is football. That is life. Every decision I made was for the good of Celtic. It was not to make a player unhappy.

'If I had to leave a player out of the team, I would tell him. But I would keep the conversation short. When you have to give someone bad news, you do not go on about it with a one-hour explanation and debate. You get it over and done with quickly – no more than two minutes. If a player was left out, I wouldn't expect him to agree with my decision. This is normal.

'There is pressure to win every game, and there is pressure to win a league. I felt we should have won the title at Dunfermline. We should have been able to win that game. We scored, and that allowed us to be a little calmer, but then we lost a poor goal. In my way of thinking, we were too deep at the free-kick. We should have squeezed up. The goal we lost was avoidable. At least we still had one chance left to do it by ourselves, and that was in the home game against St Johnstone.

'Can you change a result or a decision by shouting and swearing? You need to relax, gather your thoughts and breathe. That was my way of thinking. If necessary, I could have raised my voice, but what good would it have done? I needed to be focused, needed to be technically aware. You can speak to the players about the 90 minutes that have just passed, but the most important thing is the next game. At least you can do something about that. You can make tactical changes, and you can show a player good or bad things that you want him to build on or to erase from the next game.

'Because there was so much pressure surrounding the club that season, for obvious reasons, I felt it was important not to highlight too many of the mistakes made by my players. It was not a season for shouting at players and criticising them. They had so much to contend with, trying to stop Rangers under the most unbelievable pressure, that sometimes it was better to say nothing to them. It was all about protecting them. I felt it was best to get them to change one or two things in their game in practice sessions during the week. Based on their performance in the previous game, I would ask them to do some things, and they'd respond. So, I was correcting their mistakes without them knowing it.

'But I did have some very good players. In soccer, there are two types of footballers: those who only use their legs and those who use their brains. The ones who only use their legs will never get to the top. You have to be aware on the football pitch, have to lift your head and see what is around you. If you have players who can do that, then you have a better chance of winning football matches. Thankfully, we had enough who were able to make a difference on the pitch.'

Jonathan Gould: 'It was a rotten feeling when we drew with Dunfermline. Wim was raging when we lost that goal to them. It was a complete fluke of a header. But we had to pick ourselves up, and the old team spirit didn't take long to come to the surface. We were off on the Wednesday, so on the Tuesday after training we arranged to go to the Amber Regent in Glasgow city centre and have some good food and a blowout on the drink.

'Despite the fact it was just four days before one of the biggest games in the history of the club, I was as drunk as I'd ever been. I couldn't see straight when I walked out of the restaurant. I think Tosh McKinlay took advantage of my state and managed to squeeze my head through some railings. It was a great day and exactly what we needed. We trusted each other and just wanted to be together as much as possible that week, to share the tension and build up to the game.'

Paul Lambert: 'There was a great atmosphere inside East End Park. It was the old terracing, and there were probably more fans crammed into the ground than there should have been. We looked on our way, and then they scored. It was a huge setback. We were all over the place the next few days in training. Wim sent us home one day in the build-up to the St Johnstone game because the session was a shambles. But we knew what was at stake and knew we would produce the goods in front of our own fans.'

sixteen

One in a Row

On 9 May, Celtic were given the chance to win the title. All they had to do was defeat St Johnstone at Parkhead. However, if Rangers didn't win at Tannadice against Dundee United, then the title would be going back to Parkhead for the first time in a decade, regardless.

Malky Mackay: 'We were staying at Cameron House on the Friday night. On the morning of the game, I took a walk into Balloch with Phil O'Donnell, and we decided to attend morning mass. No more than 30 people were at the mass, and we stood at the back, out of the way, although we had our Celtic tracksuits on! The priest spotted us, and at the end of the mass he said that we should all pray for our loved ones and also that the two lads at the back of the chapel and their teammates get the right result that afternoon. Everyone turned to look at us. We were so embarrassed.'

It was a typically nervy afternoon for the Celtic players. The starting XI that had failed to wrap up the title the previous weekend in Fife were given the nod to make amends: Gould, Boyd, Annoni, McNamara, Rieper, Stubbs, Larsson, Burley, Donnelly, Lambert and O'Donnell — 11 men who in 90 minutes of football could make their mark in the history of Celtic Football Club.

That man Henrik Larsson settled the nerves of the crowd of

more than 50,000 – one of whom was John Higgins, who had just been crowned World Snooker Champion – cheering on the Hoops. It took the Swedish striker just 160 seconds to score. He received a pass from Paul Lambert out on the left-hand side of the pitch, midway inside the St Johnstone half. The Swede cut inside on to his right foot, feigned a shot and gradually got closer to goal. He had created a perfect angle to shoot from, and he let fly from 20 yards. The ball flew past Alan Main into the left-hand corner of the net. What a start.

The lead was most welcome, but after what had happened in their last game Celtic were desperate for a second goal. Craig Burley and Simon Donnelly both came close, and there was a scare when George O'Boyle should have levelled for Paul Sturrock's side, but he headed over the crossbar from just six yards.

Jonathan Gould: 'I was nervous going into the game against St Johnstone. We quickly went a goal ahead, and then they had a couple of half chances. Leigh Jenkinson whipped in a free-kick, and I managed to push it over the bar. It couldn't have looked too convincing. Then there was a cross ball, and I got the slightest of touches on it to direct it away from George O'Boyle's forehead. It hit the top of his head and went over the bar. Had I not deflected that ball, albeit ever so slightly, then who knows what would have happened.

'The pre-match nerves I had were nothing compared to how I felt at half-time. I was unbelievably nervous. I kept thinking that one mistake could cost us the title. I sat with an ice-cold towel over my head and went into my own wee world. I didn't hear a word of what Wim or the other players said during the break. There was just so much tension in the stadium, and I doubt if there has been anything like it since.'

Alan Main was in top form and denied Simon Donnelly from close range in the 56th minute. Three minutes later, Donnelly was replaced by Harald Brattbakk. St Johnstone had plenty of possession at that stage, and there was a dreaded feeling in the home crowd that Celtic were going to concede a goal. But they withstood the pressure, and in the 73rd minute there was no doubt about the destination of the league crown when Celtic doubled their lead.

Burley fed Jackie McNamara with a pass out to the right wing. McNamara looked up to see Brattbakk making a run, and the Norwegian striker was grateful to get on the end of the low, driven cross, coolly picking his spot and steering the ball beyond Main from seven yards. Brattbakk, so often ridiculed that season, ran to the corner flag at the junction of the Main Stand and the Celtic End to take a bow. Larsson jumped on his back, as if to give the player his seal of approval. The fans felt a weight removed from their shoulders, safe in the knowledge that the championship was now theirs, and the party started. Ten in a row was not going to happen. Referee Kenny Clark's final whistle made it a matter of fact. Rangers had won at Tannadice, but that was now irrelevant.

The Celtic players, led by skipper Tom Boyd, savoured the moment and stayed on the field for more than 40 minutes to party. They changed out of their green-and-white strips and replaced them with white T-shirts, specially made for the occasion. The words 'Smell the Glove' appeared on them in huge print. The media scrambled to find out exactly what was with the strange slogan, but all the players clammed up. The only piece of information forthcoming was that it was Tosh McKinlay's idea. 'Ask Tosh about it' was the standard reply whenever a player was asked for an explanation.

One theory was that Andy Goram had thrown one of his gloves into the Celtic dressing-room after an Old Firm game and had asked the Celtic players to 'smell the glove', a reference to the fact that he had had a quiet afternoon and not broken sweat, having no saves of note to make. The truth was that while on the Scotland team bus on the way to a training session at Rugby Park McKinlay had spotted graffiti on a wall. Darren Jackson was sitting next to McKinlay when he saw 'Smell the Glove' written on the wall. McKinlay repeated the words to Jackson several times and then started to use them in the Celtic dressing-room on their return from international duty.

After the match, the Celtic players spoke about the achievement of winning the league. Brattbakk, however, refused to speak to the Scottish press after the game. He preferred to remain silent. It was his way of getting his own back for the months of criticism he had taken.

Harald Brattbakk: 'I had many highlights during my time at Celtic and my career in general. I enjoyed some great times at Rosenborg and scored some massive goals for them in the Champions League. But, without a doubt, scoring the goal that helped us to lift the title was a very special moment. It was a phenomenal day in my life, and I will always remember it. We were probably expected to win the game easily, but we knew it was never going to be that way, because there was so much at stake. We found that out the week before when we only had to beat Dunfermline and drew 1–1. Simon Donnelly scored for us and then missed a chance late in the game to put us 2–1 ahead.

'It all depended on the next game, and Henrik gave us an early lead. Then it was my turn to grab the spotlight, and I can still remember the ball being played into my path for me to run on to and score. It was a perfectly weighted cross from Jackie. And it was the one chance I was never going to miss.'

Wim Jansen: 'Henrik scored the first goal, and I was happy for him. It was one of many important goals he scored for the club during his seven years there. What I admire most about him is that he worked hard to develop himself. Think about it. Compare the player that arrived at Celtic to the player that left, and you can see exactly what I mean.

'He was a special player to work with. By that I mean you didn't have to give him many instructions, didn't have to speak too much to him. He was an intelligent player and knew how the game should be played. He was creative and had confidence, and that allowed him to try things other players would not have tried. I don't know every transfer in the history of Celtic but I believe Henrik has to go down as one of the best pieces of business. For sure, he was the best signing I ever made in my career.'

Jackie McNamara: 'That cross gave me so much pleasure. What a relief when that goal went in.

'Gouldie had some incredible saves for us that season. He also had his moments, right enough. There was one game – can't remember who it was against – and a cross ball came over. He shouted to me, "Mine. Yours. Keeper. Away." The other team scored. I looked at Gouldie as if to say, "What the fuck are you playing at?" He just shrugged his shoulders and gave me that wee smile that meant you couldn't be angry at him.

'I had to attend a Celtic Supporters Club dance at Linwood after the draw at East End Park. I wasn't too sure about going and was thinking about calling off. I thought the fans would be angry and it would be a nightmare night. But I knew it was bad manners to pull out, and it wasn't fair to punish our fans even more by not turning up. It turned out to be a great night, and the supporters were positive and offered plenty of encouragement. In a way, they seemed happy we hadn't won, as it would give more Celtic fans the chance to see us finish the job at home the following weekend.

'I was a nervous wreck in the build-up to that St Johnstone game – I hardly slept a wink all week. If Rangers had won the league, they'd have been as well shutting our place down. I don't think that there would have been any chance of a recovery. It was bad enough Rangers won nine titles, but if they'd got to ten . . .

'It was great to win the player of the year award. To win that personal accolade, see the birth of my first child, Erin, win the league with Celtic and go to the World Cup with Scotland all within the space of six months made it one of the best periods of my life.

'I was surprised to win the SPFA [Scottish Professional Footballers' Association] award. I didn't have the best of starts to the season and remember watching *Scotsport* after we lost to Dunfermline on the second day of the season. Gerry McNee was critical of me, saying that I hadn't lived up to my early promise. I suppose that was the kind of kick up the backside I needed at that time. I managed to bounce back, and to have played most of the season with tendinitis made it all the sweeter. I was very honoured and proud.'

Tom Boyd: 'We were nervous before the game against St Johnstone. They were hoping to win the game to clinch a place in the UEFA Cup. So, it wasn't as if they came to our place to lie down and had nothing to play for.

'George O'Boyle missed a sitter in the first half. Had that gone in, we would have been level at the break, and our nerves would really have been shot to pieces. But Henrik settled us down. Genuinely, I was almost in tears when Henrik scored the first goal. Then Harald scored, and I knew we were over the line. I knew we wouldn't concede two goals.

'When Kenny Clark blew the final whistle, I sank to my knees on the turf. I didn't want to leave the pitch. I had waited five years to win the league with Celtic and wanted to make the most of every minute of it. I just thought I'd have won it sooner. When you join a club such as Celtic, you don't expect to go five years without a league success, but we just didn't compete well enough for it to happen.

'I think I was stripped down to my Y-fronts, or slips as we call them. I also made a fool of myself when I was handed the microphone by Tony Hamilton and started to sing "Stand Up For the Champions". It was a shocker. I couldn't hear myself, and I was off key. It was the kind of moment you get caught up in when a title success happens.

'It was a pleasure to see our fans' joy. Some of them had probably gone right through their schooldays without seeing us winning the league. They must have had to put up with a few pastings in the playground on a Monday morning. Likewise for guys going to their work.'

Alan Stubbs: 'It was a total relief to stop "ten". There was a mixture of emotions during that day, from the first whistle to the last – anxiety before, relief when Henrik scored, and jubilation when Harald got our second. It was a great achievement and right up there with anything I've achieved in the game. I got great satisfaction from winning the title.

'I hear the word "legend" used to describe the players who won the league and stopped Rangers. Yes, it was something very special, but I don't look upon myself as a Celtic legend for doing it. Jimmy Johnstone is a legend. Billy McNeill is a legend. They achieved sensational things over a number of years. I was part of a successful team, but I was only doing my job.'

Rico Annoni: 'I would socialise with Marco Negri. Sergio Porrini, Lorenzo Amoruso and Rino Gattuso would not join in. I don't think they wanted to meet with me. Marco and I would have dinner, and we shared some good memories. It was great for Celtic that he didn't play many games for Rangers in the second half of the season after he suffered an eye injury. I think that gave us a very big advantage. Marco was under the impression that Rangers didn't play him because they did not want him to beat Ally McCoist's goal-scoring record. (McCoist scored thirty-four goals in two separate seasons, and Negri had thirty-two by the turn of the year.)

'I remember everything about beating St Johnstone. The whole day is still very clear in my head. I enjoyed the celebrations afterwards and thought that the Celtic supporters were very well behaved and allowed us to share the moment with them. It must have been tempting for them to invade the pitch and try to be closer to the management and the players. It shows they are well educated and know how to behave. I then enjoyed some wine with my family and friends that night. The whole occasion was just incredible. Marco Negri congratulated me on being a part of that Celtic team and achieving the main prize.

'The only disappointment is that I no longer have my championship-winning medal. My house on the outskirts of Milan was burgled in 2005 while we were away on a winter holiday. The robbers took my medal and other things of sentimental value. I was very sad about this. It is something in life that cannot be replaced. The only consolation is that the happy memories I have of being in the Celtic team that won the league in 1998 can never be taken from me.'

Marc Rieper: 'I was very tired after we beat St Johnstone. I just felt fatigued. The last three or four games had been very draining, with so much pressure on us to deliver. Thankfully, I had some energy left to party on the pitch with my family and the supporters. I could see how much it meant to the Celtic people. Had we not won the league, I wouldn't have found it unbearable. I had not been dealing with it all my life. For some people, it would have been like the clock had stopped ticking, but it was different for me. Yes, I was caught up in it, but for me it was more important to win the league than to stop ten in a row. I had a different priority. There was a subtle difference.

'Wim never mentioned ten in a row in any of his team talks. I think it was different for the players when Tommy Burns was manager. He might have used it as a motivation. I worked with Tommy in later years at Celtic and felt his passion, his feeling for the history of Celtic.'

Simon Donnelly: 'The pressure we felt that week was unbearable. We had to switch off. We had to go somewhere, forget about the league and just get drunk together. It was ridiculous that we were all drunk a few days before the most important game of our careers. Most of us fell out of the restaurant. It's fine to talk about it now, because we won. However, imagine the flak we'd have taken if we'd blown it . . .

'I enjoyed the St Johnstone game. When I was playing, I was fine – rarely felt any nerves. I took most of the games that season in my stride. It was when I wasn't playing that I was at my worst. The most nervous I felt during the whole season was the final 20 minutes of the St Johnstone game. I had been subbed and sat in the dugout. We were 1–0 up, but I was now helpless to do anything about the outcome of the title race. I chewed my nails, and all sorts of scenarios went through my head, mainly negative ones. But Harald scored, and I was fine after that. I jumped on John Clark and gave him a massive hug.

'Rangers didn't hand us the title, and it's totally unfair to suggest that they did. We worked hard and deserve praise. Rangers were the benchmark, and we had to match them and then overtake them to stop them winning ten. We'd never have heard the end of it from the Rangers fans if we'd lost the league, and we'd have gone down in the history books as the team that failed to stop them making it ten. That would have been unbearable.

'I feel a real sense of pride at having won the league in 1998. It's my most enjoyable season in football. Yes, it was satisfying to an extent when I played under Tommy Burns and we only lost one game in 1995–96, but the bottom line is winning. A title says it all.

'I gave my three winner's medals to my grandpa Tom, my dad's dad. He passed away last year, and now my dad has them. I won the league in 1998, the Scottish Cup in 1995 and the league cup in 1997. I have the full domestic set. Some people think I should have more to show for my seven years at Celtic. That's not the way I look at it. If Celtic had been successful when I joined as a teenager, I might not have been given a chance in the first team. But when I broke through in season 1993–94, Lou Macari was the manager, and we were fourth or fifth in the league. We had less than 20,000 watching our home games, and we had hardly any money to buy players. The club was as low as it had ever been. It meant youngsters, such as Brian McLaughlin, Stuart Gray and me, were thrown in. So, I have to be grateful for the path my career took at Celtic, and I look back with fondness. But the moment that sticks out is the 1998-title success. In terms of football, nothing beats that and nothing ever will.'

Stéphane Mahé: 'Maybe because I'm a foreigner and came to Celtic slightly blinded, I didn't really feel the pressure of that ten-in-a-row season. I wasn't from the west of Scotland, so I didn't understand just what it meant to stop Rangers winning the league, what it meant to block their efforts of winning ten titles in a row.

'But I knew two things. There were definitely people in our dressing-room who knew this was a must-win season, and every single fan who paid to watch us that season knew how crucial it was. I also knew that, aside from Celtic's desire to win the league and stop Rangers from the record, I wanted a winners' medal for myself. I didn't come to Celtic to finish second best; I came to be a winner.

'That drove me on, and it drove all the other new faces on. Craig Burley came with the desire to be a winner, Jonathan Gould wanted it, Henrik Larsson had a point to prove, and so did every one of Wim's signings. He had the perfect blend, the right mix, to help us win the league.

'I knew within two or three games that we'd win the league. That sounds strange, because results-wise we didn't have the best start, but you have to look deeper than that when you are talking about a title-winning side.

'Behind closed doors, there was a real bond between the players. We all liked each other as players *and* as people, and it showed on the park.

'The fans were confident. Wim was a great believer, and we had a great motivator in Murdo MacLeod. There was a buzz around the club, an unwritten understanding that something great was going to happen, but it took until May before we proved that.'

Regi Blinker: 'Wim gave me a big lift when he included me in the squad for the game against Dunfermline. It doesn't get much better than title-winning day. Wim had faith in me and wanted to have me on the bench for such an important game. I was in good form in training during that period, giving my all, always being a team player. Yet I still felt like an outsider.

'Did I enjoy it when we won the league? The truth is that I didn't. Personally, I didn't feel a part of it all. I didn't feel that I was part of the success of stopping ten in a row, because I wasn't a regular player that season. When I won the league with Feyenoord, I played in every game and scored 13 goals. This was different. I can't put my finger on why my form wasn't good. Perhaps I underestimated the standard of the Scottish game. Sure, the calibre of player was not of top European standard, but the effort and commitment was as good as any league you want to mention.

'Some people might say that I was out on the town too much in Glasgow. I wasn't out any more often than the next guy. And when I was out, I would rarely drink alcohol. Most of the time I would have my car with me.

'I got the impression I was viewed by some as just another foreigner who didn't give a fuck about the club. I did give a fuck. It was just such a hard time for me. Because you are not performing well on the pitch doesn't mean you don't give a fuck.'

Tommy Johnson: 'I was delighted for the lads when we won the league. I was also delighted for the fans, because it didn't take me long to find out how much it meant to them to stop ten in a row.

'Wim had his own ideas, and I just wasn't part of them. You fear the worst when a new manager comes in, but I didn't think I'd have to face up to a new gaffer three weeks after signing for the club. Tommy Burns signed me, and then he was out of the door after I'd played less than a handful of games for him. I thought to myself, "Bloody hell, what a mistake you've made coming up here."

'When Celtic came in for me, I was doing well at Aston Villa. Brian Little said I was under no pressure to leave, and if I wanted to stay, we would sit down and look at a new contract. But the pull of Celtic was too great to resist. I had no attachment to Celtic but knew that they were a massive club and that I'd regret it if I didn't go.

'I was sorry to see Tommy leave, and we have remained good friends. He was great with me, as was his wife Rosemary. Lovely, lovely people. I've also been in Wim's company a few times since, and there are no hard feelings. He had a job to do, and I respect that.

'I'm not one for letting my head go down, but I did have my bad days during the season Wim was there. I had many opportunities to leave Celtic and go back down south or go to another Scottish Premier League club, but I felt I had to stay and win a place in the team.

'I suffered a lot of injuries playing for Celtic. I thought it was the end for me when I was carried off after collapsing with a knee injury as I ran in on goal against Dunfermline at Parkhead. I had ligament damage, and as I lay on the stretcher I thought, "Oh my Lord. Is this the end of my career?" It was a nightmare, but I had to bounce back. Thankfully, I did.

'Joining Celtic was the biggest decision of my career and one I'm glad I made. After the club paid so much money for me, I didn't want to be remembered as an expensive flop, a failure. I felt I had unfinished business. My decision to stay was justified in May 2001 when I scored the winning goal against St Mirren at Parkhead to win the league. I'm remembered for that goal, and the fans still mention it to me. It was Martin O'Neill's first season and my last. We won the Treble. What a way for me to bow out. Thank God I stayed. I loved my time at Celtic – even through the bad times.'

Darren Jackson: 'I was left out of the St Johnstone game. It was just another kick where it hurts. I wanted to play that day – wanted to play so much. I sat in the stand with Tosh McKinlay and watched events unfold. I was happy for Harald to score on such an important day.

'The team spirit was fantastic. Tosh, Malky, Tommy Johnson, Brian McLaughlin and Stewart Kerr were also on the sidelines that day, but we couldn't have been happier for Wim and the players. One of the first people I congratulated was Wim. He sanctioned the move to sign me, and I've got him to thank for everything. I just wish I could have played more games for Celtic that season. That's all. It's the same for every player at every club when they don't get a game. And the manager always seems to get the blame for it!

'I spoke to Wim at an SFA Hall of Fame dinner in 2006, and we had a good chat. I held no grudges. I fell out with him over his team selection, and I fell out with Murdo, too. I voiced my opinion to them on several occasions, but I always gave them my respect.'

Malky Mackay: 'It wasn't a good performance against St Johnstone. The players were nervous, and the fans were nervous. Just about every fan had a radio glued to their ear. Henrik scored a magnificent goal, but we were still worried that they would get one back and end our chances. We knew Rangers were winning at Tannadice, and it was up to us to get three points.

'Harald settled us all down when he scored the second goal. I was delighted for him, as it couldn't have happened to a nicer guy. He arrived with a weight of expectation on his shoulders, and it couldn't have been easy for him to cope with that.

'I enjoyed the lap of honour at the end of the game, and it was great to be a part of it all, no matter how small a role I had played. It was my club, my team and my teammates, and I was so proud. I would have loved to have played 40 games that season, but I had been playing amateur football for Queen's Park only a few years earlier. So, to go from that to being a part of the 1998 title-winning squad was so special and will never leave me. Seeing the faces of the fans was special. I grew up in the East End of Glasgow and recognised a few faces from Baillieston in the stands.

'We were a close bunch of lads, and there wasn't an ego in the dressing-room that season. We fought hard to win games and made sure we gave it our all. A lot of our dirty linen was washed in public, and that wasn't the way the players wanted it. It would have been easy to crumble with all the stuff that was going on behind the scenes, but we had a togetherness in the group, and we weren't for lying down.'

Davie Hay: 'I was delighted to see Celtic winning the championship. I was no longer at the club, but it meant a lot to me. I was so pleased for Wim, Murdo, the players and the supporters. On that afternoon in May, I was at a game between Livingston and Inverness. By that stage, I was doing a bit of work for Livingston. When we got into the boardroom after the game, the television was on, and the celebrations at Parkhead were being shown. Lovely scenes. It was great to see them celebrating a title win and stopping Rangers winning ten in a row.

'I was also pleased to see Harald Brattbakk score that day. I identified Harald as a potential recruit, but it was only after I left that the deal to sign him from Rosenborg for around £2 million was concluded. I think that signing caused some problems between

Wim and the Parkhead board. I thought he was better playing on the left than through the middle, and he struggled to make an impact for Celtic. I think Harald's arrival was over-hyped by the media, and he was being hailed as some kind of goal-scoring saviour. The goals didn't flow for him, and he was criticised by the Celtic fans. I don't think he was disliked by the fans, but they weren't too enamoured by him, either.

'But scoring the second goal against St Johnstone paid back every penny of his transfer fee, in my opinion. That goal calmed the nerves and put it beyond any reasonable doubt that Celtic would win the game. Had he not scored, the final minutes would have been very nervy and anything could have happened.

'Harald was one of a number of strikers we considered. Goodness, the list was endless, to be honest. We were bombarded with names from agents, and we looked at many of the them, including Juan Antonio Pizzi of Barcelona and Tony Yeboah at Leeds United. Perhaps Harald wasn't first choice, but he was the man, for a variety of reasons, that was brought to the football club. He enjoyed scoring that goal. He knew what it meant.

'It also meant a lot to Wim to win the league. He felt the pressure that was involved, the expectation level of trying to stop Rangers. He dealt with it all and delivered the ultimate prize.

'From my point of view, I was no longer at the club but still felt proud. I helped to bring in some of the players that won the championship, and that gave me enormous satisfaction. In many ways, it was more satisfying than winning any titles I had during my career as a manager.

'I had the direct line for Wim's office and dialled the number about an hour and a half after the St Johnstone game had finished. I could hear the popping of champagne corks and clinking of glasses. The backroom staff had well and truly started their own party, and it was in full swing. I offered my congratulations to Wim and his staff. They were grateful for the call. I'm not one for looking back. What's done is done, but I definitely wished I was in that room with them that day.'

Craig Burley: 'I never expected to play well enough that season to receive a personal accolade, but I won the Scottish Football Writers' Association Player of the Year award. When I arrived, I just wanted to make sure I was consistent and was accepted as a good signing by the Celtic fans.'

Morten Wieghorst: 'Tommy Burns wanted to win the league more than anyone. It was getting to him in his final season in charge. We played some fantastic football under Tommy but couldn't get what mattered – the title.

'Under Wim, it was more relaxed. I think Tommy lived and breathed the nine-in-a-row thing, but Wim found a way to switch off. When we won the league, the main thing I felt was relief. It had been such a trying two years, and it was great to get there in the end. It's hard to explain how I really felt, but it was just good to get the job done and dusted.

'It was also a credit that we managed to stay focused with all of the negative stuff that went on throughout the season. We could have easily got caught up in it all, but we reserved our energy for when it mattered – on the pitch. Of course, it wasn't long until there was chaos again.

'The 1997–98 season was my best for Celtic. I thought I played well, and it was also the season I started most games in. Clinching the title was the pinnacle, but my most enjoyable game was the Coca-Cola Cup final. I had a very good game that afternoon, and it was great to get that first piece of silverware.'

Murdo MacLeod: 'When we were on the lap of honour after the St Johnstone game, Wim gave my arm a little tug as we celebrated with players, fans and families. "Look, Murdo, look at this. It's a nice way to go." Wim's words have never left me, and they never will. The Celtic supporters still talk about how we stopped ten in a row, and it's special to know that I played a part in making thousands and thousands of people around the world happy.

'After we had a couple of drinks in the office, I went home to my bed. I was drained. The players asked us to party with them, but I had nothing left in the tank. Wim was the same. It was nice just to get home, have one quiet drink with my family and try to let what we had achieved sink in.

'There was no relationship whatsoever between the coaches and the men upstairs. When we won the league, I did not receive a handshake or congratulations from Fergus McCann or Jock Brown. I think that tells you what was going on by that stage. There was a total breakdown. It was over.

'It really annoys me when I hear people say, "Rangers threw the title away." What? Are you serious? Do you think for one moment that Gough, Goram and McCoist didn't want to write another chapter in the history books? We needed to match their mentality and adopt the winning attitude that had served them so well over the years. We needed to put a new team together, and there wasn't the luxury of a year to get it right or a year to gel. It was always going to be hard enough to match Rangers, never mind with the added pressure of what was at stake.

'Wim treated the St Johnstone match as he did any other. He didn't go over the top on tactics. And if he was in any way nervous, he hid it well from the players. Wim's team talks were always simple and to the point. When he addressed the players as a group, it would only be for a maximum of two minutes, but he'd then go round them individually to make different points. I would tell the players their roles at set-pieces, for and against.

'He was different class at half-time. He wouldn't say a thing for the first five minutes. He would let the players get a drink, sort out any treatment from the physios and make sure he was composed and focused. He would tell them the things that pleased him and the issues that were causing him concern. He would tweak little things and make subtle changes. He'd maybe say to Stéphane Mahé to move higher up the pitch and float about in the area 15 yards either side of the halfway line. But he never, ever shouted or swore. Not once. It was unusual to see such a thing in the dressing-room of a Scottish club. Some dressing-rooms at half-time and at full-time can be similar to a battlefield. But

Wim's behaviour was not a sign of weakness – it was a sign of a man in total control who knew what he was doing and totally trusted his players to get it right after listening to the instructions they were given.

'The wives were great that year. They had to put up with every emotion, try to ignore every piece of negativity and not get too high when things were going well. It was a difficult time for them, living with us for ten months, twenty-four hours a day, having to judge what kind of mood we were in. But they were able to let it all out when we won the league. They were able to breathe a sigh of relief and then enjoy the celebrations, although they were quite short-lived.'

The players wanted Wim to stay on and made their feelings very clear. The last thing they thought the club needed was another summer of turmoil and uncertainty. They would not be granted their wish. As always seemed to be the case with Celtic that season, there were problems on the horizon.

seventeen

The Aftermath

It's the Sunday morning after the night before, and the players have gathered at Glasgow Airport for their flight to Lisbon, via Heathrow, for a friendly match against Sporting Lisbon. They all have on their official club tracksuits, and sunglasses are in evidence to hide the events of the previous evening. Wim Jansen and Murdo MacLeod are there, but Jock Brown and Fergus McCann are not present. This is strictly for the 'football department'. This trip to Lisbon is a chance to continue the title celebrations. Like most good trips, the game is only going to get in the way of some serious boozing.

The Sunday newspapers have been purchased, and the front and back pages are dominated by Celtic's success. Of course, the question of Jansen's future remains unanswered, although the smart money is on him quitting at some point during the coming few days.

At that point, the players are not too concerned about the decision of their manager. There will be plenty of time for that. Their priority is to keep the party atmosphere going all the way to Portugal. On the flight from London, a few of the players stand up and chant 'Stand Up For the Champions'. The flight attendants tell them to sit down and behave.

They check into their hotel and go out for dinner to a restaurant in Estoril that night. The wine is flowing, and the singing soon follows. Many of them get on top of tables, and 'Stand Up For the Champions' starts again. This time, it is Jansen who asks the players to calm down. It is one of the few times that season that he doesn't get his own way.

Heads are thumping again the following morning, but what happens at lunchtime soon sobers everyone up. Less than 48 hours after winning the league championship, Jansen announces his resignation. It is expected but still a shock now that it is a reality.

Darren Jackson: 'I sat in the foyer of our hotel that morning and was actually thinking about Tommy Burns. I never worked with Tommy, but I felt sorry for him. I knew that he had wanted to sign me and also had the likes of Craig Burley and Marc Rieper on his list of targets. I wondered if he would have won the league had he been given one more season by Fergus McCann. Then the news about Wim came through. Nothing is ever hush-hush. It was a shame it had to end so quickly and so soon after we had won the title. But at least he left Parkhead as a winner. As a champion. A legend. Not many do that.

'A lot of the blame for Wim's departure was left at the door of Jock Brown. For sure, both are strong characters, but it's not for me to say how accurate or inaccurate that is, because only Wim and Jock know the answer. However, I take people as I find them, and Jock was first class with me and my family.'

Not every person at Celtic shared Jackson's view of Brown.

The Scottish media gathered at the team's hotel for Jansen's press conference to confirm his resignation and his reasons for walking away. Jansen firmly blamed his departure on Jock Brown, saying, 'My relationship with Jock Brown was bad from beginning to end, and it was not the best way to continue. I cannot work with him, and our relationship has been getting worse and worse. I haven't spoken with him in the last month. There was no base to work with. This is the reason I am going, because the important thing is you have to work together. I wanted to resign after two or three weeks, but they didn't allow me to do it.'

With the battle underway, Jansen's explanation quickly made its way to Brown, and from Parkhead he refuted those allegations, saying, 'Any clash there was, was in the approach to strategies and policy. It is clearly set down by the board how we are going to operate. There is a long-term strategy plan. I am in charge of putting it into place. That means relating to Wim in the correct manner, and it was clear the policies the club had didn't coincide with Wim's policies.'

The players were irate and so were the fans. A few hundred gathered outside Parkhead to voice their disgust. Fergus McCann wasn't perturbed and agreed with his head coach's decision. He said, 'The decision Wim has taken is one the board believes is also best for the club. He was quite a nice guy for whom it just didn't quite work out. We wish him well for the future.'

The players couldn't hide their disappointment and wanted to pull out of the Sporting Lisbon game as a form of protest. They also constructed a letter to let McCann know their feelings and faxed it back to Parkhead.

Wim Jansen: 'The first person I told I was going to leave was Cobi. She was the only person I told for two or three weeks. It was not an easy decision to make, as I had grown to feel part of Celtic and had an understanding of the history of the club. I also didn't want to let the players and Murdo down. Cobi was disappointed but fully understood my decision. We enjoyed living in Bothwell and enjoyed being a part of Celtic. Why did I leave? Well, you have to know for yourself when the time is right to do something, and in my way of thinking I had to go. I told Fergus face to face what I was going to do. He understood my decision.

'Of course, the people outwith the football department had a bearing on my decision. If I thought a second season at Celtic would have been a smooth one, then I would have stayed. No doubt about it. I've been a technical director of a football club, and you have to have a good working relationship with the head coach. You have to do everything for the good of the club. I felt that was not happening. Certain individuals at Celtic thought that they were more important than the club – thought that they were bigger than the coach and the players. It was wrong, all wrong.

'Jock Brown was the technical director. I didn't have a good working relationship with him. It was not the way it should have been. Jock Brown wanted credit for things that went right, but he did not make the team. He had no part in our success of winning the league and the Coca-Cola Cup. He didn't make the team, and he was no help to me. I think he put obstacles in my way. My help came from Murdo and David.

'I felt as though I didn't receive the proper backing when it came to my recommendations of players we should sign. The one that sticks out most is Kieron Dyer. Andy Ritchie scouted him and told us we should get him. I made a personal check on the player and agreed with Andy's assessment. But the club didn't want to buy him. What is the point of having a scouting staff and a head coach if you don't do your very best to back their plans?

'You know, for every club the two most important things are the short-term scouting of players and the development of young players. If you have the right scouting in place, then you will be able to develop in the long term. That is my way of thinking. Celtic didn't agree. Having both things is an all-round insurance for the football club. Feyenoord has it. They have good scouting, and they develop their own. Some of the players who have come through their youth system have left for around £10 million.'

MacLeod knew Jansen was chucking it but still hoped that he might change his mind at the last minute.

Murdo MacLeod: 'We had many problems with the board, but I still thought we might be able to persuade Wim to stay on, because there were things to be positive about. I thought that he might want to build on the foundations he had put down and try to improve the squad in the summer. The final straw for him, I think, came when he met with the men upstairs to discuss the players he wanted to bring in for the new season. Wim told them that it depended on what kind of budget was available to him. Did he have £1 million, £5 million or £25 million to spend? He wasn't supplied with an answer, not even a rough figure.

'He came out of that meeting and said to me that he wanted to sign David Beckham, Ryan Giggs and Paul Scholes. I laughed at him, but he said, "You never know, Murdo. They haven't given me an idea of what I have to spend, so maybe I will have £50 million and can bring the three of them in from Manchester United."

'Of course, we knew there was never going to be anything close to that amount available. I think it was just part of the process to sicken Wim and give him no option but to leave. It was also childish the way they came out after he had resigned to say that they would have sacked him anyway. I don't believe that. They were just jumping on the bandwagon, trying to save face. When I look back at the way Wim was treated, I think it was shameful.

'Thankfully, though, the good times of winning the league, working with an excellent bunch of players and the fantastic support from the fans made it all worthwhile for him. The good outweighed the bad.'

Some of the Celtic players were disenchanted with McCann and Brown for causing the breakdown that had ended with Jansen leaving.

Tom Boyd: 'I had an inclination Wim was going to resign, but he never let on exactly what was happening until we were in Portugal. Out of the players, he was quite close to Henrik, and he might well have given him the nod in advance, but I'm not definite about that.

'We didn't want to be in Portugal for that game. And his resignation took the whole shine off our title achievement. It wasn't a nice feeling. We were back at square one. Back searching for a manager and back to the constant speculation. It was the last thing the players needed. We would far rather have milked the whole situation. Rangers had enjoyed nine years of celebrating, and our one chance to taste how that felt was taken from us after less than forty-eight hours.

'We wanted to cancel the Sporting match. The players held a meeting, and we agreed that we didn't want to play. But Wim told us that we had to go out and perform. We were still representing Celtic Football Club and still had to uphold the great name of the club. But some players were determined not to play. Wim had to make a personal plea, and it was only then the situation was resolved.'

Alan Stubbs: 'We sort of knew Wim was leaving, but it wasn't confirmed until we were in Portugal. It saddened me. I had just started to get to know him and then he was on his way. I didn't want him to go. The club also didn't need another summer of uncertainty and more turmoil.

'Wim's departure happened very quickly, and I think it soured our achievement. When he arrived, he was looked upon as a little bit of a laughing stock. But that only goes to show how shallow people can be and how ignorant. But on 9 May 1998 he outwitted Rangers to win the league. Rangers were a solid, big-spending club, and in the space of ten months Wim had pretty much dismantled them. When you look at Wim's pedigree, it really shouldn't have come as any great surprise. He was a European Cup winner with Feyenoord and had played in World Cup finals with Johan Cruyff. As a footballer, he had done the dirty work for the ball players – a total team player. As a manager, he was the same. An unselfish team player.

'But I totally understood and respected his decision to go. He didn't enjoy the full support from the people above him, and after winning the league there was really only one way he could go as Celtic manager if he had stayed on – and that was down. He'd never have bettered the 1998 league championship.

'I also felt sorry for Murdo. He was always going to lose his job after Wim left. Murdo had a good input into our season, and I think he helped to bring the best out in Wim and vice versa. Wim allowed Murdo to have his say, and he let rip on a few occasions. But he would do it in a positive way, and it was always for the good of the team. I respected him because he had a good knowledge of the game and had Celtic's interests at heart.'

Craig Burley: 'Some guys were glad to see the back of Wim, but I was distraught when I found out that he was leaving. Really gutted. Wim's plan was to bring in three or four quality players to add to our squad. He had a good core of players, but we all knew we had to bring in extra quality, and Wim was going to do that. It was a travesty he was allowed to go. But for the ego of certain people at Celtic, who knows what might have been?'

Jonathan Gould: 'Wim never said anything officially to the players. It's not like there was a meeting called to explain developments. Wim's decision came through the rumour mill, and we took it as being a done deal. My memory of it was standing in the hotel lift with Wim, Paul Lambert and Tom Boyd, and we all asked him not to go. Paul in particular wanted him to stay.

'The players had a meeting, and we constructed a letter that we faxed back to the club to make our feelings known about what had happened with Wim. We weren't happy that he was allowed to leave and felt that the club should have been trying to get him to change his mind.

'We wanted to pull out of the game against Sporting Lisbon, but Wim told us we had to retain our dignity and professionalism. We had to do the right thing. We were due to play in Lisbon, the city of Celtic's greatest ever moment as a football club, and we couldn't just walk away.

'During the pre-match meal, Wim stood up and said to us all, "Just one more time. Let's hear 'Stand Up For the Champions'." It was a great moment, with all of us banging on the dinner table, shouting at the top of our voices. I'll never forget it.

'We were not allowed to celebrate the league win as much as we should have. Wim leaving left a sour taste. But at least we had the three or four days together in Lisbon. We'd done something very important for Celtic, and we enjoyed the celebrations that came with the achievement.

'It was a blow to see Wim go. He had restored the club back to being league champions and, under normal circumstances, would have been able to build on the success. But I'm glad he maintained his dignity. He had his reasons for going, and I respect those reasons.'

Simon Donnelly: 'We had to wear bright shell suits that season, and I think you lost a stone every time you put it on! Wim had it on when he came to meet us for the first time. This, along with his curly hair, made me think, "Who is this guy?" But he was a first-class coach, and his training was good. The ball was always out, and the furthest we had to run was the length of the pitch. I enjoyed working under him, and even though he didn't play me in every game, he wasn't the type of guy I could hold a grudge against. I think that was the good thing about our squad – we had a good spirit, and it was very rare for a player to spit the dummy out if he didn't get a game. The likes of Davie Hannah only started a few games for us, but when he was asked to play, whether it be from the start or coming off the bench, he never let the team down. His attitude was first class.

'Wim rarely joined in any of the banter. I do remember one of the boys tried to make a smart comment at his expense, and Wim just looked at him and said something along the lines of "I've played in two World Cup finals. And you?" There was no comeback.

'We were in someone's room when Wim told us that he was quitting. I don't think we could quite take it in. I think we were still trying to sober up from the night before.

'When he started singing "Stand Up For the Champions", I found it quite funny and totally unexpected. Because he wasn't one for having a laugh and joke with the boys, it came right out of the blue and made a real impact. It was so unusual to see him behave that way, but I enjoyed it.'

Regi Blinker: 'I think it was Paul Lambert who broke the news to me that Wim was leaving. I was shocked. I didn't really believe it, to be honest. I wanted Wim to stay, and I'm sure most of the players felt the same way. Paul Lambert spoke to a few of the lads and told us that we had to get Wim to change his mind. Paul was determined to put in an effort to stop Wim leaving.

'Our words were no good. Wim was going, and that was that. It was nothing to do with the players. It was to do with other people at the club. I don't know if that made us feel any better or just made it all the more frustrating.

'Wim never told me of his intention to quit. I'd be surprised if he told any player. Apart from his wife, I think he might only have told Murdo. Wim kept that kind of thing away from the players. I suppose he felt that if he told me, I might tell someone else, and before we'd know it, it would be common knowledge.

'I've said already that Celtic reminded me of Feyenoord, and this was another example. The internal wrangling. The chaos. Less than two years after we won the title with Feyenoord, we were 14th in the league. The fans went crazy and invaded the pitch several times. Honestly, terrible, terrible times. This felt similar.'

Marc Rieper: 'What happened a day or two after we won the league was a big turn-off for us all. There was a lot of unease throughout the season, and there was a bad feeling between the coaches and the people upstairs. At many times, and in many different ways, it could have got to the players, but the bond we had was so strong that we didn't let anything distract us. The players and the coaches stuck together – it couldn't have been any other way.

'But when you look at the trouble at Celtic during the season, the in-fighting, the sackings and other things, we really shouldn't have won the league. We overcame the problems that threatened to destroy everything.'

Stéphane Mahé: 'I can't remember how or when I learned that Wim Jansen was leaving as our coach, but it hit me and the rest of the players hard. We had been in an end-of-season break, celebrating the title win when the manager and directors came to the conclusion that he was no longer part of Celtic.

'Shocked, stunned and upset, we had no answers as to why he had left us, but as time passed by we picked ourselves back up and moved forward. I started to understand why I had come to Celtic. Yes, Wim Jansen was a great influence on me, but I didn't come to Glasgow for him. I didn't sign for the directors; I signed for the club. So, while Wim had left, I hadn't. I was still at this wonderful club and was determined to stick around and add to the winners' medal that he helped me achieve. We will never really know why Wim left Celtic, but he left on an almighty high, and often that is the best way to do it.

'He was only at the club for 12 months, but he achieved what he set out to do. His sole job that season was to wrestle the title from Rangers' grasp, to stop ten-in-a-row and to get Celtic back to winning things. He did it – then left. Now he's part of the club's history, and no one can take it away from him. He will always be idolised by Celtic fans, always remembered as the man who won them their pride back and blocked Rangers. Celtic have moved on without him. He is gone but never forgotten. No man is bigger than a club, but sometimes a man can really make a club tick, and for that season Wim did.

'I hope it is felt I also made a worthwhile contribution. I had my moments on the pitch and one or two memorable moments off the pitch. Remember my haircuts? My wife was fond of cutting my hair when I was in Glasgow, and she was pretty good at it, so I often left it down to her. But one day I looked in the mirror and there seemed to be more off one side than the other. The razor had slipped. It was a big mistake, and my hair didn't look right at all. I decided the best solution was to cut the other side and even things up. The more I cut it, the more my hair became a Mohican style, and I left it at that.

'I didn't tell anyone about it before I went into training, but all I heard at first was laughter. The other players couldn't believe this was my haircut, so for a few days after that they took the mickey out of me and wound me up. I actually grew to like it, so I kept it until my hair began to grow back in before I got a normal haircut again, and when I look back now it was just one of those silly things you do in life. I've still got newspaper cuttings of stories about my hair, and I often look back at them and laugh. For some reason it didn't catch on with the fans, though. Celtic fans are hugely passionate, and they love to emulate their heroes, but I wasn't Henrik Larsson – perhaps if I had been, then a lot more fans in the ground would have copied my hairstyle!

'I was just so happy to win the league. It was special and I have special memories. I also have a room in my house in which I keep newspaper cuttings, my photos, my strip and the many gifts I got from Celtic fans. I have a crystal ball given to me by the Giffnock CSC that is close to my heart, and everything I picked up during my time at Celtic and in Scotland will stay with me for life. I didn't just have a good time in Scotland, I had a marvellous time and look forward to going back there again.'

Jackie McNamara: 'Surely the guys in charge of Celtic should have tried to keep Wim – should have sat down and attempted to iron out their problems. If the roles had been reversed and Rangers had stopped ten in a row, I don't think David Murray would have allowed his title-winning manager to walk away. He just wouldn't have allowed it to happen. I'm sure Wim wasn't faultless in his dealings with the board, but there had to be a way of keeping him. We should have built from a position of strength instead of going into decline 24 hours after winning the league. When Wim activated the get-out clause in his contract, I tried to think how I would have felt as a Celtic supporter. And I have many times since. I always come to the same conclusion: I don't believe the people in charge could have been real Celtic people.'

Paul Lambert: 'It was just bizarre to lose Wim. He thought that he could build on his achievements in the first season, but the in-fighting didn't help. It drove him away. My own view is that you must get on with the people who employ you. However, you must also be allowed to run the football club. That's what they pay you for. You shouldn't be paid to accept their opinion on football matters. It has to be your way, and there shouldn't be any interference. You drive the bus, and you have to dictate who is allowed on the bus and who should get off it from the football department. You cannot allow people to influence your decision-making on team selection and players coming and going. If you're not allowed independence, then you might as well not be in the job.

'What really got on my goat about it all was that we had a very good manager in place, and we had a good squad of players, with a great atmosphere in the dressing-room. We didn't have a massive squad, and we all had to work really hard that season. Then it was all taken away in a heartbeat. I was so disappointed with the whole scenario. We should have kicked on from winning the league. It should have snowballed from there. Instead, we were back to square one, and Rangers were handed back the initiative, which they took and didn't let go of for two seasons. The people "upstairs" at Celtic were largely responsible for that.

'My own recollection is that Wim told us that he was leaving when we were having our pre-match meal. We had an idea that he was going, and the rumour mill was in overdrive. Things were always leaked out of Celtic Park. It was ridiculous, sometimes. But we had to hear the words from him. There should have been a deal thrashed out to keep him. The manager should be the most important guy at the club. You don't let him go, not after he has just won the league. The person with the most power should have sat down with him and sacrificed someone else if that's what it would have taken to keep him.

'We had to do our bit to protect the proud record held by the Lisbon Lions. If we didn't, we would always have been remembered as the team that failed to stop "ten". My goodness, Rangers would still be bringing out DVDs about it. Winning the league in 1998 has to be high up on the list of achievements in the history of Celtic. I don't think the group of players from 1998 got the credit they deserved. We helped preserve a piece of history, but it was almost forgotten about within a few days. That was very disappointing. It was just too quickly forgotten about.'

On the team's return from Lisbon, the sparks were still flying, and they became fireworks by the end of the week. Jansen called his own press conference at the Glasgow Hilton Hotel.

That afternoon, Jansen said, 'I had a problem with Brown from early on – from the Darren Jackson signing. He told the press that I saw videos of Jackson, but I never saw any videos. They [McCann and Brown] keep going on about how I would not go to look at Harald Brattbakk as one of the ways in which I neglected club policy on signing players. Well, I didn't see Jonathan Gould, Marc Rieper, Craig Burley or Stéphane Mahé. I also wanted to sign Karl-Heinz Riedle, but the club didn't even make a phone call to see if he was available. Two weeks later, he signed for Liverpool.'

Jock Brown later replied, 'I found out Riedle's age. I ascertained what salary he would require. I found out what transfer fee would be involved. I found out all the figures required. I then said to Wim, "Let's go and look at this guy and see what you think. See if he's still got it." Wim wasn't interested in anything like that. He just wanted Riedle signed.'

The tit for tat continued over the coming days.

Wim Jansen: 'There is no one in football I have ever found it more difficult to work with. Sometimes I had to fight more against my own people than against my opponents.'

Jock Brown: 'He has no right whatsoever to form an opinion of me except from the direct dealings we have had. He never ever wanted to find out anything about me and has no right to have an opinion on what I am like and what I do.'

When I met Jansen in Rotterdam almost a decade on, he was more calm than he was during those fraught few days in the aftermath of the title win.

Wim Jansen: 'I stand by everything I said back then. I believe I spoke the truth. But there is no point in going over it and over it. It is not so important now. There is no point in looking back over too much negative stuff. My only goal was to win the league. The problems I had with the club were not going to take priority over winning the league. I had to stay focused and never forget what my job was. The next game should always be the most important thing for a manager.

'We still come back to visit Glasgow, and my son and daughter enjoy it. They missed Glasgow when we left. Cobi and our children understood my decision to leave, but I don't think they liked my decision. I enjoyed my year at Celtic, and so did my family. To bring the championship to the club was so special, and to do it under the circumstances we encountered made it even more special.

'It's nice to be remembered as a "legend". Celtic supporters still come up to me and say, "Thanks for stopping ten in a row." I was recently on a flight to South America, and the flight attendant came up to me and said, "Thanks for your contribution to the history of Celtic." But I was only doing my job. A big impact was made, and the success of winning the title will never be forgotten. That is nice.

'We won it as a team. You cannot win the championship with an individual. One player never wins you the three points on his own. But we did have a solid central line in the team. We had a good defence, a good midfield and good strikers. You just try to make the team as high quality as possible. You organise the players in practice all week so they are ready for the next game. You try to make the team hard to beat and give them enough ideas to score goals to win the game. It is simple, but you need to have good players for it to work. You need to have the support of the dressing-room, and I think I had that with most of the players.

'I wasn't around to defend the title, and I would have been up against Dick Advocaat at Rangers. I had worked with Dick and never had a problem with him. He is a nice guy and a good coach. Rangers made a good signing when they brought him to the club. I think he enjoyed his time at Rangers, and he appeared to have a good working relationship with David Murray. Would we have won the league again the following season if I had stayed at Celtic? Well, we will never know.

'What I do know is that I enjoyed working with Murdo. I could trust him completely and was able to give him responsibility. We worked together perfectly. He was the ideal man for me. We were like a couple. We are still friends, and our wives remain friends. We still visit each other.

'Winning the league was special. It was lovely to see the players, their families and the supporters singing and dancing. It made me happy to see thousands and thousands of Celtic people happy and in full celebration. The pressure on us to stop Rangers winning the league was enormous, truly enormous. I don't think I had sampled anything like it in my career.'

eighteen

The Main Men

Celtic had eight or nine players who performed consistently well for them during the season. Craig Burley was voted the Scottish Football Writers' Association Player of the Year, and Jackie McNamara was given the SPFA Player of the Year award. It was the first time since 1988 that a Celtic player had won both. Paul McStay was the deserved recipient of the awards that year.

When players vote for the SPFA Player of the Year, they are not allowed to choose someone from their own club. However, they would have selected a Hoops teammate in 1998 if they had been given the choice. They have now cast their thoughts back and chosen a player of the year, nominated for their contribution to the title success on the pitch, and also a teammate of the year. The teammate of the year is for someone who was in good form around the dressing-room and off the pitch, helping to give the squad the togetherness that has been mentioned so often in this book.

Tom Boyd: 'My player of the year would have to be Craig Burley. He scored important goals and, overall, played exceptionally well in the middle of the park. He was a strong character and was not afraid to upset people, whether they be an opponent or in his own dressing-room. He played central midfield for us and enjoyed that position much better than the wingback role he was asked to perform by Craig Brown for the national team.

'My teammate of the year is Tosh McKinlay – 100 per cent. I used to travel in with him every day, and he was great company. It couldn't have been a particularly easy season for him, as he rarely played. Stéphane Mahé was first-choice left-back. Yet Tosh was the life and soul of the party and was delighted to have made some form of contribution to the 1997–98 season. He was involved in the incident with Henrik, and I felt sorry for Tosh. It was a tough time for all the players not in the top team, as they were rarely made to feel properly involved in the first-team squad.'

Darren Jackson: I think Craig Burley had an excellent season and scored so many vital goals, but Jackie McNamara just pips him to it for player of the year. It's so close between the two of them that you could virtually have tossed a coin. However, I think Jackie developed into a top player that season, and the foundations were laid for the successful career he went on to enjoy with Celtic and Scotland. He showed no fear during that campaign, neither mentally nor physically, and became a figure we relied on to help us win games. Overall, I thought he was outstanding.

'My teammate of the year is Tosh McKinlay. Tosh didn't play many games but was always professional and always wanted Celtic to win. That's what mattered most to him. Yes, there was that moment on the training ground with Henrik Larsson, but that was so out of character. On the day we returned from our end-of-season game in Lisbon, we both found out that we were in the Scotland squad for the World Cup. We just hugged each other. It was a special moment and great to share it.'

Regi Blinker: 'It's not an easy choice for my player of the year, but I would just edge towards Craig Burley. He scored important goals and had the ability to dictate the tempo of a game, which is not an easy thing to do. I also liked the way he was comfortable with the ball. He always looked to have a nice feeling in his feet.

'My choice for teammate of the year is an easier decision, and it's Henrik Larsson. We were in the hotel together in East Kilbride and knew each other from Feyenoord. We had the same agent [Rob Jansen], and when we first signed for Celtic we wondered how much the other was being paid. We used to have fun about it, and eventually we agreed to exchange wage packets. We did that for a few months and discovered that we were being paid exactly the same wage. When Henrik was given a new, improved contract the following season, he still offered his wage envelope, but I told him I did not want to see it any more.

'Henrik had a bad start to his career as a Celtic player but worked so hard to make himself appreciated. He was a help to me, and I was able to confide in him whenever I wanted. It's always good to have someone like that as a teammate.'

Marc Rieper: 'We had some quality performers, and I felt that Jonathan Gould really excelled. I gave him a hard time during games, but he responded positively and rose to a high standard of performance. Tom Boyd was also steady and reliable throughout the season. But Jackie McNamara sneaks ahead of both of them as my player of the year. The way he improved during the course of the season was a credit to him, and the effort and application he showed was top class. He looked tiny and skinny, but he turned in some giant performances and never lost a tackle against the opposition.

'The dressing-room was lively and the social gatherings even livelier. A lot of that was down to the efforts of Craig Burley. He also played very well for us during the season, but he helped with the bonding that brought us all closer together to help us win the league. That's why he is my teammate of the year.'

Rico Annoni: 'Henrik Larsson went on to have better seasons for Celtic during his seven years at the club, but I felt he was also incredible that season and is my player of the year. He scored goals and was an excellent professional. He was also a clever player and was good at educating others around him. Marc Rieper is my teammate of the year. Marc is a very good person and was very helpful and friendly towards me. I enjoyed his company and his honesty.'

Alan Stubbs: 'There's so many to choose from for both categories. But I won't sit on the fence, and I'll choose Henrik Larsson as my player of the year. Henrik was class – top class. I know he went on to greater things as a Celtic player, but I still think his first season was an excellent one. He made my job as a defender easier. Any time I had the ball at the back, I only needed one glance up and he was in line of sight. He'd make a run to give me an out-ball, and he'd then hold it up to give us a breather. Defenders couldn't switch off for a second or else he'd punish them. It was the same for me and Marc Rieper in training every day. He scored important goals and none more so than in the final game against St Johnstone. He settled us all down.

'I was also glad to see his career go on to greater heights at Barcelona when he helped them win the Champions League in 2006. He then had a spell at Manchester United and was their most influential player during a three-month period at Old Trafford. It was important for Scottish football that Henrik made a success of it at that level in Spain and in England.

'We had a great dressing-room at Celtic during that season, and I could put virtually all the names in a hat and select one. But I will go for Craig Burley as my teammate of the year. He also had a brilliant season, as he scored many important goals. However, he was a great friend to me, and his wife Sheryl was a great help to my wife Mandy. We're still all close to this day. Craig was good at helping bring the boys together for a night out, and we all enjoyed our socialising. As a footballer, you think that you make many good mates, but you don't – not really. You are just ships passing in the night. But I have a good friendship with Craig, and that's something I value.'

Malky Mackay: 'Henrik Larsson stands out for me as deserving to be the player of the year. He scored a fantastic diving header against St Johnstone to help turn our season around, and that was also a taster of what was to come from him in the air. He made an incredible impact and was a very good professional.

'The teammate of the year is more difficult to choose, as we were such a close bunch. The younger lads in the squad, such as Jackie, Phil, Stubbsy, Craig and Tommy, all got on very well, as we also did with Tosh and Boydy. People might think that because you share a dressing-room that every one of the 20 guys in it will get along very well. That's not the case, and I've been in dressing-rooms where there wasn't a great togetherness. However, that season was special, and I'd single out Simon Donnelly. Like me, he also came from Queen's Park, and we were very good friends. Our families still keep in touch to this day.'

Craig Burley: 'I've thought long and hard about my player of the year, and my choice is Jonathan Gould. He was a real unsung hero, and he came from nowhere. He told me the story of when he phoned his mate to tell him that he was moving from being third-choice keeper at Bradford to Celtic. His mate was happy and told him that it would be good for him to play first-team football again and that a bit of form might lead to him getting a move to a bigger club within a couple of months. Gouldy's reply was, "I won't get any bigger than Celtic. This is the best move of my career." His mate said, "Steady, Gouldy. Stalybridge Celtic are a decent club, but you've got to aim higher in the long run!" His mate couldn't believe it when Gouldy told him that it was Glasgow Celtic he was signing for. He pulled off some great saves, and to go from being bombed out at Bradford to the pressure-pot of Celtic spoke volumes for his mental strength and ability.

'Tommy Johnson is my choice for teammate of the year. He was my neighbour and my main drinking buddy. He was hardly selected to play by Wim, but Tommy never let it get to him. He was positive, and it was great to see him bounce back to score the winning goal that clinched the league for Celtic in 2001 during Martin O'Neill's first season.'

Jonathan Gould: 'I'm going to have to sit on the fence on this one and take the easy way out for my teammate of the year – I can't choose between Alan Stubbs and Tommy Johnson. Tommy was rarely in any of Wim's starting line-ups, but he was a chirpy character and never tried to stir things or turn any of the boys against the coaching staff. He was a good lad and someone that always brightened up the dressing-room. Alan was a great friend to me at the club, and we remain in touch. He was a good player and played a big part in bringing the players close together, making sure that we had the right spirit in the dressing-room to give us a better chance of winning games on a Saturday.

'The player of the year has to be Craig Burley. He arrived from a big club and cost a lot of money, but he slotted in well and was a strong influence in the dressing-room. He was a quality footballer who dominated games from the middle of the park and scored vital goals. I think his contribution to the team became greater after Paul Lambert arrived. The two of them worked well together – Paul would hoover up in front of the defence, and Craig would drive us on from middle to front.'

Simon Donnelly: 'There's one guy who stands out for me as someone who kept the dressing-room going: Tosh McKinlay. He made everybody laugh and was always at the centre of the banter. He didn't play that often, but he never let us see that he was down. He was so positive. He was as happy as anybody else when we won the league, because he is a Celtic man through and through. He conducted the singing in the dressing-room after we beat St Johnstone to win the league. He never touched alcohol, but he gave us a great laugh in Portugal on our end-of-season trip when he pretended to be drunk, slurring his words and getting the boys to carry him into the nightclubs. He got a few knock-backs from the Portuguese bouncers!

'My player of the year has to be Craig Burley. He scored many important goals, and I can't remember him having a bad game. He had a bit of steel in the middle of the park and a winning mentality. He came from Chelsea, and you could see he'd had a good education there playing with top professionals. My dad's brother, Robert, had coached Craig when he'd played for a youth team in Cumnock, and we spoke about that. That gave us a wee connection, but I'm sure we'd have hit it off anyway.'

Tommy Johnson: 'To win a title you need to have a good squad, and we had that. We had players with ability, and we had winners. I thought Jackie McNamara was immense that season, and he gets my vote for player of the year. He had to work hard to convince Wim that he was good enough to play every week, and he kept at it. Eventually, he became one of the first names on the team sheet and made a significant contribution to the success achieved. He was always a threat to the opposition as he worked up and down the right-hand side.

'Along with ability, you need to have spirit and a willingness to do well for the guy next to you, and we also had that. I think I could put eight or nine names in a hat and pick one out for my teammate of the year. Boydy and Tosh were great for organising things for the players and their partners. One or two others were just good at organising things for the boys! Stubbsy is my big mate, and that's why he is my shout. He is a top lad who would do anything for a teammate.'

Harald Brattbakk: 'Henrik Larsson would have to go down as our best player that season. He scored many wonderful goals and set up so many chances for the rest of us. It was the start of a fantastic relationship between Henrik and Celtic, and he continued to help bring success to the club.

'It would be easy for me to choose one of the Scandinavian players as my best teammate, but for this particular nomination I have to go for Darren Jackson. He provided the humour in the dressing-room. He had a lot of fun about him, and it was a pleasure to be in his company. He had a tough time that season with his brain operation, yet he was very rarely down.'

Paul Lambert: 'It's too difficult to single out one player. We had eight or nine guys that season who were on top form. I really put the league success down to a squad effort and the efforts of Wim and Murdo and their backroom staff.

'There are also many contenders for teammate of the year. Tosh and Gouldie were really funny. They helped to keep things lively, as both were characters. But we had a good squad, a great bunch of guys and a lively dressing-room.'

Morten Wieghorst: 'It's a tough call to choose a player of the year, as there are five or six guys who would be serious candidates. But I will go for Craig Burley. He made a first-class contribution to our success, and I don't just mean the important goals he scored. He was a leader, making sure that the other guys were up for the challenge, and I'm sure that his will to win unsettled the opposition. He was the kind of player I wouldn't have liked to play against.

'Tommy Johnson hardly played any games, what with injury and not being a first-choice striker, but he always remained upbeat. Tommy was a lively character, and that's why he'd get my vote as teammate of the year. It would have been easier for him to have been moody, but his chin was always up, and I admired him for that.'

Jackie McNamara: 'Craig Burley had a great season and is my player of the year. He drove the team on, scared the opposition and scored vital goals. For the money Celtic paid to get him, he was a bargain.

'Simon Donnelly and I were as thick as thieves that season. But it's more difficult to select a teammate of the year. We were such a close bunch, and I'm still close to Simon, Darren Jackson, Tommy Johnson and Henrik Larsson. I was over in Sweden for a party Henrik threw last year, and a few of us went over to Dublin for a charity dinner Tommy Johnson organised. Regi Blinker, Alan Stubbs and Morten Wieghorst also came to Ireland for that. Friendships were built that season that will stand the test of time.'

Stéphane Mahé: 'So many players performed to their peak that season. Morten Wieghorst was an unsung hero in midfield, Jonathan Gould made some terrific saves and of course there was Henrik Larsson – a great teammate and goal scorer. But the best had to be Craig Burley. He was a passionate Scotsman who always seemed to be there at the crucial moment. His runs into the box led to so many great goals, and every single one of them was decisive in helping us to win the title.

'Everyone at Celtic made me feel welcome, but some went that extra yard and will never be forgotten by me. Tosh McKinlay is one such player. He intricately understood the traditions and virtues of Celtic. He was also a passionate Scotsman, and I liked his attitude to life. He taught me more about the club than any book would have done, and he made me fall in love with Celtic because of it.'

nineteen

Back to Square One

Another summer of uncertainty lay ahead. Within days of Wim Jansen's resignation, names were being linked with the vacant manager's job. Martin O'Neill was installed as the bookies' early favourite. Southampton boss Dave Jones was also reported to be in the frame. As usual, Celtic refused to confirm or deny any stories linking them with managers. With the media unable to get an off-the-record 'steer', it was another few weeks of the close-season silly season. The only consolation was that Celtic were, most of the time, kept off the back pages, as Scotland were on World Cup duty in France, and the exploits of the national team dominated the press.

Celtic had eight players in Craig Brown's squad for the tournament. Rangers also had representatives in the national team, and the conversation between the Old Firm players often turned to what the hell had gone on at Parkhead with Jansen and his bosses. The Ibrox contingent couldn't believe that the self-destruct button had been hit once again at Parkhead. Rangers should have been the ones with the catching up to do, but within 48 hours of losing the title they felt superior again and that the title loss would only be a blip.

As Celtic searched for a new gaffer, Dick Advocaat was

spending lavishly to bring the likes of Giovanni van Bronckhorst, Arthur Numan, Gabby Amato and Rod Wallace to Ibrox. Andrei Kanchelskis, Lionel Charbonnier and Colin Hendry soon followed. Rangers had spent around £25 million before Celtic had even brought in someone to head the football department.

On 4 June, the inevitable happened when Celtic sacked Murdo MacLeod. He fancied staying on in some capacity, whether it was to become manager or to assist the new guy. But due to the in-fighting the previous season, both scenarios were unlikely.

Murdo MacLeod: 'When Wim resigned, I spoke to him about my position, and he said I should stay on at the club. My feelings were that I didn't want to abandon the dressing-room and leave them on their own. I wanted to give the place some form of continuity. I was willing to work with the new manager and give him advice and guidance.

'I went away on a family holiday after we returned from the end-of-season game in Portugal. During my holiday, I received one or two phone calls to mark my card that Jock Brown wanted rid of me and that I should be prepared for the worst.

'I met Jock on my return, and he told me that it was breaking his heart to tell me that my contract wasn't being renewed. He said that there was a new manager on the horizon and that he was appointing his own assistant. Jozef Vengloš was appointed, and Eric Black was promoted from his role with the youths and reserves to assistant head coach. I think that was possibly all part of Jock's plan.

'I told Jock that I felt it wasn't the right decision. Jock's response was that he believed I didn't offer him enough help and that I was always more interested in helping Wim. I told him I had no regrets about that and would do exactly the same again. I reminded him that the most important guys at any football club are the 11 on the pitch for the 90 minutes. Everything is secondary to that.

'Now, ten years on, I still feel disappointed that I wasn't allowed to help the club build on the success of that year. I was dismissed by a man who only had a fleeting association with Celtic. It will sit uneasily with me all my days that I was only allowed to stay for one year. It should have been longer.

'On the day I left Celtic, I was offered a manager's job in Scotland and was offered two more soon after that. I turned all three down for different reasons. Everton were in for Wim at that time, and I was asked through a third party if he wanted the job. I phoned him in Holland, but he told me that they were not the right club for him. He had also rejected them the previous summer so that he could take over at Celtic. In many ways, I wanted him to take the Everton job when I contacted him, as it would have been nice to go down south and work in the Premiership.

'People often ask me why I'm not in the game, and the simple answer is I've never been offered something that suited me and my family. I'm still passionate and enthusiastic about the game and enjoy doing my media work. One day I would love the chance to be involved in the professional game again, but it would have to be a very good offer.'

The first name Celtic seriously courted to become their new manager was Norway boss Egil Olsen. He was at the World Cup finals in charge of his nation and made it known that he would be quitting after that. Celtic wanted him, and it became a very public chase. Olsen then decided he wasn't interested in the job and announced that he'd be taking a complete break from football due to ill health.

Rosenborg boss Nils Arne Eggen was also discussed at length. He had an excellent record at domestic level and in the Champions League, but nothing materialised from the speculation. Swede Tommy Svensson was the next coach to be considered. He was met by Celtic and was seriously interested in the job but opted not to go to Parkhead. Things were getting desperate. The players had returned to pre-season training with Black in charge. But they were not happy at having no new coach in place. It was a re-run of the previous summer.

Gérard Houllier was the next person to be courted by Celtic. He was part of the French national team backroom staff and had a fine reputation. France wanted him to stay on, but he was also interesting Liverpool. Celtic waited and waited for him. In the end, he went to Anfield to become co-manager with Roy Evans.

Certain managers who turned down Celtic that summer never went public with their reasons, but privately they made it known that word of what Jansen had had to go through the previous season was not to their liking.

By that point, Celtic were on a pre-season tour of Holland. They played against Hollandia on 9 July and FC ASWH 24 hours later. They still had no manager. It was getting embarrassing for Celtic, and there was tension in the boardroom. The ten-week chase to find Jansen's replacement was becoming a farce.

With less than a week until their Champions League first qualifier at home to Irish side St Patrick's, McCann and Brown were now onto people who they didn't really fancy but had no option but to go for. On Friday, 17 July, they wheeled out Dr Jozef Vengloš, a 62-year-old Slovakian. The appointment of the former Aston Villa boss was ridiculed by the media and the fans. Even Vengloš found it hard to put up a decent case as to why he was given the job when he was paraded at Parkhead that afternoon. Brown thought that he was being convincing at the press conference, but he was fooling no one. He said, 'My exact brief from the board of directors was to look for someone with special qualities and talents as a coach. I'm delighted the fruits of my labour are now here in the form of Jozef. He fits the brief as well as any other person in the world could.'

When pressed on Vengloš's failures as a manager in several other jobs and the fact that he was pretty much unknown, Brown said, 'Nobody had heard of Arsène Wenger two years ago. In terms of Jozef, I was told by respected people on the Continent that this man is ten years ahead of his time.'

McCann, who sat beside Brown that afternoon, had the decency not to be so foolish as to go over the top about this appointment and said, 'Jozef might not have been top of the list at the start, but he became the best person for the job as we carried out our investigations.'

The players were completely underwhelmed with the appointment.

Craig Burley: 'They brought in Jozef Venglos as Wim's replacement, and that was embarrassing. When they appointed him, Celtic said Jozef was ten years ahead of the rest with his ideas on football. Rubbish. He was 30 years behind. Almost every player in the dressing-room was not happy with the appointment of Jozef.

'I wanted to leave, and I hoped Wim would get a job. I know Everton and Sheffield Wednesday sounded him out, but he refused to take them up on their offers. I was desperate for him to get back into football in the hope that he would come for me to play for him again. I used to phone Murdo to ask him to ask Wim to hurry up and take a job. But he was so single-minded and would not budge on anything if he didn't feel it was right.'

Darren Jackson: 'Jozef Venglos was Wim's replacement, and you'll do well to meet a nicer guy. But I'm not so sure he was right for Celtic at that particular time. Still, he brought in Lubo Moravčík, Johan Mjällby and Mark Viduka. His record in the transfer market was different class.

'But it was during his reign that my time with Celtic came to an end. We played St Johnstone at home and lost 1–0. My first touch on the ball was hopeless that night. I couldn't control a thing. My confidence had totally gone. I knew it was time to go – time to try and enjoy my football again. Jim Jefferies signed me for Hearts, and I was grateful to him for that. It was just a pity every season couldn't have been as good as the Wim Jansen season. Still, I made a contribution to one of the greatest achievements in the club's history, and nobody will ever be able to take that away from me. It was the right decision for me to leave, but it broke my heart the day I left Celtic, that's for sure.'

Jonathan Gould: 'It took a long time for me to come to terms with the fact that Wim was no longer manager. In fact, when we were waiting for Jozef Venglos to walk through the dressing-room door to introduce himself as the new manager, I was still clinging to the hope that Wim was going to take over again. No disrespect to Jozef, but I wanted Wim and Murdo back. Jozef came in under worse circumstances than Wim did, and he must have wondered what he'd let himself in for. The atmosphere at the club wasn't great. There was a hangover from Wim's departure.'

Unfortunately for Venglŏs, he ended up in the middle of a financial wrangle between McCann and the players. It was something that had been festering for a while. The players were of the opinion that they had not been given the going rate by McCann for qualification to the Champions League. The players made an agreement that they would battle him every inch of the way. Had Jansen still been in charge, the bonus-money battle would not have been as messy, and the players would have probably been more reluctant to push things so far. But Wim had left, and the players blamed McCann and Brown. They felt that they owed them nothing and that it was time for the dressing-room to stand up to McCann. Brown kept his distance from the negotiations. The players and McCann managed to keep their differences private for the first couple of weeks.

Unbeknown to McCann, the players had gathered information on the bonus money their counterparts at Rangers had earned for their Champions League qualification. They were told that it had worked out in excess of £35,000 per man, more than double what the Celtic squad were being offered.

The Celtic players were always being told by McCann and Brown that Rangers were the benchmark. Now that they had overtaken Rangers, the players felt that they should be paid the 'benchmark' rate. Although handsomely paid by the Parkhead chiefs, the Celtic players also knew that those in the Ibrox dressing-room averaged a much higher salary than they did.

Jonathan Gould: 'We had issues over bonus money. We sat up the night before we played St Pat's in a hotel room in Ireland to discuss the bonus payments. This was between midnight and one in the morning. My opinion was that the club felt we lacked the intelligence to know what was going on and how to handle the business side of things. We had to stand up for ourselves, and it got very messy towards the end. It was unfortunate that it all came out in public, but we had to do what we felt was right. I'm reluctant to heavily criticise the club, as there is no club in the land that runs itself to the full satisfaction of a dressing-room. But I did feel strongly about that incident. Unfortunately, the biggest losers out of it all were the fans and Jozef, as our minds weren't fully focused in the proper manner to play football games.'

It all became public knowledge on Monday, 10 August. Regi Blinker, Jackie McNamara and Marc Rieper were all asked by the Parkhead PR department to wear the new away kit for a PR launch to the media and fans. On the grounds that they were in dispute over bonus money, the squad agreed that they would refuse to cooperate. The three players received heavy criticism from the fans for their actions, particularly Blinker, which was totally unfair, as it was a decision made by the whole squad. It just so happened that they were the three guys chosen to model the kit.

The next two days were as chaotic as any had ever been at Celtic. McCann offered the players a pot of £280,000 to be split between them if they defeated Croatia Zagreb in their final qualifier to make it through to the Champions League proper. The players believed that they were worth more. Captain Tom Boyd had to negotiate with McCann on behalf of the players and found it to be a horrible task.

Tom Boyd: 'It was a helluva responsibility to be the captain of Celtic, especially at that time with all the pressures surrounding us. I also had distracting issues to deal with and had no idea just how stressful it was going to be for me for the next year to year and a half. I had many supporters' functions to attend, and that was, of course, never a problem. But having to deal with bonus rows took its toll. There were other tedious things that made it all a strain. It got to the stage that I felt more like a union leader than a football player. I was the guy who had to go in and organise a day off with the manager for the players. I also had to deal with Jock Brown over bonus money. We couldn't resolve it, so it was then passed to Fergus. There was no fun in that. I didn't enjoy one second of having to deal with him. The players put pressure on me to come up with the figures we were looking for, and I tried my best for the dressing-room. But Fergus just would not budge. He ran the club as he saw fit. That caused a lot of disharmony in the dressing-room. We formed a player committee, and a few of the senior guys and I had spats with Fergus. In the end, we pretty much got what we wanted, but it took a lot of time and energy to get there, and that time and energy would have been better spent trying to win football games.'

On the day of the first leg of the Zagreb tie at Parkhead, McCann stated that his players needed a 'reality check', as his offer was fair and generous. He then announced that he was deducting £50,000 from the players' bonus money and donating it to the Schiehallion Unit at Yorkhill Hospital, whether Celtic won the tie or not. The Celtic players held a meeting, and Boyd broke off from their final preparations at Cameron House to issue a statement on behalf of the squad. Boyd said that the players would walk away from the bonus row if the remaining £230,000 was donated to a charity of McCann's choice. Again, this was whether they won or lost. McCann agreed.

Alan Stubbs: 'The bonus payment was up for renewal, and the players wanted the going rate. We'd done our homework and knew the kind of money that was being paid elsewhere for winning the league and Champions League qualification. We were made an offer, and we felt we were being duped.

'Fergus was a very powerful man and deserves credit for saving the club and building a great stadium. He wiped out the huge debt and got Celtic back on a level playing field. But that didn't mean he was right every time and that his word had to be the final one. The offer he made to the squad was short of the going rate. He had a non-negotiable attitude and could have an unfortunate manner about him when dealing with the players on business matters. He told us that if we didn't like the offer, then tough. We thought that wasn't acceptable, and we dug our heels in. We didn't like being dictated to, and, rightly or wrongly, we took him on. It was a major collision and yet more unwanted negative publicity. Poor Dr Jozef was caught in the middle of it, unable to do anything.

'There was never a dull moment at Celtic. For one reason or another, I don't think there was ever a sustained period of calm. It was a roller-coaster ride, but one that I was glad to be on. In my first three years, I think the coaching staff and playing squad were dictated to by those above. It all changed when Martin O'Neill came on board. He took control and was in charge of the people who were meant to be in charge of him. Fergus had gone by that time. It would have been interesting to see Fergus and Martin trying to work together.'

Marc Rieper: 'It was poor that the players and the people upstairs couldn't agree on a deal. The bonus money should have been sorted before we kicked a ball in the Champions League. The fighting and disagreements we had were so disappointing. It ruined a lot of good things at the club. The spirit in the squad had gone from being very high to really low. We were all well paid at Celtic, and Fergus McCann was of the opinion that we didn't really deserve much more. To the people on the outside, it might have looked like we were acting like spoiled kids and that we should have dealt with it more professionally. But I knew what other clubs were paying for Champions League qualification. If we defeated Croatia Zagreb in the qualifier, it was going to generate millions and millions of pounds for Celtic. We felt we were due a portion of that income. It became a public disagreement, and it didn't help the new coach, Dr Venglos. He wasn't the type of character to help sort things out.

'I suppose an argument was a long time in the coming. The players thought that it was a major mistake not to keep Wim at the club and that others were acting out of self-interest. The good feeling we had after winning the league had virtually disappeared overnight. It ended up impossible for Dr Venglos to achieve any momentum that season. The players had just had enough of it all.'

The bonus row might well have been sorted, but it only papered over the cracks. The gap between the players and the boardroom was now wider than ever. Not surprisingly, they lost to Croatia Zagreb and didn't make it into the Champions League; instead, they had to settle for a place in the UEFA Cup.

The night they crashed out in Croatia will also be remembered for Blinker appearing to pull back from a 50–50 tackle with the Zagreb goalkeeper as he chased a pass that might well have given him a scoring opportunity.

Regi Blinker: 'I often had friends and family over to visit from Holland. They were very impressed with the stadium and the atmosphere created by the Celtic supporters. They still talk about it to this day. They'll often refer to my time at Celtic and the great memories they have. That's what makes Glasgow so special and Celtic so special. They feel very proud that I'm able to say I played for Celtic. And I mean that. That's not me talking as a foreigner trying to patronise Celtic and their people.

'Celtic is a huge club, and it's because of the supporters that they have an excellent worldwide reputation and following. Playing for Celtic is enjoyable, but it is also intense. Living in Glasgow can be a little bit suffocating for an Old Firm player. It's much more intense than playing for Feyenoord and living in Rotterdam, for example. In Glasgow, if you are out and about and a fan recognises you, they are over to you and want an autograph and a chat about football. In Holland, they recognise you but don't put demands on you. They will just nod in your direction. That's the difference.

'Yes, I remember that incident in Zagreb, and I remember the reaction to it. How could I forget? I was labelled a "shitebag" and also the "guy who cost Celtic a place in the Champions League group stages". I've never seen a replay of the incident, but it is still clear in my mind. I grew up playing football on the streets, and my skill always got me out of situations during games against players of lesser ability. I was never the bravest player, and when 50–50 balls used to come about I would go in for the challenge as if I was feigning from going for the ball, but my quick movement would allow me to steal it just before the other guy got there. I probably had about a 75 per cent success rate. That night in Zagreb, I went back to my youth. Only I didn't manage to win the ball.

'Right away I had a feeling that it might have looked bad for me, and I was then left in no doubt when Henrik shouted at me for the way I approached the challenge with the goalkeeper. Right away, I knew I'd done wrong.

'The thing I can always hold my head up about is that I played in a history-making Celtic side. I played my part, no matter how small, in stopping Rangers winning ten in a row. I'm so proud of that. I have my championship medal on display, along with my 1993 medal from the Feyenoord championship success. All of the boys feel so proud. Every time we meet up or speak on the phone, Jonathan Gould always calls me "legend". He calls all the boys that.

'I stayed for three seasons at Celtic, every last day of the original contract I signed when I joined from Sheffield Wednesday. In October 1999, during the reign of John Barnes and Kenny Dalglish, I was offered a new two-year contract. I rejected it, or more like I just put it on hold. I told them to wait until I was back in the team, and we'd see what unfolded. I was never offered another deal. Looking back, I probably wish I'd signed it when it was initially offered. It could have led to me being part of the Martin O'Neill era. Bobby Petta got the chance to shine in the first season under Martin, and he performed well. But I know if there had been a competition between me and Bobby for a place in the team, I'd have won it. And I'd say that to Bobby's face.'

Blinker had his time under the microscope from the Celtic fans, as did McCann. On the day the League Championship flag was raised, the club's owner was booed by the Celtic supporters, who were not happy with the appointment of Vengloš and also wanted more investment in the team. It was 1 August, minutes before the team kicked off the defence of their title with a game against Dunfermline. It should have been one of McCann's proudest moments, but it instead turned into something he would have been keen to forget.

Jansen and MacLeod were both present that afternoon, as guests of former Celtic director Brian Dempsey. Brown slaughtered them for turning up that day. Vengloš was more receptive and shook hands with Jansen as they met in the VIP area at full-time after Celtic had recorded a 5–0 win.

Tom Boyd: 'Fergus was booed as I unfurled the league championship flag before the new season kicked off. Wim's departure and bringing in Jozef as his replacement was perceived to be Fergus's fault. The fans obviously thought that the treatment of Wim was disgraceful and chose that time to make their feelings known. I wish they had hung fire and chosen another time, another day. We should have enjoyed celebrating the flag day, but instead of happy memories we were left with a bad taste in our mouths.

'Wim attended, and I think he was perfectly entitled to return. He should still have been in the dugout that day to get the credit and appreciation for leading the club to the title. The pressure and ill-feeling towards Fergus and Jock really started to escalate after that. The fans were not happy with the appointment of Jozef as the new manager, as they felt he was the cheap option. Over at Rangers, Dick Advocaat was Walter Smith's successor, and he was spending money like it was going out of fashion on internationally proven players. Perhaps Wim had an idea of the bigger picture, read the signs and knew the right moment to get out.

'Fergus also left the club and departed for America with a huge profit. I wish he had handed back some of that cash to be invested in a proper training facility. That would have been a tremendous gesture. But, first and foremost, Fergus was a businessman, and when you worked in the same building as him you could never forget that. One phrase you could not associate with Fergus was "He let his heart rule his head". No. Still, he built us a stadium to be proud of, and we should always be thankful for that.'

One of the reasons Paul Lambert came to Celtic was the chance to work with Jansen. He is of the opinion that the Dutchman's departure put the club on a downward spiral for two years.

Paul Lambert: 'My own view is that Celtic didn't settle as a football club until Martin O'Neill took over as manager in the summer of 2000. We had Jozef Vengloš and John Barnes after Wim, and neither worked out. But Martin put the club back on the map. He made the club the major force in Scotland, and I believe Celtic still feel they have that superiority just now. I think Rangers are still playing catch-up on Celtic because of the foundations O'Neill put down and the success he had.

'When I look back on my career, I won the Champions League and played in a UEFA Cup final. I played in the Celtic team that stopped ten in a row and also won three more titles with the club. And I played for Scotland in the opening game of the 1998 World Cup finals in Paris against Brazil.

'I enjoyed my experience at Celtic. I learned so much. But I don't feel comfortable going back to Celtic Park. The only time I've been back was when I was manager of Livingston. It's not my era any more, and you need to move on. I had great times at Celtic, don't get me wrong. I played in the league-winning side of 1998, won the Treble in 2001 and added league titles in 2002 and 2004. I also captained the club the night we played in the UEFA Cup final in Seville. My biggest regret in football is not beating Porto that night. I really wanted it. We all did. It was a roasting night, and the pitch was crap. Yet, we worked so hard, put in so much. Henrik was incredible that night. For us to get to that final was some achievement, and we had to beat some quality sides along the way. I will stand up and argue with any person who says that Liverpool, Celta Vigo and Stuttgart were not good sides. Boavista in the semi was probably our most difficult tie. We had to win over there in the second leg, and we did. Bobo Baldé was brilliant that night. But it also came at a cost, because we lost the league on the last day of the season. Had we not gone all the way in the UEFA Cup, we would have won the league. Absolutely.'

Lambert might have regrets about that heartbreaking night in Seville, but he can always look back with pride on the dramatic season when he returned from Germany and became a legend at Celtic. As Jonathan Gould repeatedly says, Lambert was one of a number of legends created by that unforgettable season. That 1997–98 team might not be remembered as one of the greatest in Celtic's proud history. But their achievement will go down as one of the greatest. Stopping Rangers' seemingly relentless march to ten in a row was fought out under incredible pressures on and off the pitch. That season wasn't about playing the traditional, swashbuckling Celtic way. It was all about winning the league and stopping the club's greatest rivals from making their own piece of football history.

That's why the Celtic team of 1997–98 will forever be part of football history – and that's why they're remembered so fondly a decade later. And they'll be revered by Celtic fans for many years to come. Stand up for the champions.

Results from the
1997–98 season

UEFA Cup	Inter CableTel	0–3	Celtic	23.07.1997
UEFA Cup	Celtic	5–0	Inter CableTel	30.07.1997
Scottish Premier	Hibernian	2–1	Celtic	03.08.1997
Scottish League Cup	Berwick	0–7	Celtic	09.08.1997
UEFA Cup	FC Tirol	2–1	Celtic	12.08.1997
Scottish Premier	Celtic	1–2	Dunfermline	16.08.1997
Scottish League Cup	St Johnstone	0–1	Celtic	19.08.1997
Scottish Premier	St Johnstone	0–2	Celtic	23.08.1997
UEFA Cup	Celtic	6–3	FC Tirol	26.08.1997
Scottish League Cup	Celtic	1–0	Motherwell	10.09.1997
Scottish Premier	Motherwell	2–3	Celtic	13.09.1997
UEFA Cup	Celtic	2–2	Liverpool	16.09.1997
Scottish Premier	Celtic	2–0	Aberdeen	20.09.1997
Scottish Premier	Dundee Utd	1–2	Celtic	27.09.1997
UEFA Cup	Liverpool	0–0	Celtic	30.09.1997
Scottish Premier	Celtic	4–0	Kilmarnock	04.10.1997
Scottish League Cup	Dunfermline	0–1	Celtic	14.10.1997
Scottish Premier	Hearts	1–2	Celtic	18.10.1997
Scottish Premier	Celtic	2–0	St Johnstone	25.10.1997
Scottish Premier	Dunfermline	0–2	Celtic	01.11.1997
Scottish Premier	Rangers	1–0	Celtic	08.11.1997

Scottish Premier	Celtic	0–2	Motherwell	15.11.1997
Scottish Premier	Celtic	1–1	Rangers	19.11.1997
Scottish Premier	Celtic	4–0	Dundee Utd	22.11.1997
Scottish League Cup	Celtic	3–0	Dundee Utd	30.11.1997
Scottish Premier	Kilmarnock	0–0	Celtic	06.12.1997
Scottish Premier	Aberdeen	0–2	Celtic	09.12.1997
Scottish Premier	Celtic	1–0	Hearts	13.12.1997
Scottish Premier	Celtic	5–0	Hibernian	20.12.1997
Scottish Premier	St Johnstone	1–0	Celtic	27.12.1997
Scottish Premier	Celtic	2–0	Rangers	02.01.1998
Scottish Premier	Motherwell	1–1	Celtic	10.01.1998
Scottish FA Cup	Celtic	2–0	Morton	24.01.1998
Scottish Premier	Dundee Utd	1–2	Celtic	27.01.1998
Scottish Premier	Celtic	3–1	Aberdeen	02.02.1998
Scottish Premier	Hearts	1–1	Celtic	08.02.1998
Scottish FA Cup	Dunfermline	1–2	Celtic	16.02.1998
Scottish Premier	Celtic	4–0	Kilmarnock	21.02.1998
Scottish Premier	Celtic	5–1	Dunfermline	25.02.1998
Scottish Premier	Hibernian	0–1	Celtic	28.02.1998
Scottish FA Cup	Dundee Utd	2–3	Celtic	08.03.1998
Scottish Premier	Celtic	1–1	Dundee Utd	15.03.1998
Scottish Premier	Aberdeen	0–1	Celtic	21.03.1998
Scottish Premier	Celtic	0–0	Hearts	28.03.1998
Scottish FA Cup	Rangers	2–1	Celtic	05.04.1998
Scottish Premier	Kilmarnock	1–2	Celtic	08.04.1998
Scottish Premier	Rangers	2–0	Celtic	12.04.1998
Scottish Premier	Celtic	4–1	Motherwell	18.04.1998
Scottish Premier	Celtic	0–0	Hibernian	25.04.1998
Scottish Premier	Dunfermline	1–1	Celtic	03.05.1998
Scottish Premier	Celtic	2–0	St Johnstone	09.05.1998